NIGHT CATS & CORSAIRS

The sleek Grumman F7F-3N Tigercat outside the company's facility in Bethpage, NY. The Tigercat was Grumman's attempt to supply the U.S. Navy during WWII with a fast, two-engine, long-range fighter. Instead, it was destined to serve as a night fighter with Marine shore-based squadrons. (Robert F. Dorr)

Alan C. Carey

NIGHT CATS & CORSAIRS

The Operational History of GRUMMAN AND VOUGHT

Night Fighter Aircraft

1942-1953

Schiffer Military History
Atglen, PA

Library of Congress Control Number: 2013955642

Printed in The United States of America
ISBN: 978-0-7643-4373-5

We are interested in hearing from authors with book ideas on related topics.

Published by Schiffer Publishing Ltd.
4880 Lower Valley Road
Atglen, PA 19310
Phone: (610) 593-1777
FAX: (610) 593-2002
E-mail: Info@schifferbooks.com.
Visit our web site at: www.schifferbooks.com
Please write for a free catalog.
This book may be purchased
from the publisher.
Try your bookstore first.

Contents

Acknowledgments

I want to acknowledge the following individuals and organizations who share my passion for military aviation history and made this book possible. The following veterans of Korean War night air operations provided vivid primary accounts of their experiences: James Brown VC-3, Garry Cleveland VMF(N)-513, and Marshall Foreman VC-3. I especially thank Eileen Bertie, daughter of VF(N)-76's John Bertie, for providing information and images about her father's squadron; and Nicholas A. Veronico for providing the story of the Navy's only Korean War ace, VC-3's Lt. Guy P. Bordelon, and the data on Latin American F4U-5 Corsairs. Also to Thomas E. Doll for providing photographs and data on Marine Corps land-based night fighter units. Finally, the Textual Archives of the National Archives and Records Administration (NARA), the Naval Historical Center, Grumman History Center, Vought Heritage, the American Aviation Historical Society, the Tailhook Association, and the Emil Buehler Library at the National Museum of Naval Aviation (NMNA) provided primary source documents, as well as images. Photo credits are included in the captions.

Introduction

Fighting in the air is not sport. It is scientific murder.

- Capt. Eddie Rickenbacker

Capt. Rickenbacker's quote was made during the era of fabric-covered biplanes, when aerial warfare was in its infancy. Twenty-five years later, sleek, fast, metal-skinned interceptors had come into their own, some equipped with the latest electronics gear of the period, so that a pilot could track his unseen quarry in the most adverse weather conditions and at night. Many times, the hunted was oblivious to the predator's existence until machine gun and/or cannon fire pierced their aircraft's thin aluminum skin—air warfare had truly become scientific.

This book traces the developmental and operational history of radar-equipped night fighter aircraft produced by American aircraft manufacturers Grumman and Vought for the U.S. Navy and Marine Corps before the advent of jet aircraft with similar nocturnal capabilities: the night variants of the Vought F4U Corsair, Grumman F6F Hellcat, and F7F Tigercat.

The first commissioned squadrons to enter combat in the Fall of 1943 performed reasonably well, despite inadequate equipment and inexperience of pilots and ground controllers participating in the new art of night aerial interception. Radar-equipped Grumman F6F Hellcats proved to be the most suitable aircraft for nocturnal work, becoming the Navy's frontline night fighter, beginning in early 1944, and it became the agent responsible for the majority of aerial kills by naval and marine night fighters during WWII. The immediate postwar years saw the development of jet aircraft, but such aircraft lacked the capacity to house period airborne radar sets, which were heavy, large systems consisting of vacuum tubes. Therefore, Grumman's F7F-3N Tigercat and Vought's F4U-5N/NL served as interim, short-term solutions until the arrival of jet fighters with night and all-weather capabilities.

BIRTH OF AIRBORNE RADAR TECHNOLOGY

The adoption of radar technology by U.S. fighter aircraft for locating, intercepting, and destroying enemy aircraft in the air evolved from research conducted by British and American scientists prior to WWII. The U.S. Navy began experimenting with radar during the 1920s and '30s, even coining the acronym RADAR for Radio Detection and Ranging in 1940. Albert H. Taylor and Leo C. Young, working for the U.S. Naval Research laboratory, built and demonstrated the first successful ship-based radar system in 1937, with the capability to detect ships and aircraft. Further trials resulted in the development of the XAF radar in 1938, capable of detecting aircraft at a distance of 50-100 miles. Testing of the system aboard the battleship USS *New York* (BB-34) in late 1938 led to the production version, designated CXAM. In May 1939, the Navy awarded RCA with a contract to produce the system, with deliveries to the Navy beginning a year later and installation taking place aboard the carrier *Yorktown* (CV 5), the battleship *California* (BB-44), and several cruisers. The Navy installed an improved version designated CXAM-1 on a number of capital ships prior to the attack on Pearl Harbor. While the U.S. Navy focused attention on ship-based radar, the U.S. Army Signal Corps, in conjunction with Western Electric, developed the ground-based SCR-268, with the system entering service in early 1941. Improvements to the -268 resulted in the SCR-270 mobile system, which was the type deployed to the island of Oahu, Hawaii, that detected the first wave of Japanese aircraft approaching Pearl Harbor on 7 December 1941.

The British were also working on similar programs, but went a step further by adapting radar to aircraft, particularly in fighters. The basis for this application began with the development of the cavity magnetron in 1940 by Harry Boot and John Randall, which was small enough to be installed on some military aircraft. Research by British and Commonwealth scientists greatly enhanced the Royal Air Force's (RAF) fighting capabilities when ground-based radar systems vectored night-flying RAF fighters towards approaching German bombers. It became quite clear to the British and Germans that by the fall of 1940, night air operations had become an integral part of the air war. German losses during the Battle of Britain from the coordination between the RAF and ground-based early-warning radar also forced the Luftwaffe into the night, while British bomber losses against German military and industrial targets during daytime raids forced the RAF to switch to night operations, as well. Therefore, the night air war over Europe created the need by both Germany and Britain to develop superior radar-equipped aircraft.

EARLY AIR INTERCEPTION SYSTEMS

The British first installed airborne radar equipment, called Air Interception sets (AI), on night fighter variants of the Bristol Type 156 Beaufighter and de Havilland DH. 98 Mosquito. However, the early AI sets were unreliable: the Mark I through IV series operated at long wavelengths (wide beams) and could only acquire targets at short range. They were often unreliable, because the radar pulse could not discriminate between returns from ground clutter and airborne aircraft. Therefore, identification of enemy aircraft at night became more of a skill acquired due to combat experience by the pilot or radar operator, who could interpret the information displayed on the set. British and American researchers found a solution to the problem by introducing the SCR-520 (British Mark VII) produced by General Electric, a system using microwave beams with wavelengths of less than 10 centimeters, which proved to be more accurate and reduced false returns and ground interference. A combined effort by the Massachusetts Institute of Technology (MIT), Western Electric, and Bell Telephone resulted in further advancement in airborne radar technology with the SCR-720 (British AI Mark X) in 1942. This system offered protection from enemy jamming with a range of 6.5 miles, and was such a technological advancement that it remained in service with the military until the early 1950s.[1]

The U.S. Navy developed its own air intercept radar systems for night fighters beginning with the ASH or AN/APS-4 (British AI Mark XV). Built by Western Electric, the AN/APS-4 had a maximum range of 30 nautical miles on surface vessels and five miles on aircraft (with continuous tracking within 300 feet); however, actual maximum effective range was less than three miles. Modifications to the AN/APS-4 resulted in the introduction of the AIA-1, also called the AN/APS-6, an improvement over the earlier model. It enabled the pilot to locate surfaced submarines within 15 miles; a 4-8,000 ton ship within 30 miles; a 75 nautical-mile range on well-defined coastlines; aircraft within a 5-mile range; and track a hostile aircraft within 300 feet, enabling the pilot to approach within gun-firing range and to aim and fire the night fighter's guns accurately without actually seeing the enemy.

NIGHT FIGHTER TACTICS

Night interception required a team effort, consisting of the aircraft's pilot and/or radar operator (R/O) working with a ground radar system called Ground Control Interception (GCI). The GCI guided friendly aircraft into position by viewing a radar screen that assessed target information on a Planned Positioning Indicator (PPI). The terrain within GCI's search sector superimposed on the PPI screen displayed all aircraft within range as little dots of lights called blips. A second display determined which aircraft the controller was guiding via Identification Friend or Foe (IFF), a transmitting device aboard the night fighter that sent a signal back to GCI. By using VHF radio, the GCI operator would vector the aircraft toward the enemy (bogey) by giving the pilot and/or RO compass headings and altitude adjustments to guide the "friendly" towards the target. Once vectored and a good AI contact was established, the airborne radar operator or pilot would use their system to close in for a kill, adjusting course, altitude, and airspeed when necessary. Once visually identified, the pilot increased speed and closed in for positive identification, and the fighter would then attack from behind or below the target. This was the general tactic used by the GCI-night fighter team with variations based on unique situations.

The British were three years ahead of the Americans in night fighter development with the Bristol Beaufighter IF going into operation September 1940. Shown here is a Beaufighter Mk IIF that went into service April 1941. (Author's Collection)

The De Havilland Mosquito NF Mk II entered service with the RAF in April 1942, and with a top speed of over 360mph, the U.S. Navy had nothing to match its performance until the F4U-2N Corsair entered operational service 17 months later. (Author's Collection)

Chapter 1

World War II Night Fighter Development

Prior to United States entry into WWII, very few American military pilots had experience in night cross-country flying or night interception of aircraft. The United States Army Air Force (USAAF) and Navy were in the process of using ground or ship-based radar as an early warning system, but neither service seriously contemplated equipping aircraft with similar systems for air interception and target location. Early Air Force involvement with night interception consisted of a few night flying exercises between 1937 and 1940, where fighter-searchlight teams guided aircraft in the interception of enemy bombers; a tactic which would have very limited success in the early phases of the Pacific War. When AAF, Navy, and Marine Corps observers arrived in the United Kingdom in 1941, it soon became obvious the U.S. armed forces lacked the training, tactics, and specialized aircraft for night air offensive and defensive operations. The British, realizing the probability of the United States entering the war, began sharing their radar technology and night fighting tactics, which allowed the AAF and Navy to apply such equipment to existing aircraft, enabling them to field the first American night fighter units. Based on British technology, American companies further advanced radar technology and, by 1944, were equipping Air Force and Navy bombers and fighters with American-designed systems.

U.S. ARMY AIR FORCE NIGHT FIGHTER DEVELOPMENT

The formidable German Luftwaffe, operating both day and night, required the AAF to establish its first night fighter squadrons for the European Theater, rather than the Pacific, since there was little concern about Japanese nocturnal capabilities. Just as the Navy realized, the Air Force required the expertise and quality of British radar technology and aircraft to establish the first such units during the summer and fall of 1942. Early Air Force night fighter squadrons deployed overseas in the European and Mediterranean Theaters flew British radar-equipped Beaufighters or Mosquitos, which did not bother the American crews, as the aircraft proved to be reliable night fighters. AAF pilots and radar operators primarily operated British-built night fighters from 1942 through 1943. In the interim, AAF crews flew, in addition to British aircraft, modified American night fighters based on existing airframes, which did not live up to expectations. One American Army pilot lamented about relying on the British: "Our procedures are 100-percent British; our equipment, our phraseology over the radio, everything but our food and personnel."[2]

The Air Force operated only two American-built night fighters on a large scale: the Douglas P-70 Havoc and Northrop P-61 Black Widow. The reason behind American crews flying

The U.S. Army Air Force (USAAF) initially relied on British-built radar-equipped night fighters, such as the Beaufighter shown here with the U.S. Army Air Force's 416th night fighter squadron at an airfield in Italy in late 1943. (USAF)

British aircraft was due to the inadequate performance of the P-70, converted from the A-20 Havoc, the Air Force's only night fighter available upon U.S. entry in the war. The AAF saw the P-70 as an interim night fighter until the advanced P-61 Black Widow became operational (throughout the 1940s and early-1950s, the Air Force and Navy continued to rely on "interim" night fighters due to development and production delays of more suitable aircraft). When the P-70 went into service, the Air Force characterized the aircraft as having poor performance and a less-than-satisfactory radar system. The aircraft's AI SCR-540 radar, which was an American-manufactured copy of the British Mark IV, had only a forward search azimuth of 150 degrees, a maximum search range of

The first USAAF aircraft modified as a night fighter was the twin-engine Douglas P-70, developed from the famed A-20 Havoc as an interim fix until delivery of Northrop's P-61 Black Widow. The Army Air Force deemed the P-70's combat performance to be very unsatisfactory. (American Aviation Historical Society)

less than five miles, and a vertical and lateral range of only 3,000 feet. The absence of engine superchargers ruled out its use as a high-altitude night fighter that required 45 minutes to reach 22,000 feet, where Japanese bombers could easily outrun it. Upgrading the radar system to the SCR-720 did not substantially improve detecting ability and by August 1944, only twelve P-70s were still serving in active combat operations.

The Air Force's first aircraft specifically designed as a night fighter was the twin-engine Northrop P-61 Black Widow, equipped with the SCR-720 radar. Two prototypes were ordered in January 1941, but due to technical issues, a prototype did not take to the air until May 1942. Labor and material shortages delayed delivery of the first production P-61A until October 1943, followed by the P-61B in July 1944 and a C-variant in July 1945. The twin-boom Black Widow armed with 20mm cannons and .50-caliber machine guns proved far superior to the P-70. Powered by two 2,000-hp

The Northrop P-61 Black Widow, after production delays, began its operational career in Europe and the Pacific in July 1944. It remained the Air Force's only night fighter until the late-1940s. (USAF)

Pratt & Whitney engines with two-speed General Electric superchargers, the aircraft had a top speed of 367mph with a rate of climb of 1,775 feet-per-minute. However, it proved to be a poor interceptor against Japanese bombers above 20,000 feet and the Black Widow's radar operated satisfactory only 81 percent of the time, making that system responsible for more abortive missions than any other malfunction. The SCR-720 had a forward search azimuth of 180 degrees with a maximum search range of 5-7 miles. The Air Force would rely on the P-61 until 1948, when the North American F-82F/G Twin Mustang became operational.

The Air Force continued its search for an exceptional night fighter during the war, leading it to the Lockheed P-38 Lightning. Modification of the twin-boom P-38 Lightning into a night fighter began with the installation of the SCR-540 radar on two single-seat P-38Fs. However, Lockheed quickly determined that it was too difficult a task for the pilot to both fly and operate the radar. In 1944, the Lockheed added

The Lockheed P-38M was a night fighter introduced during the final weeks of WWII in the Pacific. It was a far superior aircraft to the P-61, but the Air Force scrapped the Night Lightning as its postwar night fighter. (Author's Collection)

a radar operator's station aft of the pilot and installed the AN/APS-6 radar inside an external radome underneath the nose. Armament consisted of one 20-mm cannon and four .50-caliber machine guns, and the P-38M had a maximum speed of 406mph, more than 30mph faster than the P-61. However, the AFF received only approximately 80 converted L-models, with a handful reaching the Pacific only weeks before the end of the war, serving with the 421st, 547th, and 550th Night Fighter Squadrons. The Air Force made the decision to keep the P-61 Black Widow as its interim night fighter and all P-38Ms, with the exception of one, became scrap metal within a few months of VJ Day.

U.S. NAVY NIGHT FIGHTER DEVELOPMENT

The Radiation Laboratory at the Massachusetts Institute of Technology (MIT), an agency within Division 14 of the National Defense Research Council (NDRC), contracted the Naval Aircraft Factory (NAF) at Philadelphia, PA, under the code name "Project Roger" on 3 May 1941 for the installation and testing of AI radar sets in naval aircraft.[1]

The Chief of the Bureau of Aeronautics (BuAer) issued a preliminary plan on 7 August 1941 for the installation of radar on naval aircraft, including the Vought F4U Corsair. This was followed on 9 September by a formal request from BuAer to NDRC and the Naval Research Laboratory to develop an AI set suitable for a single seat, single engine fighter.[2]

Two months later, on 11 November, Doctor Lee A. DuBridge of the Radiation Laboratory reported the design for a 3-cm radar for fighters had been completed.[3] The plan for nocturnal air operations by the Navy was rather simple: install AI radar in the Vought F4U Corsair and F6F Hellcat then under development.

VOUGHT F4U-1 CORSAIR

The adaptation of the Chance-Vought F4U Corsair into a night fighter began with the search by the Navy for high speed, ship-based interceptor aircraft during the late 1930s, as the performance of carrier-based aircraft during that period lagged behind those of land-based aircraft of the Army Air Corps. Front-line Army pursuit aircraft, such as the mono-winged Seversky P-35, with a top speed of 282mph and a rate of climb of 2,440 feet-per-minute, was 80mph faster and had a better rate of climb than the Navy's bi-winged Grumman F2F-1. Replacement of the F2F with the Grumman F3F between 1937 and 1938 improved carrier-based fighter performance in terms of speed and rate of climb, but this aircraft still lagged behind contemporary Army fighters. The Navy stressed speed as the primary requirement for the new fighter, and in response, Vought engineers built an airframe around the 1,800-horsepower, 18-cylinder, air-cooled Pratt and Whitney R2800-4 engine with a three-bladed Hamilton Hydromatic propeller. The 14-foot diameter propeller required additional ground clearance, which led away from the conventional wing design for the revolutionary inverted gull wing concept. The engineering team also incorporated flush riveting and spot welding throughout the airframe to reduce drag.

The prototype took its maiden flight 29 March 1940, with testing continuing until 11 July 1940, when it suffered extensive damage upon crash landing on a golf course. It took Vought workers nearly three months to rebuild the Corsair before testing could be resumed. On 1 October 1940, Lt. Ben Kelsey broke the speed record for a single-engine aircraft when the XF4U reached 405 miles per hour on a flight from Stratford to Harford, Connecticut. During dive tests in January 1941, the

Corsair reached a maximum speed of 536mph at 10,000 feet. The first production F4U-1 Corsair rolled out of the Stratford plant and flew 25 June 1942, with the Navy accepting the first two aircraft a month later. The F4U-1 that went into production differed significantly from the prototype, with the 1,800hp powerplant replaced with the 2,000hp R-2800-8B engine. This increased the top speed to 415mph, cruising speed from 180mph to 186mph, and the service ceiling from 31,000 feet to 37,000 feet. Vought also upgraded the aircraft's armament with the elimination of the two .30-caliber nose guns and four .50-caliber guns for six wing-mounted. This change required reducing the fuel capacity of auxiliary internal fuel cells in the wings to one 62-gallon self-sealing cell in each wing and increasing the fuel capacity within the fuselage. Vought made the changes by lengthening the forward fuselage 18 inches, moving the cockpit three feet aft, and installing a 237-gallon self-sealing tank.

Carrier trials began 25 September 1942 aboard the escort carrier USS *Sangamon* (CVE 26) in Chesapeake Bay, but testing revealed the Corsair suffered from poor visibility and handling characteristics. The longer nose, bird-cage canopy, and the nose-high, three-point angle reduced forward visibility during taxiing, take-off, and landing. Leaking hydraulic fluid from the cowl flap actuators and engine oil further reduced visibility, leaving streaks on the windscreen as well as splattering the pilot's goggles while leaning out the open cockpit, trying to see down the deck.

Landing a Corsair on a carrier taxed the skills of even the best pilots, as the rigid landing gear oleo caused the aircraft to bounce on landing, causing aircraft to miss the arresting gear and smash into the crash barrier. A more serious issue was the tremendous torque created by the Double *Wasp* engine. Too much throttle and the Corsair had a tendency to flip over on its back. Those serious flaws prohibited the Corsair from effectively operating from carriers until early 1944, when Vought, along with modifications made in the field, corrected the deficiencies.

F4U-2N NIGHT FIGHTER VARIANT

The Corsair fit the Navy's need for a high-speed interceptor capable of carrying heavy radar gear, since the Grumman F6F was still in development. Even before the first production F4U-1 rolled out of the factory and was accepted, BuAer requested Vought Aircraft to develop a night fighter variant of the Corsair in December 1941. Vought responded by submitting Company Proposal VS-325 to BuAer on 6 January 1942 for the XF4U-2. An XF4U-2 mockup was completed and inspected by the Navy three weeks later on 28 January. The night fighter variant was not a new model, but a modification of the F4U-1

An early F4U-1A Corsair, possibly BuNo 02153, which Vought engineers converted to the F4U-2 prototype. The initial design for the Corsair night fighter was completed prior to the Japanese attack on Pearl Harbor, with Vought converting 32 F4U-1s to the night fighter configuration. (Author's Collection)

F4U-2 with VF(N)-101 Det B aboard the USS *Intrepid* (CV-11), February 1944. Only two squadrons operated the aircraft in combat conditions, but Vought's experimentation led to the development of the postwar F4U-5N night fighter. (Richard Hill collection via Tailhook Association)

airframe. Modifications consisted of removing the starboard wing's outboard .50-caliber machine gun and fitting an 18-inch paraboloid antenna inside a pod. Space was at a minimum, requiring placement of the AN/APS-4 in the aircraft's radio compartment by removing the radio and reinstalling it under the pilot's seat. Cockpit modifications included the installation of an autopilot and red lights for interior illumination. The engine exhausts on the bottom of the cowling were fitted with flame dampeners to avoid enemy detection in the air or on the ground.

The remaining five .50-caliber machine guns were boresighted to 250 yards, rather than the standard 300 yards, and angled slightly upward, as the standard angle of attack was made at six o'clock position. For gun aiming, the Mk-8 gyroscopic lead-computing gunsight was standard on the Corsair and F6F Hellcat. The Mk-8 projected an image with six diamond-shaped "pips" that formed an imaginary circle in front of the pilot on the windscreen. The pilot adjusted range by turning the ranging throttle grip either clockwise or counterclockwise. Range was increased by turning the grip clockwise, making the circle smaller, or decreased counterclockwise, making the circle larger. In an aerial engagement, the pilot slowly and steadily turned the throttle grip counterclockwise to keep the target tightly encircled while the sight continuously calculated range, rate of intercept, and deflection angle.

Technicians converted the first production F4U-1 (BuNo 02153) to the night fighter configuration as the XF4U-2 at NAF and afterward, it was flown to Quonset Point for service with the Navy's first night fighter squadron. Due to Vought's heavy production schedule, conversion of the F4U-1 to the F4U-2N configuration took place at NAF, with the conversion taking approximately six weeks per aircraft and modifications completed on 32 aircraft by September 1943, while two others were modified at Kwajalein Atoll, in the Marshall Islands, by VMF(N)-532. The low number of Corsairs modified for night operations was barely enough to equip three squadrons operating the F4U-2N overseas: Navy Night Fighter Squadron Seventy-Five VF(N)-75 and Marine Night Fighter Squadron Five-Thirty-Two VMF(N)-532, operating from shore bases; while VF(N)-101 became the first Corsair squadron to serve aboard an aircraft carrier.

GRUMMAN F6F HELLCAT

In June 1941, the Navy wisely asked Grumman to work on developing a replacement for the F4F Wildcat, at that time the Navy's front-line carrier fighter. Delays with the Corsair pushed production of that aircraft into the following summer, and it did not become operational in the Pacific with land-based squadrons until February 1943, and another year lapsed before it appeared for duty on carriers. It became apparent that Wildcat pilots had their hands full tangling against the nimble Japanese Mitsubishi A6M fighter, code-named the "Zeke," with its superior speed, range, and rate of climb. Grumman's answer was design number 50, the XF6F-1 Hellcat. Grumman built two prototypes of the new fighter: the XF6F-1 with the Wright Cyclone R-2600-16 engine and the XF6F-2 with the R-2800-16 with a turbo-supercharger, each producing 1,700 horsepower. Test pilot Bob Hall took the first prototype into the air on a 25-minute test flight 26 June 1942. The Wright engine could not deliver the desired speed and rate of climb, so Grumman decided to switch it out with the Pratt & Whitney R-2800-10 rated at 2,800 horsepower. Grumman installed the new engine, which was unavailable during initial prototype testing, to the XF6F-1, and thus the XF6F-3 was born, with its maiden flight occurring a little over a month later. The Navy took delivery of the first F6F-3 4 October 1942. The Hellcat was a fast, agile, and tough fighter armed with six wing-mounted .50-caliber machine guns with a maximum speed of 390 miles per hour, a rate of climb of 3,100 feet per minute, and a service ceiling of 39,400 feet. Grumman improved the design of the F6F-3, resulting in the first delivery of the F6F-5 on 29 April 1944. Modifications included R-2800-10 engines with water injection, a reinforced tail, spring assist tabs on the ailerons, additional armor plating, and an improved windscreen.

The Hellcat was superior in many performance categories over the Zeke, Japan's frontline fighter. It was faster by an average of 55 miles per hour and it could slightly exceed the Zeke's rate of climb. The only areas where the Japanese fighter remained at a distinct advantage was in initial rate of climb and its turning radius, where it could outmaneuver the Hellcat at slower speeds. Grumman's new "cat" did not have any significant design or handling issues as the Corsair did, and USN fighter squadron VF-9 took delivery of the first Hellcats 16 January 1943, only seven months after the prototype made its maiden flight. The Hellcat entered combat in late August 1943, with VF-9 firing the first shots at Japanese picket boats while on a raid against Marcus Island.

Wind tunnel testing of the second production F6F-3 (BuNo 04776) with radar pod conducted 18 March 1943 at Full Scale Tunnel (FST) Facility 643, Langley Research Center. (NASA)

Detailed views of the radar pod during testing at FST 10 March 1943. Tests were conducted to measure the amount of drag created by the pod. The study found the pod barely reduced the aircraft's overall performance. (NASA)

F6F NIGHT FIGHTER VARIANTS

The first Grumman F6F night fighter variant was the F6F-3E, equipped with the APS-4 radar and a wing-mounted radome pod which did not reduce the aircraft's performance substantially, having a maximum speed of 388mph, only three miles per hour slower than the day version of the F6F-3. Grumman produced 205 of this series before changing over to the F6F-5N, with the APS-6 radar, in April 1944. The latest night fighter variant of the Hellcat series retained the APS-6 radar, later upgraded to the APS-13, and was approximately ten mph faster than the F6F-3. The F6F-5N Hellcat became the most produced naval night fighter of the war, with 1,434 delivered between April 1944 and November 1945. The Navy and Marine Corps operated 14 ground or carrier-based Hellcat night fighter squadrons in the Pacific. Each squadron operated approximately 15 aircraft. Eight designated VF(N) operated radar-equipped F6F-3 and/or F6F-5 series in the Pacific beginning in January 1944. Typically, VF(N) squadrons were split into three to four detachments and assigned duty aboard different aircraft carriers. A considerable number of conventional VF squadrons operated the night fighter variant along with their complement of day fighters. Six Marine Corps squadrons operated the Hellcat night variant from Pacific bases beginning in May 1944.

Three-quarter view of an F6F-3E (BuNo 41302) with early radome, Patuxent River, MD, 31 May 1944. The F6F-3E had a very limited production run of approximately 18 units. This aircraft later served with VF-87 in the Pacific. The letters FT, painted yellow, stand for Flight Test. (Robert F. Dorr)

F6F-3N (BuNo 41764) at an undisclosed location features the updated radome faired into the wing, which created less drag than the earlier version mounted on the F6F-3E. (Robert F. Dorr)

A factory-fresh F6F-3N was one of 205 such aircraft modified as a night fighter by the Grumman Corporation at its Bethpage factory, New York. The -3E/5N were allotted to the first carrier-based squadrons: VF(N)-76 and -77. (Grumman Heritage)

F6F-3N (BuNo 41302) instrument panel with tubular radar scope mounted in the center. The gunsight, absent in this photograph, was mounted above the scope. Instruments beginning with the top row (L-R): clock, gyro compass, artificial horizon, and tachometer. Bottom row (L-R): altimeter, air speed indicator, turn indicator, vertical speed indicator, and manifold pressure indicator. (Grumman Heritage via Tommy Thomason)

F6F-5N (BuNo 58244) at Bethpage. Grumman produced 1,434 of the F6F-5E/N Hellcats, with the -E having the AN/APS-4 radar, while the -5 was equipped with the improved AN/APS-6. (Grumman Heritage)

Seen here is BuNo 58332 painted in the standard Glossy Sea Blue adopted for Navy and Marine fighter aircraft in March 1944, with white lettering and white-tipped radar pod. It went on to serve with VF-80 until it was lost off the Philippines 25 November 1944. (Grumman Heritage)

The cockpit layout of the F6F-5N, showing differences in instrumentation for day and night variants of the Hellcat. The serial number RN JZ-909 at the bottom right actually shows this aircraft to be a Royal Navy Hellcat NF II, the British designation for the -5N. (Tommy Thomason)

RESTRICTED
AN 01-85FB-1

Section I

The F6F-5N differs from F6F-5 in the following respects:

1. **Radio Altimeter Indicator**
2. **Radar Scope**

Figure 1-29. Cockpit—Forward View (F6F-5N)

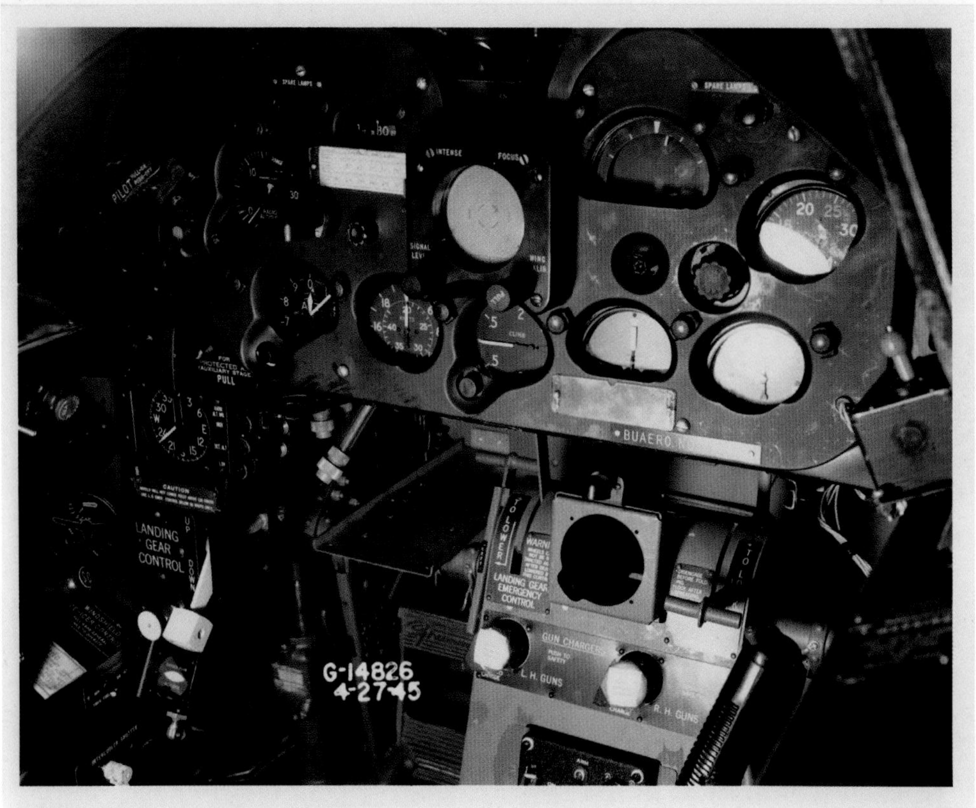

The radar screen of the F6F-5N did not protrude out like the scope of the F6F-3N. The -5N was fitted with the superior AN/APS-6 radar system. The instrument panel was painted flat black. (Grumman Heritage via Tommy Thomason)

Opposite:
Left side console of an F6F-5N. (Grumman History via Tommy Thomason)

Right side console of an F6F-5N (Grumman History via Tommy Thomason)

GRUMMAN F7F TIGERCAT

During WWII, Grumman attempted to supply the Navy with the Grumman F7F Tigercat as a long-range night fighter, but just as Vought had developmental issues with the F4U-1 which limited the carrier use of the night fighter variant, the aircraft failed to live up to expectations and did not reach the Pacific until August 1945. However, it did become the U.S. Navy's first twin-engine, single-seat fighter and the first to have tricycle landing gear. The Grumman Aircraft Company designed the F7F Tigercat to perform a variety of missions-long range fighter, close air support, bomber, torpedo bomber, and night fighter. Too late to see action in WWII due to developmental and production issues, the Tigercat might have faded into obscurity if not for Korea. The evolution of the F7F began seven years before the aircraft finally went into production in 1944. It became the aircraft of choice for Marine pilots of VMF(N)-513 and -542 during the Korean War until the arrival of the jet-powered Douglas F3D Skyknight. Remarkably, the development and production of the Tigercat took a remarkable series of twists and turns, beginning with the cancelled Grumman XF5F-1 and XP-50 projects of the late 1930s and early '40s. Data collected during development and flight tests of the XF5F-1 and XP-50, both twin-engine interceptors with a tricycle landing gear configuration, was utilized in the Model 51, the XF7F Tigercat. The use of such aircraft was somewhat satisfactory, but ideally, the Navy needed a fast, maneuverable, heavily armed, carrier-based night fighter with greater range.

The design team selected for the project consisted of designer team leader Dick Hutton, test pilot and engineer Bob Hall, and project engineer Gordon Israel. According to Gordon Israel:

> The XF7F task started with preliminary design of the airplane, which included wind tunnel testing at New York University. The next step was negotiating with the Bureau of Aeronautics on the detail specification. I then supervised the detail design to produce two flight test articles and a static test specimen.

Results from the wind tunnel tests showed the need for major modifications of the initial design, consisting of changing the aircraft design from a mid-wing to a shoulder-mounted position with the engine nacelles moved below the wing.[4]

The proposal issued to the Navy in spring 1941 identified a single-seat, conventional-style aircraft with aluminum skin, hydraulically-driven landing gear, flaps, folding wings, arresting hook with fabric-covered rudder, elevators, and ailerons. The designers abandoned the twin-rudder configuration, but kept the XP-50's twin engine, sleek and slender nose, tricycle landing gear, and foldable wings for storage on aircraft carriers. The 1,800hp Wright Cyclone GR-2600-14 engines replaced the 1,200hp Wright Cyclone R-1820 engines of the XP-50, but retained the Curtiss Electric full-feathering, constant-speed propellers. The updated engine was expected to give the aircraft a top speed of 437mph, potentially making it the Navy's fasted prop-driven fighter. Other proposed improvements included internal self-sealing full cells, the ability to carry external wing-mounted fuel tanks, and armament consisting of two nose-mounted .50-caliber machine guns (or a pair of 20mm cannons) and four .50-caliber machine guns located in the wing roots. Based on Grumman's proposal, the Navy readily signed on for the production of two XF7F-1 prototypes 30 June 1941, which coincidently was the same day as the approval for two XF6F-1 Hellcat prototypes. The entry of the United States into WWII, coupled with the Navy's need for a replacement for its F4F Wildcat in the Pacific, placed restrictions on which project Grumman could concentrate on at any given time.[5]

The XF6F-1 became the Grumman engineering team's top priority, and further serious development of the XF7F-1 did not resume until late spring 1942, with the construction of a wooden mockup. As months went by, Grumman modified or deleted some of the original design concepts. Modifications consisted of dropping the requirement for counter-rotating propellers, switching from Curtiss Electric to Hamilton Standard Super Hydromatic, constant-speed propellers, updating the engines, and increasing the armament package. By summer 1943, after discussions with the Navy, a major overhaul of engine requirements occurred with the proposal to replace the 1,800hp Wright Cyclone GR-2600-14 engines

The Grumman XF5F-1 Skyrocket program began in 1938 and was a radical departure from conventional bi-wing, single-engine naval fighter aircraft in service at the time. Aircraft's colors are aluminum with yellow-orange upper wing surfaces. (Grumman History Center via Roger Davis)

Overhead view of the silver-painted XP-50 with black wing walkways, anti-glare panel, and upper engine nacelles. Sleek knife-like forward fuselage and tricycle landing gear closely resemble that of the future F7F. (Grumman History Center via Roger Davis)

XP-50 taxis on the grass at Grumman's Bethpage, Long Island, facility near New York in the spring of 1941. This frontal view of the aircraft shows its slim fuselage and duel engines, which nearly mirror those of the Tigercat, except for the twin-tail configuration. (Grumman History Center via Roger Davis)

Wooden mockup of the XF7F-1 was ready for inspection by the Navy mid-1942. Completion of the mockup took nearly a year after the Navy ordered construction of two prototypes, since many of the company's engineers were sent to work on the F6F Hellcat project. (Grumman History Center via Roger Davis)

Completed mockup of the XF7F-1, 12 October 1942, appears to have the standard aircraft colors of olive drab upper surfaces and grey under surfaces with black propeller spinners. Mockup's stub right wing extends only to the wing-fold hinge line. (Grumman History Center via Roger Davis)

with Pratt & Whitney R-2800-22Ws, since the latter's smaller diameter could fit in the prototype's engine nacelles. However, a shortage of -22s resulted in the installation of the R-2800-27s on the first prototype, with the provision of installing the -22s on the second. This change reduced the Tigercat's high altitude performance. During the selection process for the engines, the prototype included an updated armament package. The wing-root .50-caliber machine guns were eliminated in favor of four 20mm cannons and the number of nose-mounted .50-calber mounted machine guns doubled from two to four. This armament combination gave the Tigercat unequaled offensive punch against air and ground targets.[6]

Throughout the XF7F's development, from engineering drawings to mockup and a prototype, the aircraft remained nameless. During early flight testing, the design and test team chose the name *Tomcat* for the XF7F, since such a feline conducts his work at night, as was the aircraft's intended purpose, and the name was sent to BuAer for approval, only to have the Navy reject the idea because the term denoted "feline promiscuity." The follow up name *Tigercat*, however, was accepted. Grumman resurrected the name *Tomcat* many years later for the company's F-14.

The first prototype, powered by R-2800-27s, began taxi tests in late October 1943, followed by an accidental flight test on 2 November by Bob Hall who, while conducting a high-speed taxi run, briefly became airborne. The first official flight test, again with Bob Hall at the controls, took place the following day. Hall conducted four more flights before turning flight test duties over to Corky Meyer, with successful flights continuing through 1944, which proved to Grumman and the Navy that the Tigercat had extremely impressive high speed performance and maneuverability with a rate-of-climb twice as fast as the F6F.[7]

The second prototype, with the R-2800-22W single stage, two-speed, supercharged engines was flown for the first time by Grumman test pilot Corky Meyer on 2 March 1944 and was put through an extensive series of flight and wind tunnel testing. Tests conducted at Ames Aeronautical Laboratory at Moffett Field, California, found stability and control issues involving the vertical tail assembly, in addition to identifying a potential deadly fault involving spin recovery characteristics. Bob Hall proposed redesigning the vertical tail to reduce excess dihedral drag, improve stability and control, and improve single-engine takeoff speed. A new vertical tail approximately 25 percent larger than the original was fitted onto the prototype, and Grumman test pilot George E. Cooper, in cooperation with Howard L. Turner, tested it at the facility's 40-by-80-foot wind tunnel. Testing revealed that the new tail provided the aircraft better latitude and longitudinal stability and control. Data obtained from these tests were used in future modifications for the F7F-3 variant. Further wind tunnel tests for spin recovery showed an alarming tendency for the aircraft to become unrecoverable after more than two spins, when it would suddenly assume a nose-down attitude and then enter a flat spin. Test pilot Corky Meyer, later to become Grumman's chief test pilot of jet aircraft, validated those wind tunnel tests while conducting a spin demonstration flight:[8]

> At one and a half turns from right or left spin entries, the F7F's nose tended to rise during the last portion of the spin, and it took …one-and-a-half turns for recovery after instant full anti-spin control application.

Meyer then decided to test the aircraft's responsiveness by trying two spins, but was barely able to recover after completing the second spin.

The second XF7F-1 is prepared for test runs at the NACA Ames wind tunnel. The propellers were removed and all wing and engine nacelle openings were sealed to verify the aircraft's aerodynamics. The technician under the starboard engine nacelle is installing test equipment. (Grumman History Center via Roger Davis)

Three quarter view of the second XF7F-1 prototype flown for the first time 2 March 1944 by famed Grumman test pilot Corky Meyer. Note the gun ports are sealed and the aircraft sports a nose-mounted pitot tube. The second prototype, identified by its high antenna mast aft of the cockpit incorporated in production Tigercats. The First experimental model had a shorter mast. (Grumman History Center via Roger Davis)

"The nose was definitely rising toward a flat, uncontrollable spin in the second turn before recovery controls were applied. The two turns required for recovery seemed to take ages." The Navy and Grumman, after reviewing the results of wind tunnel tests and Corky Meyer's spin demonstration flight, prohibited pilots from conducting all spins and snap rolls, and limited the Tigercat from engaging in more than a two-turn, upright spin.[9]

Even with the issue of spin recovery difficulties, the Navy was impressed with the XF7F's performance and placed an initial order for 500 Tigercats in what Grumman expected to be a total production run of 1,650 aircraft, but only 175 were delivered before the end of WWII. Grumman produced four night fighter versions of the Tigercat between April 1944 and November 1946: the F7F-1, F7F-2N, F7F-3N, and F7F-4N. The F7F-1 and -2 were delivered to Marine units prior to the end of WWII.

F7F-1N AND F7F-2N

The single-seat F7F-1 was the first series of Tigercat to roll off the assembly line beginning 29 April 1944, with production ending at 34 units (BuNos 80259-80293) on 31 October of that year, when Grumman switched over to the -2. The aircraft was initially designated as the -1 without reference to being equipped for nocturnal operations, but an F7F pilot manual dated 15 March 1945 does list the aircraft as an F7F-1N. The -1N vas equipped with AN/APS-6 air intercept radar, with the dish installed in the nose, above the nose-gun package, and with the ID-32/APS radarscope installed in the center of the instrument panel, with the main control unit C-46/APS-6 located on the right side of the panel and the auxiliary control unit C-47/APS-6 on the left. The F7F-1 was heavier, but 27mph faster than the prototype, and had greater range, but with a slightly lower service ceiling.

Grumman took the third F7F-1 off the assembly line (BuNo 80261) and converted it to the X7F-2 in July 1944 by removing the rear 80-gallon fuselage tank and installing a radar operator's station housing the APS-6 radar scope, with the C-46/APS-6 located on the left side and the C-47/APS-6 on the left. The pilot's instrument panel retained the scope and added the SA-38/APS-32 switch box. Both a single-seat day and two-seat night fighter version of this variant were produced between 31 October 1944 and 8 March 1945, with a total production run of 65 aircraft (BuNo 80294-80358), including the prototype, with the first production -2 flying for the first time 31 October 1944. Standard armament for the -1 and -2 day versions consisted of four fixed .50-caliber machine guns installed in the lower forward section of the fuselage and four M-2 20mm cannons installed in the wing panels. The M-3 (T-31) 20mm cannons were installed on one -1 (BuNo 80264) and all subsequent -2s. Ammunition capacity was 400 rounds per machine gun and 200 rounds per cannon. In contrast to the F7F-1, the installation of wing and centerline bomb and rocket launchers allowed the -2 to carry up to eight 5-inch HVAR rockets, two 1,000-pound bombs, a torpedo, or Tiny Tim rockets.

First production F7F-1 was delivered to the Navy 29 April 1944. Prop spinners shown here on the fourth production aircraft (Buno. 80262) were deleted early in production, as they ultimately did not improve performance. (Grumman History Center via Roger Davis)

Prototype for the F7F-2N Tigercat (BuNo 80261), pictured here 7 August 1944, came off the assembly line as the third production F7F-1. This aircraft, with a second cockpit for the radar operator, was completed 29 July 1944. (Grumman History Center via Roger Davis)

In-flight photo of an early production F7F-1 without prop spinners. Early examples also featured windows aft of the cockpit and lacked ventral fins located under the aft fuselage, which later became standard on production aircraft. (Grumman History Center via Roger Davis)

Three-quarter rear view of 80261, with the aft radar operator's compartment. The addition of a backseat required removing one internal fuel cell. (Grumman History Center via Roger Davis)

F7F-2N prototype in flight, displaying engine exhaust streaks across the top of the wings. Coloring was overall Glossy Sea Blue with white tail codes. (Emil B Library, NMNA)

Opposite:
The F7F-2N pilot's instrument panel of BuNo 80324 with the Mk 8 gunsight located directly above the APS-6 radar scope. (Grumman Heritage Tommy Thomason)

RADIO COMPASS
INTENSE
FOCUS
SIGNAL LEVEL
BUAERO. NO. 80324
WING FOLDING
SAFETY CONTROL
LEFT
RIGHT
FUEL BOOSTER
WATER INJECTION
OFF
AIR
DISTRIBUTOR
FEET

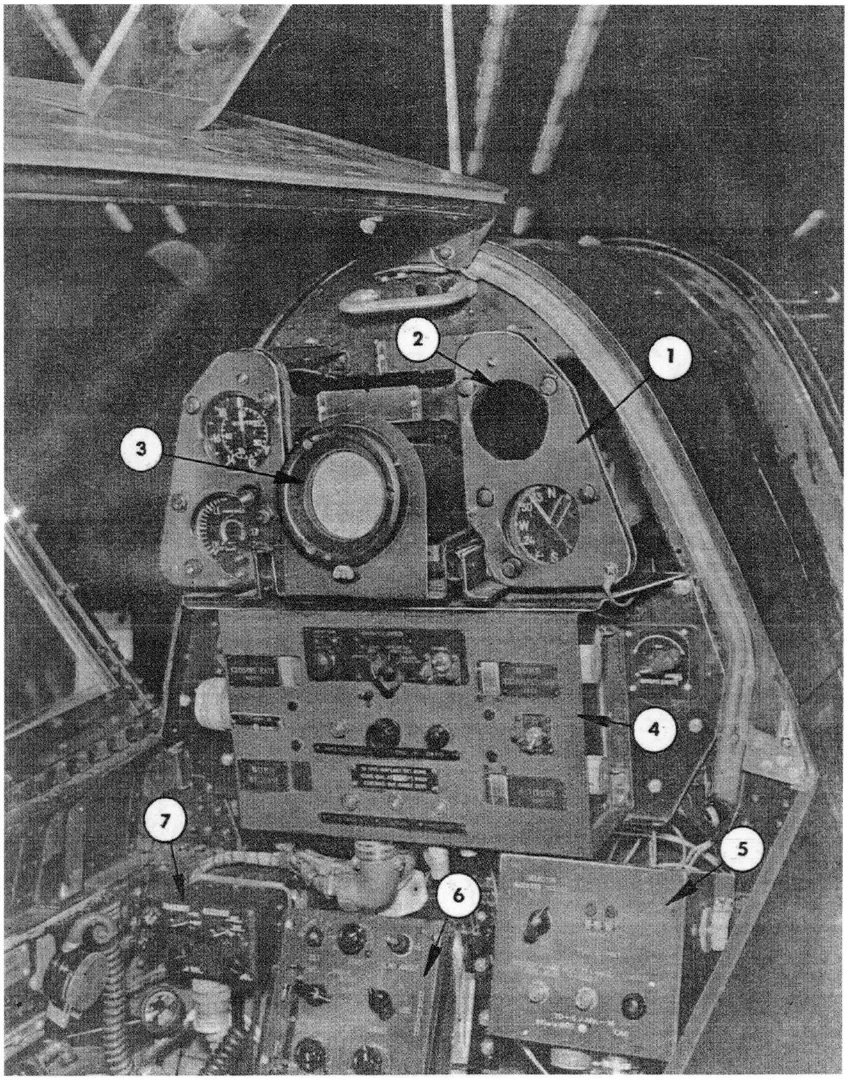

1. Instrument Panel.
2. APA Equipment.
3. ID-158/APS-19 Indicator.
4. C-275/APA-16 Control.
5. TD-6/APA-16 Control.
6. C-282/APS-19 Control.
7. C-174/AIC-4 Control.

Figure 59B—Radar Operator's Cockpit—Looking Forward (F7F-4N Only)

View of F7F-2N radar operator's compartment with the APS-6 radar equipment. The operator usually installed a removable hood over the screen to block ambient light.

F7F-1/2 Carrier Qualification Trials

In April 1944, the Navy conducted initial carrier suitability and structural integrity tests with the XF7F at NAS Mustin Field in Philadelphia, PA. Since the original plan called for the Tigercat to serve as a carrier-based fighter, a prototype was equipped with a rigid Y-frame tailhook configuration. However, the aircraft proved unsatisfactory for carrier use because of the tailhook's design and weak airframe, as it suffered structural damage even during field arresting gear testing.

The Navy temporarily abandoned the plan to operate the Tigercat from carriers and decided to equip Marine land-based squadrons with the aircraft for use in close air support. In the interim, production F7F-1s were fitted with a different tailhook, structural modifications were made, and successful carrier trials were conducted by the Ship Experimental Unit (SEU) from the USS *Shangri-La* (CV 38) in November 1944, but further ship-board use of the -1 never materialized. However, the -2N also qualified for carrier duty, with pilots of VF(N)-52 conducting carrier qualifications aboard the USS *Antietam*, 8 April 1945.[10]

Chapter 2

Project Affirm and First Combat Operations

They resented being guinea pigs in what their friends looked upon as a new experiment in suicide.

- **Lt. Cmdr. Turner F. Caldwell** *on the feelings of naval pilots selected for night flying.*

A principle advocate for the use of night fighters by the U.S. Navy was Cdr. William E.G. Taylor, a naval aviator who served with the RAF flying night interception missions during the Battle of Britain and also served as the first commanding officer of the American volunteer Eagle Squadron. In January 1942, the Navy assigned Taylor the task of establishing a training unit for carrier-based night fighters. On 18 April, the Navy formally established the program at Naval Air Station (NAS) Quonset Point, Rhode Island, under the name Project Argus, which changed to Project Affirm in August. Night fighting requirements for the Navy were fundamentally different from the Army's, since carrier operations precluded the use of large and heavy twin-engine aircraft, so they looked for a single-seat fighter to conduct nocturnal operations: the F4U and F6F. Affirm served a duel role during its existence: training pilots and fighter directors, and to research, experiment, develop, and evaluate all aspects of airborne night operations. The first aviators arrived in November 1942 for night fighting indoctrination, which coincided with the establishment of the Marine's first night fighter squadron.

On 20 January 1942, Capt. Ralph E. Davision, Assistant Chief Bureau of Aeronautics, committed BuAer: "The job of the Marines was to seize a beachhead and hold it until replaced by the Army. To do this successfully, night fighters would be an absolute necessity." Capt. Davison's recommendation was followed in May by a memorandum from Capt. Colston Dyer to the Director of Aviation urging the formation of a training unit for night fighters. Dyer was a communications specialist and one of the original American officers sent to observe British night fighter tactics a year before. The Commandant of the Marine Corps, Lt. Gen. Thomas Holcomb, followed up by issuing his own recommendation on 12 June to the Chief of Naval Operations, Adm. Ernest J. King, stating, "Air operations in Europe indicate that as our day fighter superiority is established, the enemy will inevitably be forced to resort to bombing at night. In order to meet this development, it is recommended that the dates for the formation of Marine Corps night fighter squadrons be advanced to the period 1 January-30 June 1943."[1]

General Holcomb's statement proved to be accurate several months later. After losses of aircraft and veteran pilots at the Battle of Midway in June 1942 and American landings in the Solomon Islands 7 August, the Japanese began sending fighters and bombers to harass Allied naval forces and island installations as a means to limit the further loss of aircraft, pilots, and aircrew. The necessity to defend against such night aerial attacks by the Japanese brought about the U.S. Navy's desire to provide adequate protection of friendly forces, via fighters with nocturnal ability, before enemy aircraft could get within range to strike Allied naval and ground forces. Admiral William "Bull" Halsey supported Holcomb's assessment in a 27 December 1942 dispatch and stressed that night fighters be dispatched at the earliest possible time to counter the threat. Halsey did not realize the first Marine night fighter squadron had not yet received its first night fighter, and it wasn't destined to arrive in the Pacific until the following September.[2]

However, the Marine Corps had trouble selecting an aircraft for its first night fighter, with possibilities ranging from the P-61, P-70, A-20, A-26A, SB2C, F4U-1, and PV-1 to the British Beaufighter and Mosquito. The preferred aircraft of the Marines was the P-61, which was still under development, or the proven British aircraft, but those were unavailable when the first Marine night fighter squadron formed. Lacking everything but desire, the Marines commissioned VMF(N)-531 as its first night fighter squadron at Marine Corps Air Station (MCAS) Cherry Point, North Carolina, 16 November 1942, with Major Frank H. Schwable in command. The CO of the newly established squadron had also been an early proponent of night fighters, having observed RAF operations prior to Pearl Harbor. The five officers and 21 enlisted men that initially formed the squadron operated out of an unheated hangar with two North American SNJ-4 trainers later augmented by Brewster SB2A-2 and SB2A-4 dive bombers. Establishment of a night fighter squadron proved to be an easier endeavor than actually fielding a combat-ready unit, since the Navy and Marine Corps at the time lacked experienced personnel, electronic equipment, and, above all, the right type of aircraft to do the job.

While Maj. Schwable was in the early stages of trying to deliver on Adm. Halsey's request for night fighters, the Marines sent six officers and five enlisted men to England in February 1943 for training with the RAF in all phases of night fighting. The officers were Lt. Col. Edward W. Montgomery, Majors Guy M. Morrow and Marion M. Magruder, and Captains Homer G. Hutchinson Jr., Peter D. Lambrecht, and Thomas E. Hicks, Jr. Montgomery led the group and acted as the liaison with the British. Morrow and Magruder went to study GCI operations and to acquire related electronics equipment for the Marines. Maj. Lambrecht and Capt. Hutchinson, Jr., attended training as night fighter pilots, while Hicks was selected for training as an air controller. The five enlisted men in the group went to train as airborne radar operators. Training of the future Marine night fighter pilots and radar operators began with a three-week familiarization course at RAF Station Coltishall, followed by operational training with the Beaufighter at RAF Station Cranfield. Training concluded in early May, and the Marines joined RAF Night Fighter Squadron 256 at Sussex, where they flew a number of missions over the English Channel. The experience gained in Britain sold the Marines on the concept of procuring and operating a twin-engine night fighter of their own.[3] On 9 June 1943, BuAer interviewed Montgomery upon his return to the U.S. regarding his experiences with the RAF night fighter program, including the merits of a twin-engine versus a single-engine night fighter:

Commander Harold J. Brow greets Rear Admiral Ralph Davison (left) at Naval Air Station (NAS) Olathe, Kansas, during 13 December 1944. Davison, as Assistant Chief of the U.S. Navy's Bureau of Aeronautics during January 1942, recommended the establishment of a night fighter program. (Cdr. Harold J. Brow Photograph Collection, Emil Buehler Library, NMNA)

The British have done more of this business than anyone else, and I think they've perfected beyond any other country so far. They have found out very definitely that a twin-engine night fighter is a necessity. They've put a tremendous amount of energy and money and time into training the night fighter teams and into ground control and other equipment that will do almost anything if it's properly used, and yet all that equipment and training isn't worth a cent if enemy bombers are not shot down with it.[4]

Officers of VMF(N)-531 at MCAS Cherry Point, NC, 12 December 1942, in front of an SNJ training aircraft. L-R are: Capt. Ross Mickey, Capt. Raymond George, Maj. Edward Hodgson, Lt. Col. Frank Schwable, Maj. John Harsberger, Capt. William Kellum, and 1st Lt. Duane Jenkins. Jenkins and his crew would score the squadron's first two aerial victories in the South Pacific. (Emil Buehler Library, National Naval Aviation Museum)

SB2A-4 in the air in flight near NAS Vero Beach, FL. The Navy employed the Buccaneer mainly as training aircraft, particularly at NAS Vero Beach, FL. VMF(N)-531 conducted training in the type prior to the delivery of the PV-1 Ventura. (Emil Buehler Library, NMNA)

LOCKHEED PV-1 VENTURA

BuAer held a different opinion than that of Montgomery based on testing of both double- and single-engine night fighters. It maintained that standard Navy fighters needed only minor modifications to accommodate the night fighting equipment, which would simplify the problems of training, maintenance, and the supply of spare parts. This position held by the bureau may have been the result of problems encountered a few months earlier by VMF(N)-531. Running out of time, Lt. Col. Schwable went with the only option available to him at the time: the twin-engine Lockheed PV-1 Ventura medium bomber.

The PV-1 began as the Lockheed-Vega Model 37-21-01, a heavier and faster version of the company's Hudson bomber. Powered by a pair of Pratt & Whitney R-1850 S1A4-G Double Wasp air-cooled engines, the aircraft's maximum speed was 312mph. Armament consisted of an internal bomb load of 2,500 pounds and eight .303-in machine guns: two in a Boulton-Paul dorsal turret, two in the rear ventral fuselage, and two fixed in the upper nose. The prototype, designated the Ventura I, first flew 31 July 1941, with most production units going to the British and Commonwealth forces. A change to the Pratt & Whitney R-2800-31 engines and armament resulted in the Ventura II (designated the USAAF B-34/37). Lockheed increased the aircraft's bomb capacity to 3,000 pounds, and the new model featured a Martin upper turret with two .50-caliber machine guns, two fixed .50 and .30-caliber guns in the nose, and two .30-caliber guns in the rear ventral fuselage. The Navy became interested in acquiring the Ventura as a patrol aircraft, since it was considerably faster and more heavily armed than the fleet's Consolidated PBY Catalina. To meet Navy requirements, the company installed additional fuel tanks to extend range, along with additional navigational instruments for over-water operations and the ASD-1 search radar. The navalized version of the Ventura was given the PV-1 designation. The Marine Corps selected the PV-1 by default as the service's first night fighter, since it was the only aircraft in the inventory at the time that could house the Mk IV (SCR-540) radar system. Military technicians at Quonset Point continued modifying PV-1s selected for conversion by updating the electrical system and installing radar, IFF, and VHF radio. Personnel at NAS Norfolk, Virginia, replaced the standard .50 and .30-caliber nose guns with a six .50-caliber package, added gunsights, and updated oxygen equipment. While the Marines saw fit to modify the Ventura, the Navy began the process of converting the F4U-1 Corsair and Grumman F6F Hellcat.

NIGHT FIGHTER TRAINING

VMF(N)-531 began receiving the first modified Venturas in February, but conversion of the aircraft and training, however, continued at a snail's pace, with Maj. Schwable reporting only mediocre progress during March. He cited a number of reasons for the delay, ranging from communication problems between ground controllers and aircrew; faulty electrical systems in the PV-1, along with a shortage of spare parts in radars, test equipment, radios, and aircraft. Conversion of the Ventura to a night fighter required extensive modifications, including the installation of new electrical, electronics, and oxygen systems, as well as gunsights. The squadron also lacked experienced pilots and support personnel. He reported that of the 26 pilots assigned to the squadron, all except eight were new and the majority had no instrument training, navigation, or night fighter experience. There was also a shortage of trained radar technicians and air control personnel. To remedy the latter issue, Schwable sent four officers and four enlisted men to the General Electric Company in Syracuse, New York, for instruction on the mobile SCR-527A radar system.[5]

To facilitate training, Marine Night Fighter Group 53 MAG(N)-53 was commissioned 1 April 1943, with newly-promoted Lt. Col. Schwable designated as commanding officer, while Maj. Harshberger assumed command of -531. Establishment of the night air group required splitting personnel and equipment to form two combat squadrons (VMF(N)-531 and -532), along with the formation of both a headquarters squadron and service squadron. Schwable would revert to his status as commanding officer of -531 when it deployed overseas. Subsequent Marine night fighter squadrons -532 to -544 operated under the night air group for advanced training.

The naval side of the program continued to move relatively slowly, mainly due to issues with the Corsair discussed earlier. The Sperry Corporation delivered ten AN/APS-3 radar sets to the Navy in April 1943 and Affirm technicians installed them on F4U-2s that had earlier undergone installation of the wing-mounted radar pod at the Naval Aircraft Factory. Technicians also installed the autopilot, mentioned earlier, to make it easier for the pilot to adjust the radar controls while maintaining steady flight. The arrival of the radar sets coincided with the commissioning of the first night fighter squadron VF(N)-75 on 10 April 1943 at Quonset Point under the leadership of Lt. Commander William J. "Gus" Widhelm. The new skipper, a combat veteran of Midway and Santa Cruz battles and twice the recipient of the Navy Cross, had his work cut out for him. It did not take the CO long to realize that establishing a well-trained night fighter squadron was going to take a considerable

Unlike the Air Force, the Navy and Marine Corps began their night fighter program with existing aircraft in the inventory. First was the Lockheed PV-1 Ventura, modified to carry airborne radar which went into combat in the Pacific with Marine Squadron VMF(N)-531. (Author's Collection)

amount of work. The new squadron consisted of 18 pilots, six ground officers, and 30 enlisted men. Only five pilots had instrument time and all lacked night fighting experience and electronics training. Three of the pilots were qualified in the Corsair, three in the F4F Wildcat, and the rest in SNJs. Four months would elapse before the squadron received the first radar-equipped F4U-2N Corsairs. In the meantime, Widhelm made the decision to split his squadron in two to hasten deployment overseas, leaving half to his executive officer, Lieutenant Commander Richard E. "Chick" Harmer. The night fighter program was an entirely new concept in naval aviation, and with it came problems that Commander Taylor and the newly-commissioned squadron would have to overcome.

In August, the Navy divided Project Affirm into two sections, with the research and development section moving to NAS Patuxent River, Maryland, while pilot training moved to Naval Auxiliary Air Facility (NAAF) Charleston, Rhode Island. The Chief of Naval Operations officially dissolved Project Affirm in late October 1943, as it had fulfilled its purpose of establishing the Navy's night fighter program. At Rhode Island, the training aspect of the program was renamed Night Fighter Training Unit (NFTU); Night Attack and Combat Training Unit Atlantic (NACTUANT) in turn superseded NFTU in November 1944. By the beginning of 1944, training had become better organized and equipped with the best electronics equipment and aircraft of the period. The program evolved to the point where pilots, selected for training, attended a nine-month course consisting of four phases. The first phase consisted of pre-electronics training at NAAS Kingsville, TX, for five weeks; followed by six weeks of electronics at NAS Vero Beach, Florida; then nine weeks of squadron training at NAS Boca Chica, Florida; and ending with nine weeks group training starting at NAAF Westerly, NAAF Charleston, and ending at Martha's Vineyard, Massachusetts. In the New England area, squadrons completed group training and carrier qualifications. Marine night fighter pilots, after training at Kingsville and Vero Beach, went on to either Cherry Point, North Carolina, or Eagle Mountain Lake, Texas. At Charleston, flight operations mimicked what a pilot would experience on a carrier. One runway was equipped with a catapult and arresting gear for night launching and landing of aircraft. To preserve the night vision of pilots, the entire facility was blackout from sundown to dawn. The only lights permitted outside were red runway lights and aircraft wing-tip lights, while lights in the control tower, ready room, and even the heads (bathrooms) were dimmed. Instructors stressed the importance of maintaining night vision with pilots wearing red-lensed flight goggles for 30 minutes in ordinary light or remaining in complete darkness for 30 minutes before climbing into the cockpit.[6]

EARLY LAND-BASED OPERATIONS

The first two night fighter squadrons to enter combat were VMF(N)-531 and VF(N)-75. Lt. Col. Schwable, as -531's CO, was under a considerable amount of pressure to deliver his unit to the Pacific during the latter part of 1943. Time was precious, and he did not have the luxury to wait for a suitable multi or single-engine night fighter. There was no other choice but to retain the Lockheed PV-1 Ventura with all of its inadequacies. Lt. Col. Montgomery may have been sold on the idea of a twin-engine night fighter based on his experience with the British, but the CO of -531 wasn't too thrilled about taking the PV-1 Ventura into combat for a number of reasons. It was considered too slow as a fighter, with a top speed of 312mph and a rated service ceiling of 26,000 feet; the nose guns had a tendency to malfunction; radar and radio equipment were prone to failure; and the aircraft was not allowed to fly above 15,000 feet due to a faulty oxygen system – the type installed at Norfolk. The squadron's commanding officer recorded his dislike of the Ventura in a formal memorandum dated 28 May 1943:

> If it is the desire of the Bureau to have this unit proceed to the combat zone in an aeroplane that is admittedly makeshift for the job, with guns that may or may not fire, instruments that are difficult to read, and with radar that so far has an average of one out of three working, this unit will plan accordingly and accept, without comment, the experimental installations furnished.[7]

He, along with 30 men and six Ventura bombers, left San Diego aboard USS *Long Island* (CVE 1) on 1 August, bound for the Russell Islands via Pearl Harbor and Espiritu Santos. The GCI equipment, with associated personnel, had left two days earlier, and a second group of five aircraft with aircrew and ground personnel would join the squadron 11 September. The squadron arrived at Banika, in the Russell Islands, on 11 September, and began night patrols immediately, while the CO pondered the situation with the Ventura. In a letter written to Maj. Dyer 2 August 1943 he wrote:

> It is only if the Japs are more stupid than anybody thinks they are, and come down to 15,000 ft do we even stand a chance to knock them down – if we can go fast enough to catch them! If we lack speed, expert vectoring may put us in a position to do some good, but if the Japs fly thousands of feet higher than our planes can physically be pushed up to, there's not one damned thing on God's green earth we can do about it.[8]

Schwable believed he had three alternatives to make his squadron successful: first, strip the PV-1 of its top turret and guns to achieve altitude; second, borrow an Army P-38, install a radar whose operator would sit behind the pilot; or third, write BuAer requesting single-engine fighters with radar be sent to him quickly.[9] The colonel's frustration grew as the squadron lost an aircraft and its three-man crew while on a test flight – they simply disappeared without a trace. Between 14 September and 27 October, -531 PV-1s attempted to close on 17 enemy contacts, but came up empty primarily due to the inexperience of the ground controllers and from enemy aircraft dropping small pieces of aluminum foil called "window" to disrupt American radar.[9]

Schwable's squadron would lay claim to the first Japanese aircraft brought down by a Marine night fighter, but it was not

Grumman F6F-5N Hellcats (from front to rear 7-6, 7-7, 7-8, and 7-9) over Quonset Point, RI, where designated night squadrons participated in advance training before overseas deployment. The caption on the back of the original photograph has the date August 1945, but the squadron was disestablished in October 1944. (Emil Buehler Library, NMNA)

Three F6F-5Ns from a night fighter Operational Training Unit (OTU) based at NAS Vero Beach, FL, flying in echelon formation 23 December 1944. Vero Beach was one of several facilities used for USN night fighter training during WWII. (Robert L. Lawson Photographic Collection, Emil Buehler Library, NMNA)

Aspiring night fighter pilots during training at NAS Vero Beach, FL. The pilot on the bottom left is Ensign Philip T. McDonald, who would go on to serve with VF(N)-91 and score four confirmed aerial kills and one probable 13 August 1945. (Philip T. McDonald Collection via Thomas E. Doll)

Close-up of F6F-5N 7-6 in overall Glossy Sea Blue with yellow codes on the fuselage and vertical stabilizer. The number "7" represents the last digit for VF(N)-107 and "6" the in-squadron aircraft number. (Robert F. Dorr).

Opposite:
VMF(N)-531 Lockheed PV-1 Ventura BuNo 29854 on Vella Lavella, in the Solomon Islands, 13 January 1944, with the name CHLOE. This aircraft with tri-color paint scheme and black aircraft number 53 on the cowling was assigned to Lt. Col. Frank H. Schwable. The Ventura was not Col. Schawble's ideal choice for a night fighter, who regarded it as inferior to British designs. (Tailhook Association)

the first for the naval service; that distinction went to a VF(N)-75 F4U-2 Corsair.

The first radar-guided kill for -531 occurred 13 November 1943, when Capt. Duane R. Jenkins conducted a GCI-vectored kill of a Mitsubishi G4M (Betty) bomber 50 miles southwest of Torokinata, Bouganville, on the evening of 13-14 November. Jenkins and his crew were flying Night Combat Air Patrol (NCAP) over Task Force 39, approximately 50 miles southwest of Torokinata, Bougainville, when GCI vectored him towards a single bogey shadowing the convoy. This time the air-ground team worked perfectly, with the ground controller providing updated changes in the bogey's heading and altitude. R/O Technical Sergeant (TSgt) Charles H. Stout, monitoring the onboard radar, picked up the contact at a range of a mile-and-a quarter at the same altitude of 6,000 feet with the night fighter's speed 20 knots (23mph) faster than the quarry's 160 knots (184mph). Moments later, the bogey came into sight and Jenkins recognized it as a Betty; the time was 0418 hours. The PV-1 closed from behind, and from 800 feet Jenkins gave the bomber a four-second burst with the nose guns and the enemy aircraft's engine nacelle flamed. The aircraft then went into a shallow dive, and Jenkins caught it again with a short burst into the port wing root. He fired a third burst, and Sgt. Thomas J. Glennon, in the top turret, joined in with a two-second burst into the Betty's fuselage. The Japanese bomber went into a steep dive and exploded upon hitting the water. The entire encounter had taken two minutes. Two more Japanese aircraft would fall to the guns of Marine Venturas during the remaining months of 1943. Schwable's squadron claimed another nine air-to-air kills between January and May 1944, with two crews each scoring four victories: those of Lt. Col. Schwable and his executive officer, Maj. Harshberger.

At the conclusion of -531's tour, ComAirSols Brig. Gen. Earl W. Barnes praised the unit's record, noting the dramatic reduction in enemy night air activity. Despite the squadron's success of 12 confirmed kills with the Ventura, Col. Schwable continued to hold the aircraft in low regard, and in his historical summary of VMF(N)-531, he made clear his distaste for the PV-1 as a night fighter. The PV-1 "is not and never will be a good night fighter."[10]

A crewman pushing one of the props on PV-1 Eight Ball (BuNo 29811), flown on Vella La Vella in 1944. The names painted on the middle of the nose area are a memorial tribute to Capt. Duane R. Jenkins, TSgt. Charles H. Stout, and Sgt. Thomas J. Glennon, who were killed in action 3 December 1943. (Eugene S. "Mule" Holmberg via Tailhook Association)

View of Col Frank Schwable's second aircraft (identity unknown), showing four kill markings, which tied the number of victories scored by his Maj. John Harshberger's crew. VMF(N)-531 scored 12 confirmed kills between November 1944 and May 1944. Col. Schwable supported the use of a twin-engine aircraft with a pilot and radar operator as a night fighter and believed a lone pilot in a single-seat fighter would find using radar gear too difficult to use during an interception. (Eugene S. "Mule" Holmberg via Tailhook Association)

Schwable and others who had observed and trained with the British continued to hold the view that a twin-engine fighter was far superior than a single-engine fighter. He based this view on the belief that a pilot/radar operator team would be more successful, since the pilot could focus his entire energy on the pursuit while being coached towards the target by the radar operator. The performance of the British, with their twin-engine night fighters and the Army Air Force's P-61 Black Widow, does provide ample evidence that such aircraft were highly successful in the European and Pacific Theaters. Colonel Schwable would see the Marine Corps adopt a twin-engine night fighter concept in the form of the Grumman F7F Tigercat. However, the legacy of USN and USMC night fighter operations during WWII lies with the nocturnal variants of the single-engine F6F Hellcat, and to a lesser degree, the F4U Corsair.

Chapter 3

U.S. Navy Night Air Operations (September 1943-September 1944)

Young man, you use your night fighters in the next war, I'll use my antiaircraft batteries in this war

- An unknown admiral replying to an appeal from a pilot to use night fighters.

The Navy entered night fighter combat operations when Lt. Cmdr. Gus Widhelm's VF(N)-75 arrived in the Pacific at Espiritu Santos on 11 September 1943, with six F4U-2Ns, pilots, and support personnel. Two weeks later, on 23 September, the squadron established a base of operations at Munda, with dusk to dawn patrols beginning 2 October in conjunction with -531. Heckling raids by solitary Japanese aircraft nicknamed "Washing Machine Charlies" hit Munda more than a dozen times during the latter half of October without interception from the two American night fighter squadrons. Action for the night fighters picked up considerably when the Allied forces launched Operation Cherry Blossom on 1 November, with the U.S. Marine Third Division landing at Cape Torokina, Bougainville, with additional landings occurring between 6-19 November.

The first successful destruction of an enemy aircraft by a Navy or Marine night fighter went to one of Widhelm's pilots during the night of 31 October-1 November. Several times that night, Corsairs scrambled to meet incoming enemy aircraft, but all except one failed due to malfunctioning of the airborne radar sets on the pursuing fighters. However, one Japanese bomber was not as lucky, as the VF(N)-75 scored its first kill by a radar-equipped navy night fighter. Lt. Hugh D. O'Neill's Corsair lifted off the runway at 2300 hours after ground control picked up a target located approximately 12 miles southeast of Vella Lavella, in the Solomon Islands. Visibility was excellent and O'Neill picked up the exhaust flames of his quarry, a G4M (Betty) bomber, at 10,000 feet, flying in an opposite heading. They passed each other with the Corsair 2,000 feet above the bomber. O'Neill conducted a diving turn, came up behind the Betty, and fired a short burst from 200 yards. A momentary flash of flame came from the bomber's starboard engine as the Corsair came back around for another pass at 7,500 feet. The fighter's .50-caliber guns opened up from a distance of 150 yards, sending a lethal curtain of fire towards the enemy. Both engines erupted in flames, and the stricken Betty banked sharply before diving into the water, where it exploded on impact.

VF(N)-75 suffered from six-week drought between the squadron's first kill on 31 October and its second on 11 December. The squadron stationed a detachment of F4U-2s at Torokin with -531, where hunting significantly improved over the course of six weeks; VF(N)-75 claimed five aircraft destroyed in the air along with two probables. During the evening of 11 December, Lt. O'Neill scored his second and final kill, but under bizarre circumstances. O'Neill scrambled at 2115 hours after friendly PT boats reported a Betty flying at 1,000 feet off Motupena Point, Bougainville, apparently on a mission to attack the patrol craft. The night fighter climbed to 1,000 feet, and the pilot test fired his guns when he was approximately 12 miles from Torokins. PT boats in the vicinity saw O'Neil fire his guns and then saw the Betty going down in flames. The PT boats and anti-aircraft batteries claimed they did not fire at the bomber, so O'Neill claimed he was aided by Superman.

The squadron's tally increased two days later, with Lt. J.S. Hill damaging a Nakajima A6M2-N (Rufe), a float plane version of the famed A6M (Zeke) fighter. Hill followed up by bringing down two more float planes on 15-16 December. His first kill came just before midnight, after obtaining a vector from Torokina. The Corsair's radar locked on to a bogey flying at 5,000 feet 20 miles from base. Hill came in too fast at first and had to come back around, throttling back and dropping behind the float plane. The Japanese pilot began a tight diving turn as the Corsair closed in for the kill, firing a short three-second burst and hitting the fuselage. The fighter's blinding muzzle flashes impaired Hill's night vision and he lost contact, but the float plane was confirmed destroyed. Hill's second kill came the following evening at the same altitude and nearly the exact time as the first. The Corsair closed unobserved and opened fire, with the night fighter's rounds striking the wings and fuselage of the Rufe, causing a sheet of flame to envelop the float plane's cockpit as it dove into the water.

Widhelm's Torokina detachment brought in the New Year with Lt. C.L. Penner destroying one Aichi D3A (Val) dive bomber and damaging another in a three-minute encounter during the evening of 1 January. Scrambled at 2135 when GCI picked up a bogey at 21 miles and closing, Penner climbed to 6,500 feet and made radar, then visual contact four minutes after departure. The night fighter closed within 750 feet and opened fire, with flashes seen hitting the fuselage. The Val took evasive action by climbing into a cloud bank and Penner could not reestablish radar contact. Moments later, ground control sent the Corsair towards another target. Penner rapidly gained on the bogey and saw a Val illuminated by searchlights. At a range of 250 yards he squeezed the trigger, but only one of his guns functioned; it was enough to send the dive bomber down in flames. The last score for VF(N)-75 occurred the following evening on 13 January, when Lt. R.L. Jones was vectored during patrol after GCI picked up a bogey at 15 miles, altitude 5,500 feet. Jones picked up the aircraft on his radar below him at a distance of a mile and closed in. The Corsair approach was too fast, forcing Jones to chop the throttle, and when he did, the enemy spotted the fighter's exhaust sparks and opened fire. Jones fired a short burst at 100 yards as the Val started to make evasive diving turns. He swung the fighter back around and fired another burst and the dive bomber went down in flames.VF(N)-75, the Navy's only land-based night fighter squadron of WWII, departed later in the month and returned to the U.S. for reorganization, where it reformed 25 July 1944 at NAAF Westerly. Training began with a compliment of F6F-3s; however, three months later, on 2 October, the squadron was decommissioned at NAAF Charleston.

CARRIER OPERATIONS (NOVEMBER 1943-SEPTEMBER 1944)

By November 1943, some 19 months after its establishment, Project Affirm had yet to supply the fleet with a radar-equipped night fighter unit. Several were in the advance stages of training, but would not be ready to deploy for several months. In the interim, one industrious naval pilot had enough of nighttime aerial raids by Japanese aircraft and decided to embark on a plan of his own. Lt. Cmdr. Edward "Butch" O'Hare, the Navy's first ace of the war and the recipient of the Medal of Honor, established four Hellcat-Avenger teams, referred to as *Bat Teams*, aboard USS *Enterprise* (CV 6) during the fall of 1943. It was a hunter-killer concept with a TBF-1CD Avenger, equipped with air-to-surface Type B radar (ASB), used to locate and guide two conventional F6F-3 fighters towards hostile aircraft. The first use of the team occurred off the Gilbert Islands during the American landings on Tarawa, Makin, and Apamama.

As part of Task Group 50.2 (TG-50.2), *Enterprise* arrived off Makin Atoll on the morning of 19 November and began conducting air operations. Japanese land-based aircraft based in the Marshalls began appearing on the fleet's radar screens during the afternoon when a Nakajima E8N1 reconnaissance seaplane, code-name "Dave," was shot down 23 miles from the task force. Radar tracked groups of bogies over the course of several days during pre-dawn hours, but none of them came within 50 miles of the American ships. It was decided on the 24th to allow Lt. Cmdr. O'Hare, commanding officer of Air Group Six, and Lt. Cmdr. John L. Phillips, skipper of Torpedo Squadron Six (VT-6), to attempt night airborne interceptions with their *Bat Teams*. The *Enterprise* launched two teams early the following morning: one with O'Hare in a Hellcat and Phillips in an Avenger between 0258 and 0237 hours. The Avengers picked up hostile aircraft on their screens, but they were too far out to allow the radar-less Hellcats to make an interception. It was a different story the following evening.

Fighters from *Belleau Wood* (CVL 24) intercepted and shot down a Betty at 1737 hours that was apparently shadowing the American task force. Radar began picking up multiple bogies shortly afterward and the *Enterprise* launched a *Bat Team* of two Hellcats piloted by O'Hare and Ens. Warren A. Skon of VF-2 and a TBF-1C flown by Lt. Cmdr. Phillips, with Lt. (jg) Hazen B. Rand as the R/O and turret gunner Aviation Ordnance Mate First Class (AOM1c) Alvin B. Kernan. Vectors from the carrier's Fighter Director Officer (FDO) and by Lt. Rand guided Phillips into a visual sighting of a Betty's engine exhaust. The *Bat Team* had encountered a large formation of Japanese bombers concealed in the darkness and headed towards the fleet. Ensuing chaos followed, as Phillips shot down two bombers within five minutes using his two wing-mounted .50-caliber machine guns. The team broke up the enemy formation, but O'Hare was lost sometime during the

A radar-equipped TBM-1D Avenger produced by General Motors was the equivalent of the TBF-1D. The U.S. Navy's first night fighter strategy required the use of a radar-equipped TBF/TBM-Avenger/F6F team, with the Avenger vectoring the Hellcat in for a kill. (Robert L. Lawson Photograph Collection via Emil Buehler Library, NMNA)

aerial battle, possibly from the rounds fired from a Betty's Japanese nose gunner. The hunter-killer concept of the *Bat Team* proved the feasibility of tracking and destroying enemy aircraft, but it cost the lives of the Navy's most celebrated aviators. A post-action analysis of the mission pointed out the need for carrier-based night fighters, but also pointed out the difficulty of conducting such operations in regards to fatigue and stress among the deck crew:

> The success of this night fighter section in breaking up a very formidable night attack indicates that great stress and effort should be placed upon rushing adequate equipment and specialized training of personnel for the purpose. The Japanese are apparently equipped and intend to attack our carrier task forces at night with torpedoes. The use of night fighters to combat this threat has proven to be practicable; now they must be developed in quantity and quality to meet the scale of attack. While this carrier operated the night fighters along with daytime operations, it is very apparent that the crew will be completely worn down if kept in the ready status for operations from daybreak and around the clock through the night. It is recommended that patrols of the day be regulated so that a carrier may fly all the patrols in the morning and be in a standby status in the afternoon or *vice versa*, and if the carrier has the launching of night fighters during the night, it should be a standby in the day so the deck crews can get a little rest and food.[1]

Several members of the carrier's flight deck crew suffered injuries during night operations that might not have occurred if the men had adequate rest. The problem of fatigue and stress among deck crews continued to be a major issue as the fleet began receiving radar-equipped F6F Hellcat detachments. The arrival of night air units and their specialized role ran counter to normal carrier activities and, consequently, the new arrivals encountered a considerable amount of resistance.

Carrier-borne night fighter operations with radar-equipped fighters began with the deployment of VF(N)-101 and -76 aboard carriers of TF-38 in January 1944 for operations in the Central Pacific. VF(N)-101, which was formed by splitting VF(N)-75 in half with Cmdr. Widhelm, taking his section to the Pacific and leaving what was remaining at Quonset Point to his executive officer, Lt. Cmdr. Chick Harmer. What was left were 14 relatively inexperienced pilots (13 were newly minted ensigns) and no radar-equipped Corsairs. The unit practiced flying and gunnery with conventional F4U-1s while receiving radar training in a radar-equipped SNB that was received in September, followed by two more SNBs and six F4U-2s in October. By December, ten F4U-2s had been received, along with orders for Hawaii, where it was officially commissioned as VF(N)-101 1 January 1944. Pilots practiced day and night landings for the next two weeks at NAS Barbers Point, Hawaii, with day landings on *Enterprise* and night landings on *Essex* (CV 9). Harmer split the squadron again, this time taking four aircraft and six pilots aboard the *Enterprise* – nicknamed the "Big E" – as part of Air Group 10, while his exec, Lt. Cecil "Swede" Kullberg, took the other half and went aboard USS *Intrepid* (CV 11) as part of Air Group 6.

VF(N)-76 formed the other night fighter element of the Pacific fleet in early 1944. New Yorker Lt. Cmdr. Evan P. "Sweet Pete" Aurand, Annapolis, class of 1938 and the son of an Army Major General, formed VF(N)-76 as the Navy's first Hellcat night fighter squadron 15 July 1943. Aurand was a veteran combat pilot, receiving the Navy Cross for sinking three Japanese ships off New Guinea on 10 March 1942 while

VF(N)-101 Vought F4U-2 Corsair #10 is postioned for launch from USS *Enterprise* 6 January 1944. VF(N)-101 had the distinction of being the first Navy carrier-based night fighter squadron and the only such unit to conduct combat operations with the F4U-2. (Lt. Cmdr. Robert B. Brunson via Tailhook Association)

VF(N)-101 Detachment A (Det A) Vought F4U-2 Corsair being pushed on *Enterprise's* elevator 20 January 1944 with VF-10 Grumman F6F-3 Hellcats in the background. (Dick Hill Collection via Tailhook Association).

a pilot serving aboard USS *Lexington*'s (CV 2) Scouting Squadron Two (VS-2). At Barber's Point, the Commanding Officer split his squadron into two sections of four F6F-3Ns, with Detachment A led by the commanding officer going aboard the *Bunker Hill* as part of Air Group 17, and the other led by Lt. Russell L. Reiserer going aboard *Yorktown* as part of Air Group 5. Harmer's and Aurand's squadrons formed the night fighter element for the Fifth Fleet's Task Force 58 (TF-58), built around a fast carrier force consisting of *Enterprise*, *Yorktown*, *Essex*, *Intrepid*, and *Bunker Hill*, along with four escort carriers. Carrier aircraft conducted pre-invasion strikes against Kwajalein and Eniwetok, but the night fighter detachments were not widely used during the operation, except for an occasional unsuccessful vector against enemy night intruders attempting to attack the fleet.

Most squadron commanders encountered reluctance to use their compliment of pilots and aircraft. Harmer encountered quite a bit of animosity upon his arrival aboard *Enterprise*, since night fighters meant increasing the deck crew's workload. Many viewed night fighters as an inconvenient experiment – a waste of time, since the fleet's antiaircraft guns could deal with any threat from enemy attacks at night efficiently and quickly. The arrival of night fighters onboard the ship created tension between Harmer, the air group commander, Cmdr. Roscoe L. Newman, and the ship's air officer, Cmdr. Thomas J. Hamilton. Newman told Harmer upon his arrival that the night fighters, if used at all, would fly routine day strikes. Harmer objected,

Lt. Cmdr. Evan "Sweet Pete" Aurand, in the cockpit of an F6F-3E circa spring 1944, was the CO of VF(N)-76. (Bertie Family Archives).

F4U-2 night fighters aboard USS *Intrepid* during the first attack on Truk, 16-17 February 1944. The squadron insignia is visible on the front aircraft below the windscreen. (Robert F. Dorr)

This insignia is from Robert B. Brunson, who served with VF(N)-101 on *Enterprise* from January through July 1944. (Grace Hay Neie, CV-6 Association Secretary, via Nicholas A. Veronico)

stating, "Our planes are so much more vulnerable than normal F4Us and the kids just aren't ready for day action. I believe I was sincere in recommending against it on the grounds that we may be too valuable to waste in day actions for which we are not well suited." Hamilton at first refused to allow the Corsair's off "his" flight deck at night. Harmer recounted, "The air department had about an 18-hour day, and when they had to launch night fighters it turned out to be a 24-hour day. They hated us. The ship's air officer (Hamilton) couldn't stand the sight of me."[2]

The amphibious landings on Eniwetok, in the Marshall Islands, coincided with the first strike against the Japanese base of Truk Atoll on 17-18 February by Vice Adm. Raymond A. Spruance's Truk Striking Force, comprised of three fast carrier groups. The failure of night fighters in intercepting enemy aircraft during the operation did not alleviate the reluctance to use them. At 0011 hours on 17 February, a determined Betty eluded both night fighters allowed in the air that night and the antiaircraft fire and dropped a torpedo, hitting *Intrepid*'s stern on the starboard side. The carrier limped back to Hawaii, knocking Lt. Kullberg's VF(N)-101 detachment out of the war, but still leaving the carrier group with four Corsairs and eight Hellcat night fighters. The task force, after decimating Japanese air and surface forces at Truk, moved to strike enemy bases in the Caroline group and the Southern Marianas. Slowly, Harmer and Aurand were able to improve relations with flight operations staff by proving the capability of their pilots and

Det B F4U-2 preparing for launch aboard *Intrepid*, February 1944. The *Intrepid* took a hit from an aerial torpedo during the February strike against Truk, requiring repairs which knocked VF(N)-101's Det B out of action. (Nicholas A. Veronico)

aircraft. That began with VF(N)-101 scoring the first successful carrier night fighter interception 19 February, when Lt. Cmdr. Harmer, on NCAP, damaged a Betty 125 miles northeast of Ponope, in the Carolines; however, another two months would pass before his group could claim a confirmed kill. Night fighter detachments continued regular combat air patrol (CAP) and strikes against enemy installations along with their daytime counterparts. Indeed, a considerable number of air-to-air victories by carrier-based naval night fighter squadrons occurred during normal daytime operations.

The first recorded aerial victories by a carrier-based night fighter unit, although occurring during the day, came 22 February 1944, when *Bunker Hill*, as part of Task Force 58, launched air attacks against airfields and shipping in the Mariana Islands. Lt. Cmdr. Aurand led a four-plane sweep at dawn of enemy airfields on Tinian and Saipan, catching 50-60 aircraft on the ground at Tinian. After making a fourth strafing run, the Hellcats became the targets of approximately 20 Japanese fighters, during which time, despite five-to-one odds, the VF(N)-76 group shot down five of the enemy aircraft, including three from the guns of 20-year-old Ens. John Bertie. During the twisting and turning aerial battle between Saipan and Tinian, Aurand and Lt. (jg) Norman "Doc" Davisson each claimed a Zeke; however, Ens. Robert "Bitzy" Bice presumably became the victim of an enemy fighter. The aerial duel continued as Ens. Bertie latched on to one fighter and brought it down with a short burst, but another Japanese fighter damaged the Hellcat and Bertie suffered wounds to his arm and leg. Despite the painful injuries, he shot down two more enemy fighters that crossed into his line of fire. Wounded, separated from Aurand and Davisson, and flying a damaged aircraft, Bertie managed to navigate 130 miles to the carrier without a compass. Although weak from loss of blood, he manually lowered the flaps and gear, conducting a safe landing aboard *Bunker Hill*. Ens. Bertie, who enlisted in the Navy's V-5 pilot program at 18 and had earned his naval aviator wings just a year before, was awarded the Navy Cross to go along with the Purple Heart for his wounds.

Ens. John R. Bertie of VF(N)-76 shot down three Japanese aircraft during a daytime encounter off the Mariana Islands 22 February 1944, in which the Navy awarded him the Navy Cross. Despite being wounded and his Hellcat's compass destroyed, he navigated his aircraft back to the *Bunker Hill*. (Bertie Family Archives)

Lt. (jg) Doc Davisson of VF(N)-76 at Ulithi Atoll, circa March 1944. He shot down a Zeke on the 22 February mission, but disappeared while escorting an SB2C Helldiver off the Mariana Islands June 1944. (Bertie Family Archives)

Pilots of VF(N)-76 on USS *Bunker Hill* circa February-March 1944. From L-R: officer identified only as Mitch, Doc Davisson, John R. Bertie, Marty Martenson, J.R. Jolliff, officer identified only as Uncle Willie, and Dick Slobodin. (Bertie Family Archives)

VFN-101 F4U-2 Corsairs aboard *Enterprise* being moved on the flight deck circa February 1944. Lt. Cmdr. "Chick" Harmer and Lt. (jg) Robert Holden scored all of the squadron's kills between February and June 1944. (Bob Rocker via Tailhook Association)

The 22 February attack resulted in the destruction of 168 Japanese aircraft in the air and on the ground, while American losses were five fighters. The next missions for TF-58 were strikes against Japanese installations and shipping in the western Caroline Islands and supporting the Allied landings at Hollandia, New Guinea. Harmer's Corsair detachment remained on the *Enterprise*, while Aurand split his between *Bunker Hill*, *Hornet* (CV 12), and *Lexington* (CV 16). Nearly three months of waiting for an opportunity to score for the night Corsairs ended as Lt. Cmdr. Chick Harmer made the first successful carrier-based night interception with a confirmed kill while patrolling off Hollandia on 24 April. After being launched from the *Enterprise*, fighter control vectored him to a point 30 miles from the fleet. He made radar contact on a bogey at two miles, at a bearing of 30 degrees to port and below him. The nocturnal fighter descended from 1,500 to 500 feet and picked up the enemy aircraft visually as a Betty from half a mile. He dropped his speed to 140 knots (160mph) and closed to within 300 yards. At that point, the rear gunner of the Japanese bomber spotted the pursuing American fighter and opened fire. Harmer returned fire, but lost the prey temporarily in the darkness as the Betty headed towards the deck. Harmer picked it back up again at 300 yards, closed to within 150 yards, and fired a long burst while the dorsal and rear guns of the bomber fired erratically at the Corsair. Harmer conducted an S-turn, closed to 100 feet, and fired another burst just as the bomber's pilot decided to make a controlled water landing. The Corsair orbited over the down aircraft a couple times before leaving with the Betty's tail section as the only remaining section of the aircraft above the water.

MARIANAS CAMPAIGN (JUNE-SEPTEMBER 1944)

Night air combat operations doubled in strength during June 1944 with the arrival of VF(N)-77 and -78 at the Night Combat Training Unit at Barbers Point, Hawaii, where final training for night combat was conducted before deployment to carriers. VF(N)-77, under the command of Lt. Cmdr. Robert Freeman, operated from *Essex*, *Yorktown*, *Hornet*, *Franklin*, and *Wasp*, while VF(N)-78, led by Lt. Cmdr. James S. Gray, operated from *Intrepid* and *Enterprise*. VF(N)-77 Detachment C participated in night heckling strikes against Wake and Marcus Islands during mid-May but encountered no enemy aircraft. On 6 June 1944, Task Force 58 left Majuro Atoll for the Mariana Islands to conduct pre-invasion strikes on Saipan, Guam, and Tinian as a prelude to the landings on Saipan scheduled for the 15th.

NIGHT FIGHTER AIRCRAFT ORGANIZATION JUNE 1944

SQUADRON	DET	AIRCRAFT	CARRIER
VF(N)-76	A	(4) F6F-3N	*Bunker Hill*
	B	(4) F6F-3N	*Hornet*
	C	(4) F6F-3N	*Wasp*
	D	(4) F6F-3N	*Lexington*
VF(N)-77	Det	(4) F6F-3N	*Essex*
	B	(4) F6F-3N	*Yorktown*
	C	(4) F6F-3N	*Wasp*
VF(N)-101		-(3) F4U-2	*Enterprise*

Three of the four night fighter squadrons (VF(N)-76, -77 and -101) participated in the Marshall Island Campaign by flying night combat air patrol (NCAP) to participating in daytime and night strikes against Japanese installations, with occasional encounters with enemy aircraft. VF(N)-76 and -77 participated in strikes against Guam and the Bonin Islands from mid-June to August, often operating flying radar-less F6F-3s during the day -3Ns at night. VF(N)-76 scored first on 15 June, when the *Bunker Hill* detachment intercepted a flight of dive bombers and fighters between Rota, Guam, and Saipan just before nine in the morning. Lt. (jg) "Doc" Davisson spotted a lone Yokosuka D4Y (Judy) dive bomber at an altitude of 300 feet heading towards Task Force, located 58 miles away. The bomber spotted the four Hellcats and dove to 50 feet. Davisson dove from 1,100 feet and came up behind the aircraft, firing 400 rounds into the rear cockpit and starting a fire. Lt. Cmdr. Aurand, seeing the rear cockpit was unarmed, came up from behind and fired. The Judy's tail section fell off and the aircraft crashed into the water. Aurand scored a second daytime kill four days later, downing a Nakajima B6N2 (Jill) torpedo bomber. However, in another search sector that day, "Doc" Davisson's Hellcat, along with a Curtiss SB2C-1C Helldiver of VB-8, disappeared after reporting making contact with two enemy aircraft.

Enterprise's VF(N)-101detachment of F4U-2s also scored the same day, when Lt. Cmdr. Harmer and Lt. (jg) Robert F. Holden tangled with three of five Zeros escorting ten twin-engine Yokosuka P1Y (Frances) bombers at dusk. The Corsairs were catapulted off the carrier at 1845 hours and 20 minutes later, they were vectored to a large number of bogies five miles from their position and a few minutes later spotted two formations of aircraft, with the larger group of bombers flying at 800 feet and another smaller formation ahead of them. Harmer recounted:

The three aces of VF(N)-76 sitting in a jeep on Majuro Atoll. Lt. Russ Reiserer, in the driver's seat, with Lt. John Dear sitting in the passenger side and Lt. Fred "Buck" Dungan in the back. Standing in front of the Quonset hut is J. Hunter Ewing, another squadron member. (Bertie Family Archives)

> I made a high side pass from the starboard side of the formation on the nearest wing but observed no results, other than heavy counter fire from the whole formation. It was just dark enough so that I could not pick the bombers immediately for a second pass. I told Holden to lead the attack if he could see them. His answer was that there was a fighter on my tail, and this information was confirmed immediately by twenty millimeter (sic) tracers past my wings.[3]

Harmer made a hard right turn, placing him over the bomber formation, which opened fire at the American fighter, hitting it in the right wing's leading edge and right wheel well. Harmer continued turning at full power with the Japanese fighter on his tail when Holden came to the rescue, diving and firing at the Zero, who pulled away from Holden and went into a vertical corkscrew dive. Another Japanese fighter came up on Holden's tail while another latched onto Harmer. The latter was unaware of his predicament until tracers began passing the Corsair. Both night fighters were able to shake off their pursuers and returned to the *Enterprise* with Harmer credited with damaging one of the bombers, while Holden scored a probable.

Four days later, American and Japanese carrier forces fought each other in the Battle of the Philippine Sea, also known as the Great Marianas Turkey Shoot. It was a crippling blow to the Imperial Japanese Navy, losing three carriers, over 400 carrier aircraft, and some 200 land-based aircraft; the loss of so many pilots and aircrew was irreplaceable. The number of aerial victories claimed by Navy night fighter units during the battle was minimal compared to the overall numbers, with most occurring during the daytime hours, as illustrated when VF(N)-76 joined *Hornet*'s VF-2 on the 19th for a sweep against Orote Field, a Japanese installation on Guam, during the afternoon. Three VF(N)-76 pilots flying radar-less F3F-3 Hellcats, along with five of the *Hornet*'s VF-2, surprised a flight of 50-60 Val dive bombers and escorting fighters in a landing pattern. Lt. Russ Resierer of VF(N)-76 lowered his Hellcat's landing gear and flaps to slow his fighter down and, during the course of a few minutes, shot down five of them, while twenty-two-year-old Lt. (jg) Fred "Buck" Dungan downed a Kate and Zeke. Four days later Resierer shot down three Kates, while Lt. (jg) John W. Dear downed two more during the late morning of 24 June. All of Resierer's eight confirmed victories with VF(N)-76, along with one other while serving with VF-10 earlier in the war, occurred during the daytime hours.

The following evening, *Essex*-based VF(N)-77 Hellcats equipped with flares carried out day and night bombing and strafing attacks against targets on Guam from 11 June to 1 July. During one such night heckler mission on 20 June, a four-plane flight from the *Essex* caught a half dozen Vals on a landing approach to Agana Field, Guam, shooting down three of them in quick succession. Lt. Cmdr. Robert Freedman led his flight after being capitulated off the *Essex* at 0210 hours. The two-plane section, comprised of Lt. Cmdr. Freedman and Ens. G. L. Tarleton, reached Agana Field at 0335 hours and saw the runway lights on with a blinker light on the east end of the runway sending a blinker message either as landing instructions or a challenge. The night fighters swung around towards the downwind end of the runway and began a forty-five degree strafing run, using the blinker light as the aiming point. Pulling out their five at 1,600 feet, the fighters orbited the field from a distance of five miles and waited for any additional activity on the now-darkened airfield. Ten minutes later, the runway lights blinked on again in obvious anticipation of the arrival of friendly aircraft. Fifteen minutes after the initial attack, as the fighters prepared for another strafing run, Freeman spotted two blinking lights traveling around the traffic circle:

> Just before I got into visual range of the plane, another plane behind my original target turned on wing lights and an amber tail light. I therefore joined up on this plane. It was a single engine plane with fixed landing gear. I had him on my radar at the one-mile search scale, but there was considerable land signal interference and I didn't need the radar anyway, since he had his lights on. He was circling the field in a slow left turn (about 130 knots) at 2,000 feet. I joined up on his port quarter and opened fire at about 100 feet. The display of incendiaries striking his fuselage at that close range was so surprising that I involuntarily chopped my throttle. It looked like an electric arc welder had run from his nose to his tail, completely blanking him out in blue flame. A long orange flame appeared on the starboard side and persisted for about four to six seconds, then disappeared.
>
> He decelerated rapidly, as his engine had quit, and I had to drop my flaps to stay behind. He continued his slow turn to port, nosing over into a glide of about 85 knots (98mph). Even with my throttle closed and flaps down I slid directly underneath him. I slowly dropped back to shooting position again and opened fire from directly astern at about 50 yards. I could see incendiary flashes on the fuselage, tail, and wing roots. After about six three-second bursts from this position, the Val nosed down sharply in a steep dive toward the water.

After the Val's destruction, Tarelton gained altitude and circled east of the airfield from a distance of two miles. Seeing another set of running lights in the traffic circle, he called Freeman that he was going down for the interception:

F6F-3N of VF(N)-76 aboard USS *Essex* during mid-1944. The squadron operated detachments from the following carriers between February and September 1944: *Essex*, *Yorktown*, *Lexington*, *Bunker Hill*, and *Hornet*. (Emil Buehler Library, NMNA)

F6F-3N #1 prepares to launch from *Essex*. Note the elongated bar of the U.S. national insignia wrapped around the bottom of the radome and the circular squadron insignia barely visible below the windscreen. (Emil Buehler Library, NMNA)

> I went in fast (mistake #1) (sic) and had to make a complete circle of the field when I saw some running lights at the northern end of the field. I was doing about 120 knots and was closing on him rapidly. I dropped my flaps and was about 200 feet astern of the target when I fired from below and about 15-20 degrees to his port. He was in a left turn. I fired a short burst and didn't observe hits. I felt my lead was too great for the range (mistake #2) (sic), so I pulled my nose up and fired a five-second burst. I observed several hits on the wings and belly. He leveled his wings and then he nosed over and crashed into the water.

The engagement took Tarelton in a circle again and he was at the northern end of the airfield when he spotted the running lights of another aircraft at the opposite end. He raised the Hellcat's flaps and gained airspeed:

> I closed on the lights much too fast (mistake #3) (sic) and before I knew it I was "on top of him." I dropped my flaps again, but not soon enough. I was afraid to chop my throttle completely, as it makes too much flame from the exhaust. I was in a good position for a no deflection shot. I fired a burst and again felt that I had too much lead. I pulled up sharply and fired again. He rolled over on his back and his nose dropped. He did not have enough altitude to recover.[4]

Tarleton circled the field a few more times but saw no additional targets. He rendezvoused with Freeman over the southern tip of Rota and returned to the ship, landing at 0550 hours. After the Marianas Turkey Shoot, the fast carriers of TF-38 turned their attention to eliminate Japanese air and naval forces in the Bonin and Volcano Islands, with additional strikes conducted against Pagan Island and Iwo Jima.

The team of Harmer and Holden of VF(N)-101, who nearly ended up on the losing side of an engagement with enemy fighters on the 15th, scored on 27-28 June while operating independently of each other. At 2015 hours, after the *Enterprise* picked up bogies on radar at a distance of 100 miles, the carrier launched Holden, who climbed to 10,000 feet. Twenty miles from the task group, fighter control gave him a new heading that allowed Holden to establish radar contact at three miles. Two Mitsubishi Ki-21 (Sally) twin-engine bombers appeared in front of him a few minutes later. Holden slowed down and maneuvered behind the wing-man and opened fire at 200 yards. Incendiaries struck the fuselage and port wing and the port engine caught fire. Holden followed the stricken bomber down, firing another burst. Then the section between the port engine and fuselage became engulfed in flames and it hit the water and exploded, not far from the task force. The following evening, the team scored again, bringing down three Bettys in separate incidents, with Holden downing two of them after a vector guided him to a bogey 60 miles at 10,000 feet from the task group. A couple of course corrections followed before his own scope picked up a blip. He recounted:

> Making a contact at three miles, I closed in and made a visual at 800 feet. It was a Betty. After closing in to about 200 feet dead astern I fired a very short burst, hitting his starboard stub wing. He blew up with a terrific explosion and hit the water almost immediately in flames. I was so close I could feel the heat from the flames.

Holden resumed patrol and was vectored to another bogey 15 minutes later; the chase began with the second Betty taking violent evasive action in course and altitude to get away from the night fighter. Holden caught up with the bomber at 1,000 feet, but before he could fire, the bomber changed course and climbed a few hundred feet. Holden fired as the Betty dived, hitting it in the wing and engine area and causing it to flame and crash into the water. The carrier launched Harmer at 2130 hours, and he met up with Holden after the latter had

VF(N)-76's squadron insignia belonging to John Bertie, with the Latin phrase that roughly translates to, "We have become so much greater than we were." (Bertie Family Archives)

shot down his second aircraft. After making a practice run on Holden's Corsair, and apparently with no adversaries in the air at the time, the two headed back to the *Enterprise*. The Corsair pilots were unaware that a Betty was tagging behind them before breaking away until the fighter direction asked why they broke formation. Harmer replied they were still in formation. Holden, short on fuel, returned to the ship while fighter control ordered Harmer after the Betty following them.

Harmer's radar picked the target at three-and-a-half miles and tracked it to half a mile. Determining its altitude at 1,000 feet, Harmer dropped down to 500 feet and continued his approach, making visual contact at 400 feet at the 2 o'clock position.

Dropping his dive brakes to keep from overshooting his quarry, he slid the Corsair directly under the Betty. With the Corsair's speed under control, he picked up his dive brakes, throttled back, took aim at the bomber's port wing stub and fired a short burst. Hit in the fuselage and port engine, the aircraft banked sharply and struck the water with a terrific explosion. The destruction of the Betty marked the last aerial victory by VF(N)-101 pilots, with the squadron victory board standing at five confirmed kills with one probable and three damaged, all by the team of Holden (3-1-2) and Harmer (2-0-1). Thus ended the radar-equipped F4U-2N's brief career as a ship-borne night fighter, but one land-based Marine Corps squadron continued to operate the aircraft for several more months. The *Enterprise* returned to Pearl Harbor for repairs and replenishment, where it brought aboard a new air group (Air Group 20), along with Lt. Cmdr. James S. Gray and his VF-78 detachment and their radar-equipped Hellcats.

TF-58 continued to pound the Volcano and Bonin Islands during July in an effort to neutralize any remaining Japanese air assets in the area. Lieutenants (jg) John Dear and "Buck" Dungan of VF(N)-76 participated in one of the most spectacular aerial engagements of the Pacific War during a predawn strike against enemy installations on Chichi Jima, in the Bonin Islands. The entire engagement occurred during dawn and without the use of radar. After launching from the *Hornet* at 0400 hours on 4 July, they went on a 60-mile search northwest of Chichi Jima but saw nothing. Four hours later, they returned to the island and began strafing and bombing attacks against enemy shipping lying in the harbor. No air opposition was expected as the two split. Dungan began a run, only to see nine to ten Rufe float planes coming up towards him. He swung the faster and more agile Hellcat towards one of the enemy aircraft, dropping his single 500-pound bomb slung under his wing to gain additional speed and maneuverability. Coming up from behind one of the Rufes, its pilot, realizing he was the intended victim, vainly tried to climb and out-turn the Hellcat. Dungan fired a few short bursts, sending it down in flames. Dear made a strafing and bombing run on a destroyer coming in from 7,000 feet, dropping a bomb towards the warship from 300 feet, but it missed by 50 feet. He pulled to the left and started to circle back towards the harbor.

VF(N)-76 Hellcat coming in for a landing on *Bunker Hill* during daytime operations circa mid-1944. The squadron scored 36 aerial victories over the Japanese, most of them occurring during daylight and without the use of radar. (Bertie Family Archives)

Dungan called his wingman over the radio for help, saying he was under attack by several aircraft five miles northwest of the island.

Dungan, seeing the other Hellcat coming to the rescue, lured two of the float planes that were chasing him into the path of Dear's Hellcat, who proceeded to fire two short bursts into the engine compartments of both Rufes, causing both to crash into the water. The Hellcat pilots were no longer on the defensive, as they dove on two more enemy aircraft, with Dungan downing another and his wingman damaging one more. The aerial duel continued, as the two chased after another float plane. Dungan chased it into a cloud formation, and a few moments later, the Japanese aircraft streaked out of the clouds and crashed into the water, for Dungan's third for the day. Dungan then chased after another, but before he could close in for the kill Japanese antiaircraft fire from the island shot their own plane down. He shot down his fourth aircraft after splitting up with his wingman, but in turn another float plane attacked from above. One enemy pilot managed to get on Dungan's tail and fired. A .30-caliber bullet entered the Hellcat's cockpit, missing the armor plating, and struck the pilot in the left shoulder, fracturing his clavicle. In intense pain and barely conscious due to blood loss, he headed for the carrier and made a safe landing aboard the *Yorktown* instead of the *Hornet*. The battle over Chichi Jima made Lt. (jg) "Buck" Dungan an ace and the recipient of the Navy Cross.

Dear was off Ani Jima, busy making a sketch map of shipping in the cove on the southwest side of the island when he saw a flash to his right. At first, he thought the flash was the rising sun off his cowling, but when he looked up he saw a Rufe right on his tail with guns blazing. Dear pushed over into a dive with oil spouting over the left side of his cockpit canopy. In order to see he rolled back the cover, resulting in the wind tearing his helmet off. He dove 2,000 feet and pulled out. Then, by poking his head out and back in the cockpit, he was able to see where he was going. Getting on the float plane's tail, he fired a short burst and shot down his fourth aircraft of the day. He landed on the *Yorktown* with 36 holes in his aircraft and less than two minutes of oil remaining. Dear's downing of three Rufes, along with the three Kates on 24 June, doubled his overall score to six, establishing him as the second ace of the day.

By the end of July 1944, American air activity in the Central Pacific was largely confined to mopping up operations on Saipan, Guam, and Tinian, with regular neutralizing blows against bypassed islands in the Marshalls and Carolines. VF(N)-77 finished up its tour with the destruction of one enemy aircraft in July and another in September. Ensign Solderlund, flying from USS *Wasp* (CV 18), was vectored to a bogie at 0502 hours on 12 July and, after a couple course corrections, intercepted and shot down a Betty 72 miles from the carrier. The squadron's last kill came at 0330 hours 1 September 1944, 80 miles east-southeast of the Bonin Islands, when Lt. Anthony C Benjes, Jr. shot down a four-engine Kawanishi H8K (Emily) flying boat.

Five pilots of VF(N)-76 pose for a group photograph circa summer 1944 with Lts. John Dear front center and "Buck" Dungan rear left. They were jumped by approximately 10 Japanese Rufe float planes off Chichi Jima, in the Bonin Islands, 4 July 1944, with Dungan shooting down four and Dear bagging three others. (Tailhook Association)

Chapter 4

Philippine Operations (September 1944-January 1945)

Man was never meant to fly no how. And if he was meant to fly, he wasn't meant to fly from a ship. And if he was meant to fly from a ship, he sure wasn't meant to fly from a ship at night!

- Steward's mate on *USS Independence*, 1944.

September 1944 marked the beginning of American plans for the re-occupation of the Philippines, beginning with the First Marine Division landing on Peleliu, in the Palau Islands, on 15 September 1944. General MacArthur saw Peleliu as a potential threat to the Philippine campaign, and thus believed the island had to be taken. The Marines suffered appalling loses (1,252 killed and 5,274 wounded or missing) in a battle that lasted until the end of November, when the U.S. Army's 81st Infantry Division wiped out the last pockets of Japanese resistance. The Peleliu operation coincided with the U.S. Army's 31st Infantry Division taking the island of Morotai, in the Netherland East Indies. Morotai became a major military base and played an important role in the liberation of the Philippines, unlike Peleliu, which languished as a minor staging point for raids against bypassed Japanese-held islands.

The Task Force's mission during this time was to destroy enemy aircraft, shipping, and ground installations at Palau, Yap, Ulithi, and the Philippines. The VF(N)-78 detachment aboard *Intrepid* scored two air-to-air victories during the opening days of the campaign, both occurring during the daylight hours. The first occurred on 12 September, near Limasawa Island, off Southern Leyte, at 0945 hours, when Lt. William H. Miller and Ens. Donald Matheson joined in shooting down a P1Y Frances bomber. The Second kill occurred just after dawn, when a four-plane flight spotted two Zeke fighters ten miles west of the Task Force (80 miles east of Balar, Luzon), with Lt. Miller damaging one Zeke, while Lt. William B. Thompson brought down the other. Less than two weeks later, the squadron was disestablished and its assets were absorbed into VF-20 on the *Enterprise*.

"Sweet Pete" Aurand and Lt. (jg) J.E. Conner, launched from *Bunker Hill* on the afternoon of 13 September, flew escort for an OS2U float plane from the USS *Miami* on a ResCap of a downed pilot from VF-8. They spotted a Betty flying over Albay Gulf, Luzon, and shot it out of the sky, giving VF(N)-76's skipper 3.5 confirmed kills. The last kill for VF(N)-76 occurred nine days later on the twenty-second, when Lt.(jg) Dear, operating from the *Hornet*, destroyed a B6N2 Jill just before dawn 40 miles west of the Task Force and southeast of Cape San Ildefenso, Luzon. Dear and Lt.(jg) William E. Levering were launched at 0530 hours during a rain squall and in total darkness.

Dear turned on his radar, but a bright return from the heavy clouds and sea blurred the set, along with strong buffeting in the air making it difficult to stay on target, so he turned off radar and relied on his instruments and *Hornet*'s fighter director to direct him to the target. An hour later, orbiting some 25 miles at 18,000 feet from the Task Force, the *Lexington*'s fighter director took control and vectored Dear to a bogey two miles away at 1,500 feet. Dear spotted the Jill below him a mile away and dove towards it, firing only 40 rounds as he came into range; the torpedo bomber's engine emitted a puff of smoke and it banked away and hit the water.

USS *Independence*, in port with its complement of F6F Hellcats circa 1944, was home to Night Air Group 41, comprised of VF(N)-41 and VT(N)-41 from August 1944 to January 1945. (Emil Buehler Library, NMNA)

Pilots of VF(N)-41 aboard *Independence* circa late 1944, with the squadron's scorecard showing 38 kills. The squadron would claim another three Japanese aircraft before its tour ended in January 1945. (Emil Buehler Library, NMNA)

NIGHT AIR GROUP 41

Light Carrier Night Air Group 41 (CVLG(N)-41), the first such organization dedicated to nocturnal operations, was established through the drive and persistence of Lt. Commander Turner F. Caldwell, a native of Narbeth, Pensylvania, and an Annapolis graduate Class of 1935. He commissioned VF(N)-79 in January 1944, training at NAAF Charlestown, Rhode Island. Caldwell conceived a plan of having a "pure" night air group and tried to sell the idea to anyone who would listen. With the availability of the light carrier *Independence* (CVL 22), nicknamed "The Mighty I," Caldwell got his wish. After further training at Pearl Harbor, VF(N)-79 boarded the *Independence* in July, where it was dissolved in August and reformed as VF(N)-41, with an enlarged TBM contingent designated VT(N)-41. Total size of the Air Group was 16 F-5Ns, five F6F-5s, and nine TBM-1D Avengers. Refresher training for night operations continued through the first two weeks of August before the *Independence* set sail to join Task Group 38.2 for the first phase in the invasion of the Palau Islands, but Caldwell's group flew only routine patrols during the operation before heading to the Philippines for pre-invasion operations in the Visayas.

Higher authorities had different plans for Caldwell's Hellcats, and night operations gave way to daytime strikes against Japanese airfields and shipping in the Visayas area. It took until October for the squadron to score its first true night kill. Ensigns George Obenour and Robert Klock chalked up the squadron's first aerial victory during daylight on 12 September, when each was credited with bagging a Betty at 0755 hours 200 miles northeast of Leyte. Later that day, *Independence* launched eight F6F-5Ns split into two divisions to provide CAP for the fleet. At 1824 hours, fighter direction advised Lt. William "Bill" Henry's group of two high-flying bogies flying almost directly over the Task Group. Henry and his wingman, Ens. Jack "Berky" Berkheimer, who at 20 years of age was the youngest ensign and pilot of the air group, climbed to 24,000 feet and headed for an interception. At 1835 hours, Henry spotted a Mitsubishi Ki-46 (Dinah) reconnaissance aircraft two miles away and 1,000 feet below; however, contact was lost when the aircraft ducked into a cloud bank. He immediately spotted another Dinah below his fighter, which must have thought the Hellcat was his wingman, as it blinked a red join-up light several times. The Hellcat dove and made a rear run firing as he approached to within 750 feet, with rounds striking the aircraft's starboard engine, drawing smoke. Berkheimer, flying between 700-1,000 feet above and 2,000 feet off Henry's starboard quarter, dove and fired a short burst. Henry swung back around and fired another burst at a range of 500 feet, spraying the entire center section of the Dinah from engine to engine, with pieces flying off in the process. The engines began to flame as the Hellcat pulled over and up in his recovery, barely missing the Japanese aircraft as he did so. Berkheimer

Flight deck crewmen assembled on the *Independence*'s deck, listening to the carrier's commanding officer, Capt. E.C. Ewen, with F6F-5N Hellcats lashed to the deck in the background. (Emil Buehler Library, NMNA)

came down firing three short bursts, scoring additional hits on the starboard engine and wing root, with additional pieces of the Dinah's wing and tail flying off. Henry came in for the third and final time on a level attack from the rear, firing at 200 feet. The Japanese aircraft pulled up, rolled over on its back, and exploded. The two pilots shared credit, setting the stage for both becoming aces and the squadron's top scorers.

Caldwell's disappointment regarding his group's use intensified when he formally received word that the night air group's mission would change to fit the needs of the fleet operating off the Philippines. Beginning the 15th, a significant number of his night fighter complement was either converted or exchanged to a regular daytime configuration. With four of the original 16 fighters converted for daytime operations by removing the AIA gear, another four were exchanged for F6F-5s from *Bunker Hill*. The group obtained four additional fighters each from the USS *Barnes* (CVE 20) and USS *San Jacinto* (CVL 20). The fighter composition of the air group changed from having all radar-equipped Hellcats to eight F6F-5Ns, 13 F6F-5s, and three F6F-3s. Operating off Luzon between 19-24 September, VF(N)-41 claimed a dozen enemy aircraft destroyed or damaged in the air, all during daylight hours by non-radar-equipped Hellcats, including four during the morning of 22 September, with Henry bagging two Vals, Jack Berkheimer getting a Zeke, and Ens. Joseph F. Moore downing another Val.

NIGHT FIGHTER ORGANIZATION SEPTEMBER 1944

SQUADRON	DET	CARRIER
VF(N)-41	-	*Independence*
VF(N)-76	A	*Bunker Hill*
	B	*Hornet*
	C	*Lexington*
VF(N)-77	A	*Essex*
	B	*Franklin*
VF(N)-78	1	*Enterprise*
	2	*Intrepid*

October 1944 brought a reorganization of night fighter operations, with VF(N)-41 remaining as the only independently operating night fighter squadron of the fleet, as VF(N)-76, -77, and -78 were disestablished, with most of their pilots and aircraft absorbed into conventional VF squadrons of the U.S. Third Fleet. Additional dedicated night fighter squadrons would not reappear until the arrival of Night Carrier Division Seven in January 1945. The prelude for the invasion of Leyte on 20 October involved TF-38 air groups destroying enemy air forces, shipping, and ground installations on Okinawa, Formosa, and the Philippines. VF(N)-41 claimed 10 nocturnal victories during the month, beginning with strikes on Formosa, with Bill Henry and Jack Berkheimer bagging half of the total.

Independence launched an eight-plane CAP as TF 38.2 approached Formosa at 1615 hours on 12 October; they were divided in two sections, with Lt. Cmdr. Caldwell leading one and Henry leading the other in an operation that would claim the lives of two VF(N)-41's pilots. A little over an hour later the CAP was ordered back to the ship, with the Commanding Officer landing first, followed by Emmett R. Edwards' aircraft, which suffered damage to the prop and starboard flap upon landing, fouling the deck, and the two other aircraft in Caldwell's section were forced to orbit as the task force came under enemy air attack. Ensign J.S. Allen was vectored to a possible bogey by the fighter director aboard light carrier USS *Cabot* (CVL 28), while Ens. George Obenour, who shared the squadron's first aerial victory a month earlier, continued orbiting, awaiting landing instructions, as he was running low on gas. His radio could transmit but not receive messages, and several times he asked permission to land on a carrier. Finally, after changing frequency, he received a message to land in the water near one of the destroyers. Reports came in later of seeing float lights, rafts, and hearing cries for help, but Obenour remained missing.

Henry's section continued to orbit when fighter control sent it towards a pair of low-flying Bettys ten miles out and heading for the task force. Henry picked up the contacts on his scope ten minutes later at a range of two miles and made a visual on one of the bombers at one mile. The Hellcat was closing too rapidly, so the pilot sharply throttled back while maintaining a visual, finding it difficult, as rain had begun to fall on his windshield. Henry made the decision to open fire with his four inboard guns, since the outboard guns, loaded with tracers, could potentially ruin his night vision. The Betty's port wing stub caught the burst, starting a small fire. Henry fired another burst and the bomber's engines flamed. The aircraft went into a shallow glide and exploded as it hit the water. Two more contacts appeared on the fighter controller's radar screen and the Hellcats went to intercept, with Ens. J.A. Barnett joining Henry; they made a visual on two Bettys flying off their port side at 500 feet. Henry slipped in behind and opened fire with all six guns, causing the bomber's engines to burn. Firing again, the aircraft flamed and went down. Barnett went after the second Betty and dropped down to 100 feet to get his quarry, now flying at 150 feet and silhouetted against the sky. Barnett came up behind and fired as the bomber climbed and leveled off at 200 feet, drawing fire from the port engine. Three more short bursts started a fire in the Betty's starboard engine and then the aircraft began to burn fiercely. The bomber turned slightly and then dove into the water as Barnett passed over his victim. Henry and Barnett, along with another pilot of the section (Ens. F.A. Ficher), landed aboard *Independence* at 2045 hours, but the fourth member, Ens. Joseph Moore, who had downed a Val 22 September, went missing, presumably to enemy action. Caldwell's night fighter element claimed three Emily flying boats the following morning during a predawn heckling and bombing mission of enemy airfields on Southern Formosa. At 0345 hours, four F6F-5N and four TBM-C Avenger torpedo bombers of VT(N)-41 were launched, with the night fighters carrying one 500-pound bomb and the torpedo bombers with 12 100-pound bombs. The group was divided into four teams of one Hellcat and one Avenger with the mission of hitting various airfields. Jack Berkheimer lost track of his Avenger and proceeded to the coast alone; shortly before 0500 hours, he spotted three flying boats anchored in a lagoon and began a strafing run. On his descent, he saw the wing lights of an Emily pass by to his port wing. Executing a wingover, he pulled quickly onto the flying boat's tail and fired a burst, hitting both inboard engines, and after another short burst, the burning aircraft crashed into the lagoon. Berkheimer realized he needed to dump his bomb as soon as possible, dropping the ordnance among the aprons and hangars of a seaplane base from 300 feet. On his track back to the carrier, he saw the wing lights of another Emily and latched onto its tail and dispatched it in the same manner as the first, leaving him one-half a kill away from achieving ace status. Berkheimer would later receive the Navy Cross for this mission, posthumously. Another -41 pilot scoring that day was Ens. R.W. Klock, who also lost the Avenger he was teamed up with. He found another Emily and fired two short bursts into the engine area, and the burning plane spiraled into the water and exploded.

NIGHT FIGHTER ORGANIZATION OCTOBER 1944

SQUADRON	AIRCRAFT	CARRIER
VF-7	F6F-5N (4)	Hancock
VF-8	F6F-3N/5N (8)	*Bunker Hill*
VF-11	F6F-3N/5N (4)	*Hornet*
VF-13	F6F-3N/5N (2)	*Franklin*
VF-14	F6F-3N/5N (4)	*Wasp*
VF-15	F6F-3N/5N (4)	*Essex*
VF-18	F6F-5N (5)	*Intrepid*
VF-19	F6F-3N/5N (3)	*Lexington*
VF-20	F6F-3N (4)/F6F-5N (2)	*Enterprise*
VF(N)-41	F6F-5N (14)	*Independence*

BATTLE OF LEYTE GULF

The last major offensive action by the Japanese Imperial Navy took place in a series of engagements known as the Battle Leyte Gulf, involving four separate naval battles between 23-26 October. American surface forces and carrier aircraft power decimated the Japanese, beginning with an attack off Palawan by the submarines *Darter* and *Dace* on the 23rd, resulting in

F6F-5Ns of VF(N)-41 warm up their engines off the Philippines, October 1944. The white in-squadron aircraft number is shown within a circle on the vertical stabilizer and without a circle on the fuselage. (Emil Buehler Library, NMNA)

TBM-1D #26 of VT(N)-41, with the name *Hedy* on the engine nacelle, prepped for launch from *Independence*. The torpedo bomber element of the carrier's night air group participated with the fighter complement in dusk and night attacks against Japanese shipping, installations, and airfields in the Philippines, Formosa, and China. (Robert L. Lawson Collection, Emil Buehler Library, NMNA)

VF(N)-41 pilot receiving last minute instructions before lifting off from *Independence* during Philippine operations. (Emil Buehler Library, NMNA)

the sinking of two enemy cruisers *Atago* and *Takao*. Yet, the battle marked the first full-scale use of the kamikaze suicide planes, which alarmed the Navy brass to such a degree that it caused a near panic. The attacks were successful enough that the Japanese employed the tactic on a much larger scale six months later off Okinawa. Caldwell's night torpedo bombers provided an invaluable service during the battle by spotting the movements of the Japanese Central and Northern Forces and preventing Japanese search planes from tracking Third Fleet forces during the evening of 24-25 October.

Ens. "Berky" Berkheimer of VF(N)-41 appears to have fired the opening shots of what was to be known as the Battle of the Sibuyan Sea while flying NCAP over TF 38.2 on the 24th. He and his wingman, Ens. Harry E. Johnson, took off from the *Independence* at 0130 hours and climbed to 12,000 feet. Johnson headed for one bogey, but had to break off after his communications and radar went out. Berkheimer initially lost contact with his quarry, but at 0205 hours, he picked it up on his scope at a distance of a quarter mile at 10,500 feet before spotting the engine exhausts of an Emily. His first burst hit the inboard starboard and port engines of the flying boat. A second and third burst raked the now-burning Emily's hull, as both hunter and hunted dropped to 7,000 feet, where the flying boat exploded, the flaming remains falling into the water.

Berkheimer, while orbiting 50 miles from the carrier waiting for further instructions, was vectored to the bogey that Johnson was forced to abandon. An hour and a half after the destruction of the Emily he picked up the target (a four-engine Kawanishi H6K (Mavis) flying boat) on his screen three miles away and approximately 1,000 feet. The pilot of the flying boat was shrewd and conducted radical evasive tactics by changing altitude and making sharp turns, but the night fighter hung onto him by keeping him on his scope. The Hellcat closed to within 200 feet astern of the Mavis and he fired, hitting the flying boat's wing and two inboard engines. The two victims elevated him to ace status, raising his total to six and one half confirmed kills.

Adm. Takeo Kurita's Center Force was spotted earlier in the day by one of VT(N)-41's Avengers, and planes of TF 38.2 proceeded to sink the battleship *Musashi* and damage *Yamato* and *Nagato*, along with one cruiser and three destroyers. Another snooping Mavis tracking the Third Fleet during the early morning of the 25th became the target of an F6F-3N flown by Lt. Cmdr. James S. Gray of VF-20. The former skipper of VF(N)-78, and now the new CO of VF-20, had the distinction of shooting down the second Japanese plane of the war by a U.S. naval aviator on 1 February 1942, during a raid against the Marshall Islands. He assumed command of VF-20 during the Battle of Leyte Gulf, when the squadron's Commanding Officer, Lt. Cmdr. Fred Bakutis, went MIA for a week before being rescued by a submarine, but he did not return to the squadron. At 0100 hours on 25 October, the fleet detected

By October 1944 most fleet carriers had 2 to 6 Hellcat night fighters as part of their air groups. F6F-5 Hellcats of VF-80 aboard USS *Ticonderoga* (CV-14) with two F6F-Ns as the leading aircraft prepare for strikes against Japanese targets on Luzon, Philippines circa November 1944. (Emil Buehler Library, NMNA)

a single bogey at 0100 hours approaching the task force at a range of 92 miles. *Enterprise* launched Gray at 0135 hours, who made visual contact with Mavis twice, but lost it each time, until finally getting a firm lock on it by radar a third time. He closed to 300 yards and shot it down in flames 40 miles from the task force at 0215 hours. Adm. Halsey commended Gray for his mission, since the flying boats would have spotted the American fleet and reported the position.

Adm. Kurita's Center Force, which narrowly escaped annihilation during the Battle of Sibuyan Sea, caught elements of TG-77.4 off Samar. Outgunned American destroyers and destroyer escorts charged the Japanese force and, along with aircraft from the escort carriers, managed to disrupt the Japanese ships from destroying the entire task group. U.S. planes sank three of the Japanese cruisers, but two U.S. escort carriers were lost: USS *St. Lo* (CVE 63) took a hit from a kamikaze, causing heavy explosions and fires which eventually sank her; while USS *Gambier* Bay (CVE 73) sank after taking hits from the Japanese cruiser *Chikuma* and the battleship *Yamato*. The Americans also lost two destroyers, while three other CVEs (*Kalinin Bay*, *Fanshaw Bay*, and *White Plains*) suffered serious damage. Meanwhile, Adm. Ozawa's Northern Force of 17 ships built around the fast carrier *Zuikaku* and three light carriers *Chitose*, *Chiyoda*, and *Zuihō* (with 116 aircraft) engaged the far more superior TF-38 of 93 ships built around nine fast carriers and eight light carriers with over 1,000 aircraft. In the north Battle of Cape Engana, the Japanese launched most of their remaining aircraft for an attack during the late morning of the 25th, but they were quickly dispatched by American CAP and anti-aircraft fire. American planes launched the following morning found and sent the Japanese carrier *Zuikaku*, *Chitose*, and *Zuihō* to the bottom of the sea, while U.S. surface forces subsequently sank the *Chiyoda* damaged from an earlier air strike.

At the conclusion of the Battle of Leyte, TF-38 set their sights on suppressing enemy troop movements, destroying aircraft, and shipping in the Visayas and on Luzon. The *Independence*, with CVLG(N)-41 aboard, took part in the action as part of TG-38.2. VF(N)-41 collected five more night victories during 18-19 November, with Bill Henry leading off this series of air-to-air victories, destroying an Emily at 0205 hours on 19 November as it neared the task group. It was his eighth overall victim, making him the first Navy pilot to achieve five or more confirmed night time kills. A few hours later, Ens. F.A. Fisher destroyed two Mitsubishi Ki-57 transports (Topsy) in the air, while Jack Berkheimer joined the ace club by flaming a Nakajima Ki-43 (Oscar) fighter over Luzon.

The mission that morning began at 0305 hours, when VF(N)-41 received orders to launch a heckling mission against Japanese-held airfields on Luzon, and by 0430 hours, six F6F-5Ns were in the air. Cmdr. Caldwell had radio trouble and headed back to the carrier, leaving his wingman, Ens. Fisher, to continue towards his target, Clark Field. Caldwell, during the return leg to the *Independence*, found that a small piece of paper wedged in his earplug line was responsible for his radio trouble, and after clearing it continued on to Clark Field, where he strafed several twin-engine aircraft parked along the south end of the strip. Meanwhile, Fisher also approached the area alone and, even in the darkness at a quarter to six in the morning, visibility was extremely clear; the sharp eyes of a night fighter pilot, accustomed to searching for prey in the darkness, did not require the service of the Hellcat's radar set. Flying due south at 5,000 feet, he spotted the running lights of two Topsy transports on a northerly heading at 3,000 feet. Both aircraft broke away in opposite directions, one east and the other west, indicating the approaching night fighter had been spotted. Circling around in a shallow dive to make a rear attack, Fisher chose the one on the westerly course, dropped his flaps to slow his airspeed, dropped into position against the unarmed transport, and opened fire. The transport's starboard engine burst into flames that quickly spread across the fuselage and the aircraft fell to earth. Almost immediately after the destruction of the first Topsy, Fisher saw another set of blinking lights of a large aircraft far to the south, some 15 miles away. He quickly gained on the slower-moving target, now identified as another Topsy, and executed the same angle of attack as the first. A short burst caused the transport's port engine to briefly burn, while a second burst hit the starboard wing root and created a dull glow that crept along the aircraft's belly, which erupted into a massive sheet of flames. Swinging sharply to starboard to avoid colliding with the doomed transport, Fisher watched as the Topsy fell to the ground. Afterward, he headed back to Clark Field, his primary target of the mission, and dropped the two MK-54 depth bombs his aircraft carried onto a couple buildings, then headed back to the carrier.

The third Japanese aircraft to fall to a VF(N)-41 pilot went to Jack Berkheimer as he made an approach to Lipa Field, located west of the town by that name, shortly before 0545 hours. Circling the field, he saw the lights of an Oscar fighter taxiing onto the main runway. By the time the Hellcat could swing into position, the Japanese aircraft was 300 feet off the ground, heading northeast. He opened fire at a range of 1,000 feet and kept firing his four inboard guns until the Oscar started to flame between the cockpit and wing sections, then it nosed over in a steep glide and blew up as it hit the ground. It was 0548 hours as he orbited to search for other targets and watched a large aircraft fall into a valley a few miles south of Lipa Field; it was probably Fisher's second Topsy.

Two other pilots from the squadron possibly saved the fleet from an enemy torpedo attack that evening. It was decided to stage heckler missions against Japanese airfields on Luzon to interfere with the probable launching of dusk torpedo attacks against TF-38 as it retired to the east. Two night fighters from the *Independence* were assigned to attack Aparri airfield, on the northern coast of Luzon, since this base, lying nearest of all the Philippine fields to Formosa, was an important stopover point for aircraft being sent down to the Manila area. The two pilots assigned the mission were Ensigns Wallace "Wally" E. Miller and Reuben "Rube" F. Peterson, who took off at 1700 hours, with each Hellcat carrying two MK-64 500-pound bombs. They climbed to 5,000 feet and took a 320-degree heading towards Aparri, 230 miles away. An hour later, 120 miles away from the fleet, they spotted five Betty bombers ten miles ahead of them, flying low on the water in the opposite direction, directly towards the task force. Peterson called the *Independence*, requesting permission to attack, which was promptly granted; the bombers in the meantime had passed below them at 2,500 feet. Peterson turned the F6F-5N around, closed in on the rearmost bomber, and fired several bursts, causing no apparent damage. To maintain a good firing position, Peterson pulled up to port in an S turn, pulling behind the formation again. This time the Hellcat's guns jammed and they could not be successfully recharged, so he had to abandon any further runs. Miller had lost sight of his wingman and decided to begin his own attack by entering into a steep, banking turn, as the bombers increased speed and began gaining altitude. The bombers unleashed heavy 12.7mm fire from their waist hatches, but none accurate enough to hit the approaching fighter. Pulling up to the tail of the last bomber, Miller put a long burst into the engines, wing roots, and fuselage, causing a fire to begin in the starboard engine; the Betty, fishtailing, dove towards the water, where it flew along for a few miles until it went out of control and struck the water.

Miller's aircraft, still loaded with two bombs, requested permission to dump them, which was granted, and he jettisoned the ordnance and quickly turned towards the next target. A long burst fired from 6 o'clock flamed the Betty's engines, but it found cover in a thick cloud bank. Looking down, he saw the same bomber far below enter into a tight, diving port turn before hitting the water. A third bomber appeared slightly above and off to starboard, passing from one cloud to another attempting to flee towards land. Miller waited until the Betty reappeared and fired four short bursts into the engines, flaming both of them. However, it eluded the Hellcat by entering into another cloud and visual contact was lost. He tried to pick it up on the radar scope, but it was still daylight and the screen could not be read without a viewing hood. The search continued as the fighter climbed to 5,000 feet, but he was unable to flush out the remaining two Bettys out of the five-plane formation. The two night fighters joined up and headed back to the carrier, landing at 2,000 hours.

F6F-5E came to rest in the catwalk after an errant landing aboard the *Independence*. This aircraft is identified as an -5E based on the type of radar pod slung underneath the wing. (Emil Buehler Library, NMNA)

Another landing accident took out three of VF(N)-41's Hellcats. The aircraft's tail on the left rests in the catwalk and is missing its radar pod's nose cone, while the Hellcat in the center is missing its tail section. The F6F-5N on the right has been pushed up against the island, but appears to have suffered less damage, outside of a bent prop and dents. (Emil Buehler Library, NMNA)

OPERATION OBLITERATION

Task Force 38.2, consisting of CVs *Lexington*, *Hancock*, and *Hornet*, CVLs *Cabot* and *Independence* supported by three battleships, five cruisers, and 20 destroyers sortied from Ulithi lagoon 10-11 December for the Philippines. The mission, code name Operation Obliteration, was to support the assault and occupation of Mindoro Island by neutralizing enemy air power on Luzon and attacking enemy shipping and installations. The *Independence*, with a screen of four destroyers, operated independently of the main force as TF-38.2.10 during the approach to prevent enemy detection on the approach. The pre-dawn CAP maintained by the *Independence* on 14 December as the task force neared eastern Luzon probably prevented the enemy from being alerted when Lt. Bill Henry shot down an Emily at 0415 hours, only 18 minutes after the *Hancock* picked it up on radar. At 400 hours, the *Independence* received orders to launch two night fighters to cover the first airstrikes at dawn. Henry and Ens. Barnett were catapulted at 0353 hours, with the latter ordered to maintain CAP at 1,000 feet 20 miles from the carrier, while fighter control sent Henry south to intercept the approaching Emily some 38 miles distant. The night fighter closed the distance, with Henry's radar scope picking up the flying boat. The pilot reported "Bogey at two miles, twelve o'clock." Shortly afterwards, he made a visual on the exhaust flames of the four-engine Emily, flying low at 1,000 feet at a speed of 125 knots (144mph). Losing altitude and speed, the Hellcat pulled up behind at 6 o'clock and fired three successive bursts into the Emily's engine area. The flying boat immediately began to lose altitude in a turning glide and crashed into the water, exploding on impact; it was his ninth victim.[1]

Henry's radar became inoperable shortly after bringing down the Emily, and Lt. Frederick Hankins was launched to relieve him. The CAP stayed up until 0720 hours, when they were called back to land. Henry and Barnett were brought safely aboard, however, Hankins made his approach too low and was waved off by the Landing Signal Officer (LSO). His plane apparently lost speed and went into a stall, and when he pulled his nose up to clear the ramp, the Hellcat spun off to the starboard side of the ship and crashed into the water, the fighter buckling just aft of the cockpit's armor plate as it struck the water. An immediate search failed to find the pilot. Hankins was the first of four VF(N)-41 pilots to lose their lives during the next few days as the night air group's Hellcats, in conjunction with VT(N)-41 TBM-1D Avengers, conducted all-night heckler missions against Luzon's airfields and shipping off the coast.

The squadron lost another two pilots during the first such mission on 14 December, when Cmdr. Caldwell led six F6F-5Ns, each loaded with two 500-pound bombs, against airfields and shipping during the early evening. The group orbited off Luzon until sunset, when it broke up into three sections, with Caldwell heading alone to hit shipping in the Lingayen Gulf, while Ensigns J.S. Allen and G.V. Williams targeted Clark field and I.H. Lee, H.E. Johnson, and Rube Peterson headed southwest to cover areas south and north of Manila. The last group encountered enemy AA fire 10 miles north of Manila and Johnson's plane was hit. He radioed the others, telling them his cockpit was full of oil and that his oil pressure was dropping. Lee joined up with him as Peterson continued southward. Dropping his bombs, Johnson headed east, only to have his engine seize up. He saw a shallow lake and made a graceful water landing, then climbed out of the plane. He waved to Lee, indicating he was all right, and waded ashore, where he managed to evade the Japanese and meet up with friendly forces. Meanwhile, Lee strafed a small airfield and headed towards Clark to rendezvous with Williams and Allen. The Clark area was, according to him, "a solid sheet of AA," as he noticed a plane crash about two miles south of the airfield, followed shortly thereafter by a second plane going down and exploding as it hit the ground. Williams returned to the carrier, but Allen did not, and it appears he may have shot down an enemy plane, only to be brought down himself by withering AA fire.[2]

VF(N)-41 scored again when Lt. B.A. Bradenbaugh shot down a Nick near Clark field while participating in a four-plane sweep against airfields and shipping. The *Independence* launched the aircraft at 0230 hours, with the group breaking off into separate two-plane sections. Bradenbaugh and his wingman, Ens. Fred A. Hunziker, headed towards the eastern Luzon coast, but became separated when over the Sierre Madre Mountains. The lieutenant proceeded alone to drop the pair of 500-pound bombs he carried on aircraft dispersal areas at two auxiliary airfields. He then saw the blinking wing light of a twin-engine Nick in the air, moving northwest at 1,000 feet off his starboard wing. The night fighter latched onto the Japanese plane, and two quick bursts of machine gun fire started the port engine afire; it then slipped into a steep glide, struck the ground, and exploded.

Ensigns Jack Berkheimer and Rube Peterson went aloft at 2300 hours on 16 December after a flight of VT(N)-41 Avengers reported enemy aircraft airborne in the Manila area. They split up, with Peterson heading for Manila Bay and Berkheimer going to investigate the Clark field area. Peterson arrived over the bay at 0135 hours and noticed the city was blacked out. A few minutes later, an aircraft's running lights were observed circling Cavite and he pointed his Hellcat towards them. Making out the silhouette of a Jake float plane in the darkness, one short burst from the night fighter's guns sent it burning towards the water. Ten minutes later, an unidentified enemy fighter appeared nearby with its red and blue running lights on. Peterson jumped the unsuspecting Japanese plane, put a burst into it from 7 o'clock, and sent it crashing into the bay. At 200 hours, Berkheimer called from the Clark field area,

Wearing foul weather gear during night operations, a landing signal officer (LSO) aboard the *Independence* guides one of the carrier's approaching aircraft circa late 1944. (Emil Buehler Library, NMNA)

VF(N)-41 Hellcat #5 in the background prepares to launch while a deck handler waits in the foreground to take the wheel chock away of another F6F-5N so that it can move into position. (Emil Buehler Library, NMNA)

The teamwork of a carrier deck crew is shown as they move #13 F6F-5N BuNo 58723 of VF(N)-41 into position. Carrier-based night fighter squadrons operated around the clock, flying day and night heckling mission, CAP, and NCAP. (Emil Buehler Library, NMNA)

VF(N)-90 entered combat operations aboard the *Enterprise* with the F6F-5N in December 1944, with strikes against Japanese-held airfields in the Philippines. Between December 1944 and May 1945, they would account for the downing of 31 enemy aircraft. (Scrapbook of Cmdr. William H. Balden, Emil Buehler Library, NMNA)

saying there was no activity and would head towards Peterson. Fifteen minutes passed when Berkheimer called again, saying he was approaching Manila; two minutes later the sky lit up as some 15 searchlights situated around the city were turned on, followed by a barrage of intense anti-aircraft fire. Peterson heard his fellow night fighter pilot utter "Peter..." and then, looking towards Manila, there appeared a brilliant explosion on the ground near the city's center. The searchlights went out as Peterson repeatedly called the other pilot, but there was only silence. At 0220 hours on the morning of 16 November 1944, the young 20-year-old night fighter pilot from Staten Island, New York, was gone. He was the squadron's second top scorer with seven and one-half kills, including five and one-half at night.[3]

As Peterson headed for home, *Independence* launched another flight of VF(N)-41 Hellcats for a heckling mission against airfields in central Luzon, with each fighter carrying a pair of 500-pound bombs. Ensign L.E. Diskosky flew alone, as his wingman became lost on the approach to the Clark field area and proceeded to drop his ordnance on the southern and western ends of the airfield's number two runway. A few minutes later, while cruising at 5,000 feet, he picked up the lights of what he later determined to be a twin-engine Nick flying 1,000 feet below to the northwest of his location. Diskosky dropped down to the same altitude and circled around to get on the intended victim's tail. Both engines of the enemy fighter burst into flames as he squeezed off a short burst of only 35 rounds. The Nick turned into a steep glide and crashed into the northwest slope of Mt. Arayat, an extinct volcano located in the central plains of Luzon.

Enterprise arrived off the Philippines as the second element of the fleet's night carrier group, with VF(N)-90 and VT(N)-90 joining *Independence*'s VF(N)-41 and VT(N)-41 as part of TF-38.5. The primary mission of the task force was providing air cover for landing forces on Luzon, in the Lingayen Gulf, against Japanese naval and air forces launched from Formosa and the Ryukyus Islands. *Enterprise*'s night fighter squadron was formed when it absorbed the personnel and aircraft of VF(N)-103 and -104, which were decommissioned in August 1944. VF(N)-90, under the command of Lt. Cmdr. Robert J. McCullough, entered combat 6 January 1945, leading a dozen Hellcats (10 F6F-5Es and 2 -5Ns) on a dawn rocket and strafing attack strike against Clark Field. Three of the planes received serious damage from intense, accurate AA fire. McCullough, with his controls and hydraulics shot out, returned to the *Enterprise*, but the Hellcat crashed through the barriers and tumbled over the side and into the water. A destroyer fished him out and he returned to the carrier.

Enterprise and *Independence* each catapulted a group of four Hellcats at 1500 hours for CAP over the airfields of northern Luzon, with the sortie resulting in the destruction of eight Japanese aircraft, all occurring during the daytime without the use of radar. The *Independence* group of four F6F-5N fighters arrived over the coastal town Appari, at the mouth of the Cagayan River, at 1615 hours, and the flight split up into two sections: Lt. K.H. Morris and Ens. Emmett Edwards joined up with the *Enterprise* fighters. South of Tuguegarao town, Morris spotted three Oscar fighters at 2 o'clock flying level in a tight V formation at 2,000 feet, approximately four miles away. One of the Japanese fighters peeled away and headed towards the Hellcat; Morris anticipated this and when the Oscar came into range, he put a burst into him that blew the starboard wing off as the Oscar exploded and spiraled into the ground. Morris then saw the other two fighters make a feint move away from him, but quickly whipped around and got onto the Hellcat's tail. Making a sharp port turn, he pushed his throttle forward to outrun the enemy as they lobbed ineffective shots at the retreating American fighter. Morris pulled up into a cloud base and made a quick wingover back out, hoping for a head-on shot at his pursuers, but the sky was empty. He continued south, searching for the Oscars, and saw an unidentified aircraft hit the ground, followed by what looked like an Oscar crashing about a mile southwest of the river. Morris turned back north, flying at 1,500 feet, and ten minutes after claiming his first kill, he spotted a trio of Nakajima Ki-44 Japanese fighters (Tojos). The Hellcat pilot decided to engage the enemy and began a shallow port turn towards them, but just before getting into firing range, one of the Tojo pilots, obviously aware of the Americans' presence, attempted an interception of his own. Morris, with an advantage in speed, simply leveled out and put a long burst from six o'clock into the other fighter's wing roots. After some 20 seconds of intermittent bursts from the Hellcat's guns, the Japanese fighter began a shallow turn to port, continuing it until crashing into the ground. The remaining Japanese fighters continued straight and level away from the American without attempting to seek revenge for the loss of their comrade.

Lt. Carl S. Nielson, operating in the same vicinity as Morris as part of *Enterprise*'s four-F6F-5E element, scored VF(N)-90's first three aerial victories during a brief but intense ten-minute engagement. Nielson arrived over the Japanese airfield at Alliminao at 1700 hours, when it was still daylight, and spotted a Dinah flying west of the field at 500 feet and shot it down. Recovering from his dive, he spotted a Zeke at 4,000 feet making a turn for him. Nielson turned into the Japanese fighter and fired, but his first burst missed. However, the second burst went into the Zeke's cockpit area and the fighter dove into the ground and exploded. A moment later, a Ki-43 Oscar fighter appeared in front of him and Nielson quickly dispatched his third enemy plane of the day. The rest of the mission was uneventful and the *Enterprise* group returned to base, however, that was not the case for Morris and Edwards of VF(N)-41.

Shortly after Lt. Morris shot down the Tojo, he heard Edwards calling, requesting him to join up for the return to base. The tone of Edwards' voice indicated there was something wrong. On the way another three Tojos attempted to engage, Morris but he was able to elude them and made the rendezvous with Edwards near the eastern Luzon coast. As he pulled up alongside, he saw his counterpart make a hand signal to him not to fly too close, and then Edwards called, telling him why: a Japanese fighter had rammed into his Hellcat. The impact severed five feet of the starboard wing, including the radar pod just outboard of the flap, leaving behind about a foot of the

VF(N)-90 F6F-5N with white in-squadron number 21 applied to the engine nacelle, fuselage, and within the arrowhead on the vertical stabilizer. (Author's Collection)

main wing spar protruding beyond the point of separation. He could maintain control as long as he kept the aircraft's speed above 180 knots (207mph) and, as they headed towards the carrier, he told his wingman about shooting down a Betty and another aircraft, the name of which Morris did not catch.

The Hellcats flew back 200 miles and were at 2,000 feet, with the carrier *Lexington* visible some four miles away, when Edwards said he was going to bail out by rolling the aircraft over and dropping out. Morris saw him roll his canopy back and heard him say, "I'll never make it." Morris called him back, "Roll over and hit the silk," but there was no response as he watched Edwards' aircraft violently snap over onto its back, a white flight helmet and yellow Mae West life preserver flew from the cockpit, and the Hellcat plummeted into the water. Morris circled the oil slick where the aircraft went down as the destroyer USS *The Sullivans* conducted a search, but there was no sign of debris or Edwards.[4]

Aircraft from the night carrier groups continued maintaining round-the-clock CAP and air strikes against enemy targets on Luzon for the next three days with little interference from enemy aircraft. However, VF(N)-90 suffered its first casualties in the combat area when two Hellcats piloted by Ensigns Charles W. Glbson and John G. Sowell collided after returning from a strafing and rocket attack on Clark Field. Glbson was able to report after the incident that his right wing was on fire, but nothing was heard from him again. Sowell apparently was able to maintain control of his aircraft, climb to 5,000 feet, and bail out over the water, as the American cruiser *San Diego* reported flares from a Very pistol near his last reported position. A subsequent search failed to find the missing pilot.

NIGHT FIGHTER ORGANIZATION JANUARY 1945

SQUADRON	AIRCRAFT	CARRIER
VF-20	F6F-5N(3)	*Lexington*
VF-11	F6F-5N(3)	*Hornet*
VF-7	F6F-5N(2)	*Hancock*
VF-80	F6F-5N(3)	*Ticonderoga*
VF-81	F6F-3N(1)/F6F-5N(3)	*Wasp*
VF(N)-41	F6F-5N(9)	*Independence*
VF(N)-90	F6F-5E(16)/F6F-5N(16)	*Enterprise*

TF-38 moved to suppress Japanese naval and air forces from launching attacks from French Indo-China, Formosa, Canton, and Hong Kong by hitting airfields, installations, and shipping in those areas. VF(N)-41 continued racking up air-to-air victories, with three more Japanese aircraft falling, this time guided by radar, during a pre-dawn vector on 10 January.

TF-38, after conducting all-day strikes on Formosa on the 9th, began a run through the Bashi Straits into the China Sea, with the intention of attacking shipping off French Indo-China.

The force picked up a bogey at 0453 hours on its radar screens at 98 miles out coming from Luzon and headed for Formosa, its intended flight path taking it almost directly over the American ships. The *Independence* was ready to launch, with Lt. (jg) Robert R. Fegraeus and Ens. Hansen waiting on the flight deck in their fighters, but they did not receive permission until 0514 hours, when the bogey had closed the range to 27 miles. The carrier launched both fighters, with Fegraeus told to orbit 20 miles from the force, while Hansen climbed to 8,000 feet and headed towards the bogey. Thus began a series of complicated series of events where Hansen made and lost radar contact with the target for nearly an hour before making a firm lock that guided him to a yet-unidentified twin-engine aircraft in front and slightly above the fighter at 8,300 feet. He closed the range and identified it as a Mitsubishi Ki-21 (Sally) bomber by flying directly under the unsuspecting aircraft and observing the wing pattern. Dropping back 250 feet, he opened up with all six .50-caliber guns, with the tracers showing hits to the fuselage and both wing roots. The bomber's starboard wing began to burn, the reddish glow of the flames providing a perfect aiming point for Hansen as he fired another burst into the starboard engine. The Sally started a spiraling turn to port through the clouds, flames spreading back across the wing, with the Hellcat following. The bomber continued its death spiral and Hansen put one more burst into the now-flaming mass in front of him. The night fighter pilot pulled his aircraft out of its dive and saw a massive flare-up among the clouds, indicating the Sally had disintegrated – the time was 0610. It was the longest night interception in squadron history, and it had taken the Hellcat and its pilot near the southern tip of Formosa, nearly 100 miles from the task force.

While Hansen was returning from his successful hunt, a second contact showed up on radar at 0621 hours, distance 90 miles. The *Independence* sent Fegraeus, circling 20 miles from the task force, after the bogey closed to approximately 45 miles south of the force. The Japanese aircraft continued on a collision course, taking it dangerously close to the fleet. The Hellcat's radar picked up the bogey initially at three-and-a-half miles as the night fighter turned, but the signal was weak, however, and the contact faded from the screen. A moment later, the blip reappeared three miles ahead and cruising 155 knots (178mph) at an altitude of 9,400 feet. Fegraeus, at 9,200 feet, closed to one mile and switched his screen to the one-mile scale. He looked outside to gain a visual and saw a twin-engine aircraft appear a third of a mile away, slightly above the Hellcat. Closing to 200 feet on the bogey – now recognized as a Sally, the same as Hansen's victim – he fired a burst from the fighter's four inboard guns, since the other pair were loaded with tracer rounds that would ruin his night vision. The

Flight of VF(N)-90 Hellcats from Enterprise. Night Air Group 90 consisted of F6F-5N Hellcats of VF(N)-90 and TBF/TBM-3D Avengers of VT(N)-90. (Scrapbook of Cmdr. William H. Balden, Emil Buehler Library, NMNA)

Lt. William "Bill" Henry was VF(N)-41's executive officer and the Navy's top night fighter ace with 10.5 kills, with six and one-half victories occurring at night. (Emil Buehler Library, NMNA)

rounds tore into the Sally's engines; both began burning, with the port mount exploding a moment later. It went into a death spiral through the low overcast, plunging into the sea close to the carrier *Hancock* – time 0647 hours.

Meanwhile, Ens. Hansen was on his return leg to the ship when the *Hancock* sent him towards another contact to the south. The time was 0627 hours; seventeen minutes had elapsed since he downed the Sally, and several course and altitude changes would follow during the next 45 minutes before he could destroy his second aircraft. Hansen called "contact" at 0653, but lost the blip on his scope three minutes later after diving to 5,000 feet after his scope indicated the target was at that level, although the *Hancock* had told him the altitude was 8,500 feet. Two additional course corrections reestablished radar contact, and when the night fighter closed to a half-mile, he saw the exhaust pattern of a twin-engine Nick flying directly ahead. The approach of dawn increased the chance of the Hellcat being spotted, so Hansen decided to use the clouds as concealment, allowing him to close within 300 feet, where he opened fire. Only one starboard gun out of the six actually fired, and it ran dry after only a few rounds; however, it was enough to cause the Nick's starboard engine to burst into flames. The Japanese aircraft did not attempt to take any evasive action as Hansen recharged his guns and fired again. This time only one port gun worked, firing only some 20 rounds before stopping. It was enough, as the Nick burst into flames and then exploded as the Hellcat pulled up and directly over it in a sharp port turn.

Pilots of VF(N)-41 and -90 scored again six days later while participating in heckling Hong Kong and Canton on the 16th. *Enterprise* and *Independence* each launched four Hellcats at 1630, with Lt. Bill Henry acting as flight leader and the group proceeding in bombing, rocketing, and strafing Hong Kong's Kai Tak airfield. The Hellcats spotted one unlucky Japanese L2D Showa/Nakajima (Tabby) transport on its landing approach, and it became the focus of several 5-inch HAVR rocket; it was left burning just as its wheels touched down. Lt. James J. Wood and Ens. Robert C. Wattenburger of VF(N)-90 then spotted a Tojo taking off and, diving from 7,000 feet, proceeded to dispatch the enemy fighter with a series of well-aimed bursts from both Hellcats. Lt. Wood would score again five days later, when he shot down a Frances coming in for a landing at Tainan airfield, on Formosa.

The group reformed and headed towards Canton. Bill Henry spotted an Oscar fighter 20 miles southwest of Canton, and latching onto his tail, fired a series of bursts, hitting the fighter's wings and fuselage. The Oscar continued in a shallow glide, and as the pilot attempted to pull into a tight loop to get onto the Hellcat's tail, Henry fired another burst that apparently killed the pilot. The plane continued into the top of its loop, then nosed down and crashed into a rice paddy. The destruction of the Oscar brought Henry's total to 10.5 victories, with six and one-half of those occurring at night; it also marked the last claimed by VF(N)-41. Operations continued for nearly two weeks before *Independence* withdrew from combat operations. VF(N)-41 destroyed 46 enemy planes in the air between September 1944 and January 1945, thus establishing itself as the Navy's highest scoring night fighter squadron.

Chapter 5

Carrier Operations (February-August 1945)

The night fighter must be cool, precise, methodical, self-confident, and persevering.

- Cmdr. Turner F. Caldwell

Independence's night air operations ended 28 January 1945, and it was replaced by the *Saratoga*'s Night Air Group 53, comprised of VF(N)-53, VT(N)-53, and VF-53, with the fighter element led by Lt. Cmdr. Alphonse Main. Third Fleet assets were reassigned to the 5th Fleet 26 January, and TF-38 became TF-58, with *Enterprise* and *Saratoga* operating as Task Group 58.5. On 16-17 February, the task force struck the Japanese home islands with the intent of destroying enemy aircraft in the air and on the ground, and conduct bombing, strafing, and rocket attacks against airfield installations and aircraft manufacturing facilities. The Night Air Groups on *Enterprise* and *Saratoga* participated in such attacks, but were unsuccessful downing enemy aircraft. The task force retired and proceeded to support the Iwo Jima landings, with the night carrier group operating northwest of the island, providing dusk and night CAP, along with observing for naval gunfire. Lt. James Wood of VF(N)-90 shot down a Nakajima Ki-49 twin-engine bomber (Helen) on the 19th, which was attempting to shadow the task force.

Task Force 58.5 dissolved on the morning of the 21st, with *Enterprise* leaving to join TG-58.2, while *Saratoga* joined TG-52.2.4 and its escort carriers to provide air support for the Iwo Jima landings. *Saratoga*'s involvement was short-lived. The carrier was detached, along with three destroyers, and sent to Iwo Jima to provide NCAP and support of amphibious forces. Radar picked up a large formation of enemy planes shortly before 1700 hours heading towards the carrier and her three escorts. VF(N)-53 Hellcats, in their only aerial combat of the war, managed to shoot down a pair of Zeke fighters, but on their return to *Saratoga* they found themselves homeless.

Fourteen F6F-5N Hellcats of VF(N)-53 were scheduled for launch from *Saratoga* at 1700 hours: twelve to provide dusk Target Combat Air Patrol (TCAP) over Iwo Jima and two to provide dusk CAP over TG-52.2.4. Radar picked up incoming bogies approaching from the north and launching was expedited, with the first Hellcat becoming airborne at 1653 and the last at 1703 hours. As rapidly as each aircraft became airborne, they were vectored by *Saratoga*'s CIC, both to attempt interception and to get them beyond range of the task group's antiaircraft fire. The last Hellcat left the deck as the first Japanese suicide aircraft emerged from the heavy overcast and struck the carrier, and in rapid succession, *Saratoga* suffered four bomb hits. None of the defending aircraft managed to make a successful interception, mainly due to the confusion created by the hasty launching and the presence of an almost solid high overcast that descended into a thick but broken lower cloud cover at 2,500 feet. At 1730 hours, nearly 30 minutes after the initial attack on the carrier, Lt. (jg) Charles W. Horne, as part of a four-plane division, spotted a single Zeke crossing in front of them approximately 25 miles north of the carrier. Horne fired, scoring hits on the Zeke's fuselage and wing root, and the Japanese fighter fell off in a steep starboard dive, losing a wing as it plummeted through the low overcast and into the water. An hour later, Lt. William C. Reinhardt and Ens. V.A. Kellenbeck encountered a Judy 30 miles northeast of *Saratoga* flying a reciprocal course at the same altitude of 7,000 feet as the Hellcats. They overtook the

Night Air Group 90 (CVG-(N)-90) aircraft with F6F-5N in the foreground spotted on *Enterprise's* flight deck at sunset. Cmdr. William I. Martin led the night group, with Lt. Cmdr. Robert J. McCullough as CO of the fighter squadron. (Scrapbook of Cmdr. William H. Balden, Emil Buehler Library, NMNA)

F6F-5N Hellcat VF(N)-53 on the deck of USS *Saratoga* (CV-3) while under enemy attack off Iwo Jima, just seconds after the carrier suffered the first bomb hit. The *Saratoga* suffered extensive damage from bomb and kamikaze hits between 1700 and 1900 hours 21 February 1945. (Robert L. Lawson Photographic Collection, Emil Buehler Library, NMNA)

aircraft, which made no significant attempt to evade, except for a gradual dive towards the water, and both fired from a distance of 1,200 feet. Reinhardt's rounds struck the fuselage near the cockpit and the starboard wing. The Judy's wing tip blew off and it went into a 60-degree dive into the sea.

Recovery of aircraft after the battle was difficult, as the carrier had sustained serious damage to the flight deck and the communication system was in shambles. Nine of the 14 VF(N)-53 Hellcats landed on two escort carriers: four on USS *Rudyard Bay* (CVE 81) and five on USS *Makin Island* (CVE 93). The remaining five pilots landed aboard the *Saratoga* between 2042 and 2102 hours. *Saratoga* limped home and out of the war, taking most of its air group with it, except for a few pilots and aircraft who were absorbed by other carrier units.

The *Enterprise* took up the slack left by *Saratoga*'s loss by providing continuous air cover of amphibious forces off Iwo Jima and supplemented strikes against the Bonin Islands. The night of 24 February, Lt. Kenneth D. Smith, flying a lone wolf patrol, spotted a Helen over Chichi Jima, came in behind it, opened fire, and followed it down almost to the water, where another burst sent the enemy plane down in flames. The ship remained in the area until 2 March, when it retired to Ulithi for replenishment. Its night fighter complement had downed only two enemy planes during five weeks of operations off Japan and Iwo Jima. That would change when the *Enterprise* took part in the invasion on Okinawa, however Adm. Mark A. Mitscher, Commander of Task Force 58, took note of *Enterprise*'s night air group activities during Iwo Jima operations and wrote a letter dated 7 March 1945 to Adm. Spruance, requesting that the night carrier group be discontinued. He stated:

> It is recommended that the night carrier project be discontinued. In lieu of it, increase the complement of day CVs to six VFN and 10 pilots, and three VTN and five projects, reducing the number of day VF and VT accordingly.

He viewed the use of such a group as somewhat ineffective and draining the offensive power of day carriers.

> A night carrier task group requires day carrier protection, since even though day planes are aboard night carriers, the night carriers cannot be worked continuously day and night. Such day carriers as would be assigned to the protection of a night carrier task group would be used for defensive purposes only, and thereby lost to the task force for offensive purposes. The night carrier task group has not yet demonstrated that the damage night carriers can inflict on the enemy compensates for the loss of the offensive power of the day carriers required for the protection of the night carrier task group.[1]

VF(N)-90 Hellcats #17 (foreground) and #15 in flight over the Pacific. Number 17 has the bar of the U.S. national insignia wrapped around the radar pod. (Scrapbook of Cmdr. William H. Balden, Emil Buehler Library, NMNA)

An F6F-5N banks away from VF(N)-90 #17 (right) and #15 (left) as taken from a VT(N)-90 Avenger circa early 1945. (Scrapbook of Cmdr. William H. Balden, Emil Buehler Library, NMNA)

Spruance responded to Mitscher's desire to end the night carrier project in an undated letter to Adm. King. Spruance stated that no carriers could withdraw far enough to be safe from enemy attack and still function as an offensive tool, and that day carriers with night fighters could no more operate more conveniently or effectively during the day and night than a night carrier. Spruance endorsed continuing the program in the letter's last paragraph, but voiced concern regarding the tactical deployment of night carriers:

> It is believed that the idea of having one or more carriers with the force specialized in night work is sound enough theoretically to warrant further work and investigation of the problems involved, although at this state of the war, the assignment of all these night carriers to one task group is believed to have been proven to be unsound.[2]

OKINAWA (MARCH-MAY 1945)

Allied preparations for Operation Iceberg, the invasion of Okinawa, began with TF-58 aircraft hitting airfields on Kyushu and Southern Honshu between 17-19 March. Okinawa, only 350 miles from the southern tip of Kyushu, was well in range of enemy land-based aircraft, and the Americans expected the Japanese would throw everything at the invasion force. Japanese reconnaissance aircraft monitored the arrival of TF-58 and in response, *Enterprise* sent night fighters after them, resulting in the Japanese losing five planes, three of them at night. The first "splash" was rung-up by Lt. (jg) R.E. Wattenburger at 0100 hours on the 17th when, after an hour long chase through heavy cloud cover and rain, he caught up to a Helen and shot it down. Lt. (jg) Wesley R. Williams, on the same NCAP, closed on a Nakajima C6N (Myrt) reconnaissance aircraft after a three-hour chase and flamed it at 0320 hours. The night fighters claimed two more enemy aircraft between 0400 and 0445 hours (a Tabby and Jake), while Lt. (jg) W.J. Squires brought down a Jake over Kagoshima Bay during a pre-dawn intruder mission against Kyushu airfields. Daylight brought the task force under attack, and Ens. G. R. Earl brought down a Frances that was attempting to make a run at the the ships.

Four of VF-17's night fighter contingent conducted a similar mission that morning after launching from the *Hornet* at 0410 hours, resulting in the destruction of six enemy aircraft. Led by Lt. J.A. McIntyre, the flight made landfall at Ariake Bay and the planes split up, with each pilot independently seeking targets of opportunity around the Kanoya area. At 6,000 feet, McIntyre spotted a light blinking about 5,000 feet below him. He dropped down and found it to be a wing light from what he believed to be a heaving four-engine plane circling for a landing. After following the plane around the traffic

An errant Avenger torpedo bomber of VT(N)-90 crashed into parked aircraft aboard *Enterprise*, shearing off the vertical stabilizer of another Avenger, which in turn was pushed into Hellcat #29. (Scrapbook of Cmdr. William H. Balden, Emil Buehler Library, NMNA)

circle, he maneuvered into position and fired a burst, causing the inboard port engine to catch fire. The plane continued descending in an attempt to land, but another burst from the night fighter hit the cockpit area and the plane spun into the ground and exploded.[3]

Cruising over Ariake Bay, Ens. J.H. Thomas spotted two planes below him sending blinker messages to each other. He executed a 360-degree wingover and slid behind the tail of one of the planes – identified as a Myrt – and fired, sending it spiraling down into the water. Thomas regained altitude, saw more lights moving out to sea, and caught up to a Jill carrying a torpedo. He dropped back 150 feet and fired a four-second burst into the wing roots. The Jill flamed, nosed over, and dove straight into the water with a terrific explosion, possibly caused by the torpedo. Ens. W.J. Idelson bagged another Jill east of Kanoya airfield, followed by a Dinah, while Ens. Robert J. Humphrey scored by downing a Mitsubishi Topsy transport. It was Humphrey's first of five and one-third enemy planes destroyed in the air during a three-month period, including two and one-third victories in March. His total tally besides the Topsy was one-third of a Myrt on 23 March, an Emily and a Jill on 27 March, a Betty on 16 April, and a Paul on 24 May.

Damage control team aboard *Enterprise* fight fires fed by aviation fuel and ammunition after the carrier was hit by "friendly" fire from a destroyer 20 March 1945 off Japan. The heat from the fire appears to have warped and burned the fabric of Hellcat #28's rudder. (Scrapbook of Cmdr. William H. Balden, Emil Buehler Library, NMNA)

Enterprise night fighter pilots continued to raise their squadron's score, with Lt. (jg) L. F. Harrison and Lt. Layton E. Robinson claiming VF(N)-90's fifth victory in three days on the 19th by intercepting a Betty at 0500, four miles southeast of Saeki Airfield, on Kyushu. The Japanese launched several air strikes against the massive U.S. fleet assembled off Honshu and Kyushu that resulted in knocking two U.S. carriers out of action. On the 18th, an enemy plane dropped a 500-pound bomb that ricocheted off *Enterprise*'s forward elevator but failed to detonate. USS *Franklin* (CV 13), operating only 50 miles off the Japanese mainland with its flight and hangar decks full of gassed-up and armed planes, took two bomb hits from a dive bomber. Explosions and massive fires followed, killing over 800 men and wounding nearly 500 others. Miraculously, the crew managed to get the fires under control and regain steam, then headed for Ulithi for emergency repairs before heading back to the U.S.

Enterprise followed *Franklin* in leaving the forward area the following day, when well-meaning gunners aboard another ship and trying to protect her succeeded in knocking it out of action when two of their five-inch antiaircraft shells exploded over the carrier's flight deck. Shrapnel from the shells punctured the fuel tanks of two Hellcats, and the leaking fuel spread across the flight deck and ignited. The burning gasoline ignited two more Hellcats and 40mm ready service ammunition, with the ensuing fires and explosions burning out two 40mm gun mounts, along with communication systems. The carrier was laid up for two weeks at Ulithi, undergoing repairs before returning to the fleet off Okinawa in early April. The *Enterprise*, before heading to Ulithi, had 14 of the air group's night fighter pilots selected by lottery to join units aboard other carriers to supplement night air defense. Lt. Robert J. Smith and Lt. (jg) William G. Piscopo, while attached to VF-82 aboard USS *Bennington* (CV 20), shot down three planes between them during the first week of April, all at night, while Ensign Waldo West, with VF-84 on the *Bunker Hill*, downed three planes during the month. However, one of the pilots, Lt. James Wood, serving with a unit aboard the *Randolph*, failed to return from a mission on 2 May and was declared missing in action.

The first escort carrier to carry night fighters into combat (USS *Sangamon* (CVE 26)) arrived off Okinawa on 23 March as part of TU-51.13. The carrier's air group (CAG-33) consisted of VF-33 and VT-33, and included a contingent of F6F-5E/N aircraft and pilots; they began operations two days later. The first *Sangamon* night fighter kill occurred the evening of the 26th, with a radar-guided kill of a Val 40 miles from the ship. From 9-22 April, *Sangamon* aircraft struck Japanese airfields on Miyako and Ishigaki, islands of the Sakishima Gunto Group lying south of Okinawa. During this operation, *Sangamon*'s night fighters participated in the downing of seven Japanese fighters. On 22 April, a group of VT-33 Avengers and escorting fighters of VF-33 arrived over Nobara Field, on Miyako, and caught 25-30 enemy aircraft, most of them twin-engine bombers, warming up for a strike against Allied shipping. The American aircraft began their attack, sending rocket and machine gun fire into the group of aircraft on the ground. Overhead, seven Oscar fighters appeared and began a run against the attackers, only to be stopped by the Hellcats

Deck and damage control crews aboard *Enterprise* wade through fire-fighting foam spread after suppressing fires, while the burned carcass of Hellcat #33 is hauled away. (Scrapbook of Cmdr. William H. Balden, Emil Buehler Library, NMNA)

Damaged F6F-5N Hellcats of VF(N)-90 wait for disposal after the 20 March 1945 fire. *Enterprise* suffered severe damage in three separate incidents between March and May 1945 that shortened her operations during the last few months of the Pacific War. (Scrapbook of Cmdr. William H. Balden, Emil Buehler Library, NMNA)

An F6F-5E of VF-33 piloted by Lt. (jg) William Bailey smashes into barrier on USS *Sanganon*, spraying fuel from the wing's ruptured fuel cell on 26 February 1945 when the tailhook failed to catch the wire. The pilot was uninjured. (Tailhook Association)

F6F-5E of VF-33 on the catapult of escort carrier USS *Sangamon* (CVE-26) as the ship heads towards Okinawa 22 March 1945. Between late March and early May, VF-33 day and night fighters supported the Okinawa landings and struck Japanese airfields on the home islands. (Robert L. Lawson Photographic Collection, Emil Buehler Library, NMNA)

and losing five of the seven during the ensuing dogfight. The VF pilots had their hands full, as four more enemy fighters appeared. Night fighters from the *Sangamon* arrived, shooting down two of the four just as night fighters from the *Sangamon* arrived, and two more Japanese aircraft went down. The carrier's operational life was cut short two weeks later when a kamikaze struck her. The ensuing explosions and fires wiped out the entire complement of CAG-33 aircraft.

Preliminary ground operations prior to the main landings on Okinawa began 26 March 1945, with elements of the 77th Division (USA) landing on Kerama Retto, a group of islands 15 miles west of Okinawa. While American troops captured the outlying islands, aircraft of TF-58 focused their attention on softening up Okinawa, flying 3,095 sorties between 23 and 29 March. The prelude for Operation Iceberg becoming the bloodiest campaign of the Pacific War transpired the morning of 24 March, after the task force retired from a pre-invasion bombardment of the island. Seven suicide planes from Kyushu survived the combat air patrol and AA and struck the ships at dawn, damaging the battleship *Nevada*, the cruiser *Indianapolis*, and four destroyers.

A week later, the full-scale landings on Okinawa began, with the III Amphibious Corps and XXIV Corps landing relatively unopposed on 1 April, Easter Sunday. By mid-afternoon, Kadena and Yontan airfields were in American hands. Japanese forces on Okinawa allowed the Americans to land relatively unmolested, but their brethren in the air made their presence known, launching sporadic strikes against the transport area and damaging three ships. Five days later, the Japanese staged the largest kamikaze attack of the war, launching 350 planes against the Allied fleet and targeting landing support forces, American and British carriers, and destroyers on picket duty. The expected all-out effort by the Japanese to contest the invasion of Okinawa developed on the morning of 6 April, and continued throughout the day and into the next. The air battle became a miniature Marianas Turkey Shoot, with American fighters and antiaircraft fire downing 236 Japanese planes to the loss of only two American fighters. VF-83, with USS *Essex*, alone accounted for 65 enemy aircraft during the day, with its night fighter detachment, led by Lt. Donald E. Umphres, claiming another eight destroyed in the air during the early evening hours.

Umphres, leading Ensigns William K. Somers and James M. Barnes on a dusk CAP over Okinawa, spotted a Corsair and Hellcat chasing an Oscar fighter, both of which overran their intended victim. Somers lined up on the Japanese fighter's tail and stayed on him for three minutes before his hits finally flamed the Oscar and it went down. Three Val dive bombers flying low above the water became the Hellcat's next targets, with Umphres latching onto the "Tail-End-Charlie," knocking it down with just a couple short bursts of machine gun fire. Barnes came up on another Val from behind and splashed it, then went after the third plane heading for an American destroyer, bagging it just short of its intended target. The Hellcats then vectored 15 miles and spotted three Oscars 3,000 feet below them, flying in a loose formation abreast. Umphres made a high side run on the middle plane and flamed it with a long burst into the engine, with the pilot bailing out before the Oscar crashed (the after action report failed to disclose whether the Japanese pilot bailed out with a parachute). He then made a pass on a second one at close range and the enemy fighter disintegrated. The third Oscar made a head-on run at both Somers and Umphres, and as he did so, Barnes jockeyed himself behind and fired several long bursts into the Japanese fighter. The Oscar's pilot bailed out at 150 feet and, according to the Hellcat pilots, he landed safely in the water. Moments later, another Oscar came out of the clouds at 3,000 feet and made head-on runs against Somers and Umphries before Barnes was able to maneuver in for the kill. The trio returned to NCAP duty after downing the last of eight Japanese planes. Ens. Barnes previously destroyed a Sonia in the air at 0430 hours on 4 April, and the four credited to him on this mission made him an ace. He would finish with six confirmed victories before an operational flying accident took his life 2 July 1945. The Navy, in recognition of Somer's actions on 6 April, awarded him the Navy Cross posthumously.

Enterprise returned to combat operations off Okinawa 7 April, after undergoing repairs at Ulithi. VF(N)-90 would claim another seven enemy planes during the next five days, with Lt. Dallas Runion scoring first by bagging a Frances during the afternoon of the seventh 50 miles west of the Task Force. Late in the afternoon of the ninth, four of *Enterprise*'s Hellcats flying CAP near Okinawa became involved in a highly confusing situation involving Marine land-based fighters returning to base. Some 20 Marine fighters based at Yontan were having extreme difficulty finding their way back to base due to extreme adverse weather, waning sunlight, and were also low on gas. Radio channels were crowded with their transmissions and ground control trying to assist in bringing them in. At the same time, the enemy decided to launch several air raids against the landing support forces. Lt. (jg) Squires homed in on flashes of AA fire and saw a Val in the last light of day about to start a dive from 6,000 feet towards a radar picket destroyer stationed northeast of Okinawa. Smoke was billowing from the destroyer's bow, apparently from an earlier attack. Squires closely followed the Val as the latter dove through the destroyer's concentrated AA fire. The Hellcat's pilot fired a long burst into the dive bomber's engine and fuselage before pulling out of his dive at 800 feet. The burning Val continued on its dive, crashing into the water just ahead of the destroyer's starboard side.

Enterprise became the target of another air attack for the third time in as many months during the afternoon of 11 April, with one plane diving into the ship's port quarter, hitting two 40mm mounts before falling into the sea, where a bomb it was carrying detonated beneath the ship. Another plane crashed within 45 feet of the ship and its bomb exploded. The shock of the bomb blasts wretched her hull and broke loose number 3 and 4 generators from their foundations. Flight operations continued through the evening temporarily, despite the damage, with five pilots each scoring a victory off Okinawa's northern tip; Lt. Runion started off by bagging a Tony 90 miles off Zamba Misaki. Runion and his wingman, Lt. (jg) Purcell, had been orbiting off Okinawa for nearly two hours when fighter control vectored them to a bogey. Thirty miles into the interception all communication with the controller was lost, and Runion nor his wingman had radar or visual contact, so they reversed course and headed towards Zamba Misaki. Runion was sitting back and taking it easy when he saw the Tony 2,000 feet away, flying in the opposite direction. He called "Tally Ho" over his mike and turned into the Japanese fighter at the same time the Tony turned into him and fired, sending a burst of fire into the cockpit, and the fighter dove straight into the water.

Lt. Kenneth Smith, on NCAP over Okinawa, was vectored to a Betty approaching the landing support forces on the western side of the island at 2105, but Smith was forced to break off, as the bomber approached the fleet and the ships began to fire. The Betty broke away and headed back towards the island followed by Smith, whose radar kept him on track until making a visual and identifying the bogey as an enemy bomber. He closed to 500 feet and fired from slightly below the Betty, causing the entire starboard wing to burst into flames and the plane dove into the water. Lt. (jg) Joseph C. Gallant was vectored onto a Betty at 0200 hours 70 miles from Zamba Misaki, and closed underneath the bomber and fired. Both engines caught fire, and the plane nosed over into a steep glide and crashed into the sea, exploding on impact. Thirty minutes later, Lt. James Wood caught a Peggy in the same area, and after overshooting it a few times he finally closed and fired, sending the plane into its death dive, which ended with it hitting the water, where it exploded, burned, and sank. There was a nearly three-hour lull before Ens. James Perkins caught a Jack dropping a flare, chased it, and caught it on a maneuvering turn to send it crashing into the extreme northern tip of Okinawa at 0510 hours. The battle was not one-sided, as the squadron lost one pilot and plane on the 13th, when Ens. Fred Hunziker, who previously served with VF(N)-41, went missing in action while chasing a Betty. The damage created by the two near misses from the Kamikaze attacks on the eleventh forced the *Enterprise* once again to withdraw to Ulithi for repairs; she would return to action three weeks later.

USN NIGHT FIGHTER ORGANIZATION APRIL 1945

SQUADRON	AIRCRAFT	CARRIER
VF-5	F6F-5N (4)	*Franklin*
VF-6	F6F-5E (2)/F6F-5N (4)	*Hancock*
VF-9	F6F-5E (2)/F6F-5N (4)	*Yorktown*
VF-10	F6F-5N (4)	*Intrepid*
VF-12	F6F-5E (2)/F6F-5N (4)	*Randolph*
VF-17	F6F-5N (4)	*Hornet*
VF-82	F6F-5E (2)/F6F-5N (4)	*Bennington*
VF-83	F6F-5E (2)/F6F-5N (4)	*Essex*
VF-84	F6F-5N (4)	*Bunker Hill*
VF-86	F6F-5E (2)/F6F-5N (2)	*Wasp*
VF(N)-90	F6F-5E (11)/F6F-5N (19)	*Enterprise*
VF-33	F6F-5E/N (?)	*Sangamom*

The compliment of night fighting Hellcats aboard USS *Essex* and *Yorktown* shot down four enemy planes on 4 May, with the *Yorktown*'s Ens. John Orth of VF-9 bagging three Bettys between 0345 and 0455 hours. The 23-year-old reservist had three previous aerial victories off Okinawa, with the destruction of a Nakajima J1N1-C (Irving) reconnaissance aircraft on 5 April followed by another Irving and a Betty on the 30th. *Yorktown* launched Orth at 0300 hours, who headed for his assigned sector northwest of the task force, but before reaching his station, USS *Randolph*'s (CV-15)fighter director vectored him to a Betty flying 60 miles away at an altitude of 14,500 feet. His radar picked up the blip at a range of two miles. Experience told him to drop the Hellcat's landing gear and flaps to lower his airspeed to avoid over-running the target, and then raised them after reducing sufficient speed. Orth picked up the Betty visually a quarter mile away, flying 300 feet above him. He dimmed his gun sight, closed in, and fired, scoring hits on both wing roots and port engine. He continued to fire short bursts as the Betty weaved back and forth, trying to evade the night fighter. The bomber's starboard wing and fuselage began burning as Orth lowered his wheels and flaps and chopped his throttle in order to stay behind and watch the plane hit the water.

The battle had taken both hunter and hunted down to 4,000 feet, when fighter control almost immediately told the Hellcat pilot to climb to 8,000 feet as another blip appeared on the screen. Orth picked up another Betty on his radar after a couple course changes at 0422 hours. His first contact was weak, but showed the enemy to be below him and slightly to port. He put his fighter into a dive, watching the scope until the two dots on his set showed the bomber at a distance of a mile-and-a-half. He switched his radar setting for the two-mile

An F6F-5N Hellcat of VF-25 9 April 1945 crash landed on escort carrier USS *Chenango* (CVE-28) off Okinawa, starting raging fires among the fully-loaded aircraft on the flight deck. The crew successfully put out the fires and the ship continued operations. (Robert L. Lawson Photographic Collection, Emil Buehler Library, NMNA)

range and followed the Betty in a gradual turn to port, with the moon behind him, and finally got a visual with the bomber 400 feet above a quarter mile away. Orth pulled up until he was level with the bomber, and within a range of approximately 300 feet fired a short burst. The Betty pushed over and Orth fired another burst into the tail; the bomber pushed over in a steeper dive, but Orth pulled up and fired again. The Betty started to burn almost immediately in the port engine as Orth fired again. The bomber did a wingover to the left and went straight into the water. Thirty minutes later, USS *Randolph* (CV 15) vectored Orth to his third Betty flying at 13,000 feet, 72 miles from the task force. He pulled up to the six o'clock position and fired, scoring hits in the wing roots and engines. Orth looked up and was about to fire again when the Betty burst into flames and spiraled into the water and exploded. His air-to-air victories earned him a place among Navy aces and the Navy Cross, placing him as the Navy's second highest night fighter ace, only second to VF(N)-41's Bill Henry's six and one-half kills.

TG-58.1 and 58.3 struck Kyushu airfields, again in an effort to destroy planes being used to stage attacks against allied shipping off Okinawa, with *Enterprise* returning to action. At 0230 hours on the 12th, the *Enterprise* launched a seven-plane raid against the airfields of southern Kyushu. Making landfall at Tanega, the Hellcats split up to cover various airfields on southern Kyushu, and by the break of dawn, the flight would bring down eight enemy planes. Lt. C. D. Young spotted the exhaust flame of a plane and soon identified it as a Tony. After overshooting the Japanese fighter twice, he finally sent it flaming into the water. Observing lights of taxiing aircraft on Kanoya East airfield, one section of night fighters began strafing runs. During a strafing run, Lt. Kenneth Smith lost control of his port aileron, but was able to pull out in time; the loss of the aileron forced him to abandon the mission. On his return trip to the *Enterprise*, a pair of Tony fighters jumped him. One fighter overshot the Hellcat, and despite the difficulty in controlling his plane due to the damaged aileron, Smith shot it down, while the other, seeing his comrade go down in flames, beat a hasty retreat home.

Meanwhile, as dawn approached, Lt. Young and Lt. (jg) Charles H. Latrobe, in a thirteen-minute series of engagements near Kanoya and Kagoshima Bay, bagged three Jakes and two Petes, with three-and-a half of those going to Young, bringing his total to 4.5 kills for the day. Lt. (jg) J.R. Kenyon finished the morning's work by bagging an Oscar near Kanoya airfield.

That evening, VF(N)-90 pilots brought down two more enemy aircraft while participating in NCAP duty. Lt. (jg) G.A. Oden, after being vectored for over an hour by three different FDOs, caught and splashed a Dinah at 2300 hours, and Lt. (jg) Latrobe, who had a day before been credited with 1.5 kills over Kyushu, intercepted and shot down a Betty in flames at 0100 hours. The squadron scored two more daylight kills during a sweep of Kyushu between 0530 and 0615 hours, before returning to the *Enterprise*, where they found the task force under air attack by two dozen enemy planes. One of the planes penetrated the curtain of antiaircraft fire and CAP shortly after 0700 hours and plunged into *Enterprise*'s flight deck just aft of the forward elevator. The ship remained on station for another day before withdrawing from combat and would not return until after the war. VF(N)-90 was credited with 31 confirmed air-to-air kills, placing it second behind VF(N)-41 as the top-scoring Navy night fighter squadron, during which time it lost nine pilots to enemy action and operational accidents.

The typical carrier-based night fighter pilot often experienced a different set of emotions than his daytime counterpart, characterized by frustration, isolation, and loneliness. Some probably felt a bit frustrated observing some of their counterparts achieving a tremendous number of aerial victories. Fellowship and camaraderie typically found in an air group was difficult to form, since nocturnal operations required different periods of rest for the four to six pilots assigned to night duty. An addendum issued by VF(N)-90's Lt. Cmdr. McCullough 15 April 1945 disclosed some of the feelings felt by his pilots regarding flying night combat missions:

Ships at anchor at dusk as seen from *Enterprise*'s flight deck, with an F6F-5N in the foreground. (Scrapbook of Cmdr. William H. Balden, Emil Buehler Library, NMNA)

There exists among many members of this squadron an antipathy for or dissatisfaction with night combat flying operations. Operations at night, I believe, have been proven sound by the fine performance of this squadron. Anxiety, worry, and being generally on edge will always be a mark of a night pilot, but does not necessarily make for poor performance or the dislike for night operations. It is the confusion, uncertainty, and lack of results that make the pilots dislike the night work. Unreasonable requests and below minimum weather flights have caused many a good pilot to lose his confidence. In judging these complaints, keep in mind that they are coming from qualified night pilots that have proven their ability in combat operations, and have carried out their assignments 100 % (sic).

Opposite:
A Japanese suicide plane hits the water and the bomb it was carrying explodes just off *Enterprise's* port quarter 11 April 1945. The shock from this hit and another one severely damaged the ship, forcing an early withdrawal for the second time in a month. (Scrapbook of Cmdr. William H. Balden, Emil Buehler Library, NMNA)

Enterprise's Number One elevator is blasted some 300 feet into the air from a Kamikaze hit 14 May 1945 off Kyushu, Japan. (image from an album of photographs collected by Captain Carlos W. Wieber during his command of the aircraft carrier *Essex* (CV 9) during 1944-1945. (Emil Buehler Library, NMNA)

By summer 1945, the Japanese offered little air opposition, as they were intent on conserving aircraft, pilots, and fuel for an all-out defensive stand against the expected Allied invasion of the home islands, except when combined American and British forces launched strikes against Kure naval base and the Tokyo area in late July through mid-August. Meanwhile, the Japanese continued to launch small-scale air attacks against Okinawa and the ships offshore. The last naval night air group arrived off Leyte aboard USS *Bon Homme Richard* (CV 31) 28 June 1945 and joined TF-58 for strikes against the Japanese home islands of Kyushu, Hokkaido, Honshu, and Shikoku. Night Air Group 91, composed of VF(N)-91 and VT(N)-91, was formed at NAF Westerly, Rhode Island, on 5 October 1944, under the command of Lt. Cmdr. A. Minvielle.

The group's night fighter component's first victories came on 25 July while on a ResCap mission off the Japanese coast. Ens. Kenneth J. Baldwin scored first at 1830 hours off Kyushu, shooting down a K5Y-1 (Willow) trainer and damaging another, while Lt. R.M. Klose shot down a Aichi B7A (Grace) attack bomber. On 9 August, during the beginning of his NCAP, Ens. J.C. Stires, at 1835 hours, shot down a pair of Judys. On 13 August, during sweeps against targets in the Tokyo area, two VF(N)-91 night Hellcats splashed five enemy aircraft in less than 40 minutes, four of them became the victims of one pilot. A destroyer's FDO vectored Ens. Phillip McDonald and Lt. R.T. Kieling to a pair of bogies 25 miles west of Mito, Honshu. Kieling spotted two Nicks below at 4,500 feet at 1835 hours and the dogfight began. Two bursts

The remains of an VF(N)-90 Hellcat caught in the blast of a Japanese suicide plane and a gaping hole remains where *Enterprise's* Number One elevator was just a few minutes before this photograph was taken. (Scrapbook of Cmdr. William H. Balden, Emil Buehler Library, NMNA)

F6F-5N of VF(N)-91 with "SS" tail code flying over California before deployment aboard USS *Bon Homme Richard* (CV-31). The squadron began combat operations off Japan in July 1945. (Emil Buehler Library, NMNA)

Loading .50-caliber ammunition into an F6F-5N of VF(N)-91 aboard *Bon Homme Richard*. Clearly visible are the flame dampeners used to prevent exhaust flames from ruining the pilot's night vision and to prevent enemy detection. (Emil Buehler Library, NMNA)

The WWII squadron insignia of VF(N)-91 from the Philip T. McDonald Collection via Thomas E. Doll.

VMF-511 F6F-5N launched from USS *Block Island* (CVE-106) 6 February during training exercises off California before departing to the forward area. Marine night fighter aircraft were commonly identified by the code F(N) followed by the in-squadron aircraft number. (Robert F. Dorr)

Ensign McDonald (second from right) and other pilots with VF(N)-91 stand by one of the squadron's F6F-5N Hellcats. Between 25 July and 13 August 1945, the squadron scored nine confirmed kills while operating from USS *Bon Homme Richard* (CVA-31). (Philip T. McDonald Collection via Thomas E. Doll)

Images from VF(N)-91's Ens. Philip T. McDonald's gun camera showing one of his four kills that occurred 13 August 1945 off Japan between 1835 and 1915 hours. (Philip T. McDonald Collection via Thomas E. Doll)

VMF-511 F6F-5N being recovered aboard *Block Island* during exercises off California. A deck crewman is removing the aircraft's tailhook from the arresting cable. (Emil Buehler Library, NMNA)

from McDonald's guns dispatched one fighter, while Kieling pursued his prey down to the water and splashed it. Back on patrol, McDonald spotted a Frances three miles away, caught up to it, and fired a short burst into the starboard engine. One of the crew parachuted out just before the aircraft hit the water. McDonald scored again by flaming another Frances that was on an apparent collision course with his Hellcat. The plane's wreckage was still burning on the surface when he went after another Frances, scoring hits on the port engine, but he lost it in the clouds before he could deliver the final blow. Climbing back to Kieling on patrol, McDonald saw a Nick crossing in front of him a few miles ahead. He overtook the Japanese fighter and dispatched it with a couple of well-placed bursts, making it his fourth confirmed kill, a record for an American night fighter for one mission. The Nick's demise marked the last aerial victory by a naval night fighter in WWII.

Marine Carrier Air Group One (MCVG-1), which included a fighter element (VMF-511), operated from USS *Block Island* (CVE 106) beginning in February 1945. VMF-511, led by Maj. Robert C. Maze, operated eight F6F-5Ns, along with eight standard F4U-1D Corsairs, and two F6F-5P photographic reconnaissance Hellcats. The air group arrived off Okinawa on 4 May, and during the next six weeks flew over 1,200 missions, primarily close air support and heckling missions. Maj. Mize was lost in a rocket attack against piers at Ishigaki Island when his Corsair was hit by AA. The carrier was then sent to the waters off Borneo to support the Australian landing at Balikpapan in July 1945. The squadron's only kill occurred at 0300 hours on 3 July 1945, when 1st Lt. Bruce Reuter downed a Jake float plane. One additional carrier-based naval night fighter squadron (VF(N)-63) arrived in the Pacific at the end of hostilities aboard escort carrier *Kula Gulf* (CVE 108), while a few American carrier-based fighter units in the Mediterranean operated the Hellcat during the invasion of Southern France, but only VF-74 had a night fighter detachment, consisting of eight F3D-2Ns with nine officers and nine enlisted men. The squadron's day fighters, operating from USS *Kasann Bay* (CVE 69) between 15-21 and 24-29 August, conducted 60 combat missions, yet it appears none of the night fighters engaged in such operations. Instead, the radar-equipped planes briefly operated from Corsica under the command of the 63rd Wing, Mediterranean Allied Coastal Air Force. One radar contact was made, but the bogey outran the Hellcat near the French coast. They also provided NCAP for Task Group 88.2 before returning to Corsica at dawn. When their services were no longer needed on Corsica, the aircraft returned to the carrier 24 August and were stripped of their radar gear.

The deck crew untangles VMF-511 F6F-5N "BUTCH" from *Block Island's* barrier net circa summer 1945. This aircraft is marked with the carrier identification symbol consisting of a white block with a blue I and M. The M identifies the Hellcat as a Marine aircraft. (Emil Buehler Library, NMNA)

Lt. L. W. Roberton personalized his F6F-5N Hellcat aircraft of VF-83, shown on USS *Essex* (CV-9) in the Western Pacific area. He reportedly was a former drummer in Jack "Big T" Teagarden's jazz band. He painted "Blues in the Night" with a teddy bear drumming on the nose of his night fighter. (Robert L. Lawson Photographic Collection, Emil Buehler Library, NMNA)

An F6F-5N fighter of Marine Corps squadron VMF-511 flipped after attempting to land on the deck of USS *Block Island* (CVE-106). (Robert L. Lawson Photographic Collection, Emil Buehler Library, NMNA)

USS *Yorktown*-based F6F-5 and -5N Hellcats of VF-88, nicknamed the "Gamecocks," off the Japanese coast 22 August 1945, shortly after the end of hostilities. (Robert L. Lawson Photographic Collection, Emil Buehler Library, NMNA)

Opposite:
Block Island's catapult officer gives the pilot of VMF-511 "HANGER QUEEN" the signal to launch during operations off Okinawa. Mechanics dubbed the fighter because she had been "down" several times one week for minor repairs. (Emil Buehler Library, NMNA)

Chapter 6

U.S. Marine Corps Operations: Central Pacific (February 1944-August 1945)

...the Marines on the atolls felt they were prisoners on a pinhead. Alternately baking and steaming in the equatorial weather, blinded by the aching glare of the cloud-white coral and the brilliant blue of the skies, the air Marines moved through the doldrums of their daily existence

- **Capt. John A. De Chant**, USMCR

Six Marine Corsair and Hellcat night fighter squadrons (VMF(N)-532, -533, -534, -541, -542, and -543) operated from airfields across the Pacific, where some of them fought mostly a battle against boredom, while others would achieve fame over the skies above the Philippines and Ryukyu Islands. The first Marine single-engine night fighter squadron, VMF(N)-532 arrived in the Central Pacific in late February 1944 with its F4U-2N Corsairs. Capt. Ross S. Mickey commissioned the squadron when MAG(N)-53 was formed at MCAS Cherry Point, resulting in the division of VMF(N)-531 into two separate combat units. The following month, Mickey turned command of the squadron over to Major Everette Vaughan, a Marine reservist and former TWA pilot. Eight months of training followed, with pilots initially flying the Brewster SB2A Buccaneer and North American SNJ-4 before the arrival of the F4U-2N. The squadron left Cherry Point via San Diego for the Pacific on 26 December, arriving in Hawaii New Year's Day. By the second week of January 1944, the squadron was operating from Mullinix Field on Ella Island, part of Tarawa Atoll in the Gilberts.

Tarawa had been the target of 30 attacks from enemy aircraft based in the Marshalls prior to VMF(N)-532's arrival; therefore, the pilots eagerly anticipated their first combat mission. Two days later GCI picked up Japanese bombers heading towards the island. Major Vaughn, on NCAP, attempted to intercept, but he failed to find the enemy. It was the beginning of a very frustrating period for the squadron, as poor communication, a breakdown of equipment, and lack of experience in both GCI and pilots prevented successful interception. For the next several months, boredom and disease were the squadron's worst enemies.

Vaughn, along with eight Corsairs, were sent to the island of Roi, on Kwajalein Atoll, 15 February, after the island was bombed at night by a dozen enemy aircraft three days earlier, in which six men of Marine Air Group 31 (MAG-31) were killed and over 70 wounded. Marine squadrons typically worked in conjunction with Marine Air Warning Squadrons (AWS) manned by technicians and equipped with radar gear for providing early warning and GCI for both day and night fighters. To prevent such an attack from happening again, Air Warning Squadron One (AWS-1), commanded by Capt. William D. Felder, Jr., with nine officers and 218 enlisted men, arrived 20 February with its two SCR-270D long-range radars, two SCR-527 GCI radars, and SCR-602 radars, along with radio transmitters and direction finders.[1]

A detachment of eight aircraft from -532 arrived on Engebi, in Eniwetok Atoll, on the 27th, with the expectation that the night fighters and AWS-1 would prevent another such attack from occurring again – they didn't. AWS-1 picked up a formation of enemy aircraft at 0332 hours on 8 March, but two night fighters scrambled failed to make an interception. Eight Japanese fighters, part of a 20-plane group from Truk, struck Engebi, with the first bomb falling at 0407 hours. Casualties were one killed and seven wounded. The Marine night fighters failed in their mission that night, but growing experience and persistence in the

A radar-equipped F4U-2 Corsair from VMF(N)-532 at Roi Island, Marshall Islands. This is Major Everett H. Vaughan's plane "Shirley June." (Robert L. Lawson Photographic Collection, Emil Buehler Library, NMNA)

VMF(N)-532 F4U-2s lined up on Roi Island during 1944. The squadron had the responsibility of providing night protection of Eniwetok and Kwajalein between January and June 1944. The squadron earned its first and last kills 14 April 1944, downing a pair of Mitsubishi G4M "Betty" bombers. (U.S. Navy via Thomas E. Doll)

VMF(N)-532 #212 F4U-2 at Kagman Field, Saipan, during summer 1944. The aircraft has the tri-color scheme with black codes and a white-tipped radar pod. Tape has been applied to the aircraft's fuel access panel seams to prevent leakage. Early Corsairs were known for leaking fuel and oil, which would flow back and obstruct the pilot's view. (Frank C. Lang via Robert F. Dorr)

relatively new art of night fighting paid off the following month when the Japanese launched 12 Bettys from Truk against Engebi a little before midnight on 14 April.

Five of the squadron's Corsairs were airborne that night, with 1st Lt. J.E. Bonner being the first, lifting off at 2316 hours. Ground control of AWS-1 picked up the enemy force at 0013 hours and vectored Bonner, orbiting at 20,000 feet, to intercept the approaching enemy, which were flying at the same altitude 30 miles from Engebi. GCI guided the Corsair to the target, with Bonner making radar contact from a distance of two-and-a-half miles. He spotted the enemy from 400 yards, but could not establish a positive ID. Bonner approached and sat 20-30 feet directly underneath the bomber for two seconds until confirming it as an unfriendly. Bonner raised the Corsair's nose and shot a five second burst, hitting the Betty's fuselage and starboard wing root. The bomber fell off sharply to starboard with the night fighter closely behind. The bomber's rear gunner responded to the attack and returned fire, hitting the Corsair's engine. The fighter lost all power and Bonner bailed out at 5,500 feet, landing in the water, where he was eventually picked up 16 hours later by destroyer escort USS *Steele*.

First Lieutenants Donald W. Spatz and Frank C. Lang scrambled at 0030 hours, but both failed to find the enemy. Capt. Howard W. Bollman was scrambled at 0045, reaching his assigned altitude of 20,000 feet and 40 miles from base while 1st Lt. Edward A. Sovik followed five minutes later and began orbiting at the same altitude ten miles from base. Sovik picked a contact on his scope flying above him

3,000 feet at a range of two-and-a-half miles; he made a 180-degree turn, increased power, and climbed. The Corsair rapidly closed the distance and Sovik made a visual on the Betty when his fighter was 250 yards away. He came up to a firing position behind, slightly below, and to the left of the unsuspecting bomber and fired a series of short bursts. Sovik remembered, "The tracers showed that the aim was good; sparks showed up immediately as the aluminum caught fire from incendiaries. I cut speed, slid over to the starboard and fired at the other engine; another hit, another fire. The work was done in seconds."[2]

The Betty caught fire and began a shallow dive before exploding at 12,000 feet. A minute later a blip appeared on Bollman's scope and he gave chase, coming in fast and dead astern of the Betty 150 feet away. His first two bursts during his first diving run caused the bomber to burn. Swinging back around the Corsair delivered a final three-second burst and the bomber disintegrated in a ball of fire. Four of the five night fighter pilots returned safely to Engebi, but Donald Spatz became lost, ran out of gas, and possibly bailed out somewhere north of Eniwetok. A four-day search failed to find him. The downing of two enemy bombers by Bollman and Spatz, along with a probable given to Bonner, were the first and last victories for -532.

The -532 detachment on Engebi returned to Roi in June, where it joined the rest of the squadron on heckling missions against Japanese installations on Wotje, in the Marshall Islands. Vaughn moved moved the squadron to Isley Field, Saipan, where it flew NCAP and heckling missions against Pagan and Rota Islands. Heckling bypassed Pagan Island had a tendency to be dangerous, as Capt. Edward Sovik found out when Japanese antiaircraft fire shot up his Corsair during a mission. The pilot sustained facial injuries and a concussion when he crash-landed his damaged Corsair on return to base. Saipan was declared secured by the time of -533's arrival on 13 July, but isolated pockets of resistance continued for some time, resulting in a few American casualties, including two from -532. On the 16th, a Japanese grenade wounded Cpl. Walter C. Warzecha in the arm and enemy rifle fire wounded Pfc. Gaylord Woodard, Jr., in the shoulder. Routine NCAP patrol, supplanted by an occasional foray to Pagan and Rota, continued until 20 September, when it ended combat operations and turned over its Corsairs to MAG-21 on Guam. The squadron embarked on its return trip to the U.S. ten days later. The Navy phased out of F4U-2N in January 1945 and a new Corsair night fighter would not enter production until 1947.

The first Marine Hellcat night fighter squadron arrived on Eniwetok 6 May, under the command of Lt. Col. Marion M. "Black Mac" Magruder. Nicknamed "Black Mac's Killer," VMF(N)-533 was commissioned 1 October 1943 at Cherry Point as part of Marine Air Group 53 (MAG-53). The 33-year-old native of Lexington, Kentucky, was an early advocate for the establishment of night fighter units, having previously served a three-month tour in Britain to learn about RAF night fighter technology and tactics. Returning to the United States, he was instrumental in establishing the night fighting training doctrine for the Navy and Marine Corps. On Eniwetok, "Black Mac" and his men settled down for a life of routine patrols that lasted for nearly a year. The monotony was broken up at Magruder's insistence on maintaining a high level of readiness by establishing a rigorous training schedule that would ultimately pay off a year later.

THE ODYSSEY OF VMF(N)-534

When Maj. Ross S. Mickey and his men departed Espiritu Santos 2 June 1944, neither he nor the men under his command realized they were beginning a two-month sea voyage. Mickey, who was briefly the skipper of VMF(N)-532 between April and May 1943, assumed command of VMF(N)-534 at Cherry Point on 15 February 1944. Two months later the squadron departed San Diego on 19 April aboard USS *Breton* and arrived at Espiritu Santos 4 May, where they remained until June. While there, -534 Mickey was told the squadron would participate in the invasion of the Marianas and then based on Guam as part of the defensive force after the island was recaptured. The squadron's fifteen aircraft and pilots, along with 133 enlisted men, departed on USS *Santee* 2 June, while the support group, along with most of the gear, would follow later aboard the cargo ships USS *Cetus*, *Young America*, and *Typhoon*. The *Santee* arrived at Kwajalein five days later and stayed at anchor for another week before arriving off Eniwetok 16 June. They remained at anchor for 65 days, through the remainder of June through July. Except for a few hours (an average of four to five hours) on Espiritu Santos, the pilots hadn't flown in three months, and while at anchor off Eniwetok, the aircraft of VMF(N)-533 were offered, but permission from higher authorities was denied. The pilots did manage to log an additional one hour flying time on 14-15 July by borrowing F6F-3Ns from -533 and flying off Engebi strip. Frustration set in from boredom from inactivity, as the men spent week after week aboard the ships. They had to make do with makeshift living conditions, with enlisted men and junior officers sleeping on cots on the hangar deck beneath the aircraft. Conditions aboard the cargo ships was a different story, with 400-600 men crowded into holds with very little water or fresh air. Finally, the three cargo ships set sail for Guam on 23 July; however, the *Santee* remained in place for another nine days before it departed 1 August, arriving off Guam three days later.

VMF(N)-532 F4U-2s line up to depart for Saipan from USS *Windam Bay* (CVE-92), 12 July 1944. Squadron operations began at Tarawa in January 1944 and from there, during its 10-month tour, it proceeded to the Marshall Islands and then to Saipan. Its first and only confirmed kills came the night of 14 April, when a pair of G4M (Betty) bombers were shot down off Engebi Island. (Nicholas A. Veronico)

Lt. John Thistlehwaite of VMF(N)-532 leaves the deck of USS *Windham Bay* (CVE-92) in F4U-2 number 204 12 July 1944, during the squadron's transfer to Saipan from Roi. (USN/ National Archives via Thomas E. Doll)

Smith

10

Opposite top:
Pilots of VMF(N)-534 at MCAS Cherry Point prior to departing for the Pacific with squadron commanding officer Major Ross Mickey standing in the back (center). (Lt. Col. John E. Shields Collection via Mark Leonard)

Opposite bottom:
VMF(N)-534 F6F-3N #10 warming up at Orate Field, Guam, during August 1944. Barely visible is the squadron's triangular insignia of a light blue cat wearing a black tophat perched on a white cloud and holding a tommy gun. The triangle is dark blue with yellow trim. (USMC)

F6F-5N of VMF(N)-534 on *Windham Bay* in May 1945 prepared for launch during carrier qualification operations off Guam. The squadron by that time had been regulated to conducting heckling strikes against by-passed islands held by the Japanese. (Emil Buehler Library, NMNA)

At 0952 hours on 4 August 1944, the first VMF(N)-534 Hellcat, with Maj. Mickey at the controls, catapulted off *Santee*, with the last of the squadron's aircraft becoming airborne at 1017 hours. At 1130 hours, Mickey became the first Marine to land a fighter on Orote Field, Guam, where he and his squadron became part of MAG-21. Once again, a Marine night fighter squadron would operate in an area void of any significant enemy air power, and so began months of routine CAP interrupted by participating in occasional strikes against Rota. Unfamiliar territory and adverse weather conditions probably led to the disappearance of Capt. Paul. H. Todd, the squadron executive officer, who was lost on an NCAP during the evening of the seventh. Combat operations began within hours of Todd's disappearance, with Mickey and Capt. Charles. F. Finnie conducting the first of six bombing and strafing missions against Rota. The mission of night fighter squadrons was to intercept and destroy enemy aircraft, but no such action materialized for -534 throughout the remainder of 1944. The squadron's only interception and kill occurred the morning of 2 February 1945, after receiving a message that a Japanese VIP would be a passenger on a seaplane from Truck to Iwo Jima. Mickey sent four of his Hellcats to Saipan, while a destroyer took aboard controllers from AWS-2 to direct the fighters. Lt. Brett E. Roueche picked up the seaplane, identified as a Myrt, on radar, and shot it down 110 miles northeast of Saipan. For the remainder of the war, the squadron was split between Guam, Eniwetok, and Saipan, during which time command of the squadron was handed to Maj. James B. Maguire, Jr., on 24 May, and then to Maj. Clair C. Chamberlain.[3]

VMF(N)-541: THE BAT EYE SQUADRON

Lt. Col. Peter D. Lambrecht's Bat Eye Squadron (VMF(N)-541) made its combat debut on 24 September 1944, when eight of its Hellcats landed on Peleliu to begin operations under MAG-11. (Lambrecht was one of the original group of Marine Corps officers to attend night fighter orientation training in England in early 1943.) The squadron arrived nine days after the First Marine Division invaded and fighting was still raging on the hotly-contested island. The battle would claim the lives of approximately 2,000 Americans, with another 8,000 wounded or missing, while nearly the entire force of 11,000 Japanese defenders would perish on an island that held little strategic value. Meanwhile, the ground echelon was pressed into evacuating Marine infantry casualties and reinforcing ground forces fighting the Japanese on the island. Six men loaned out to the First and Second Marine Battalions were wounded in action, another was evacuated due to combat fatigue, and another went missing in action. Remaining pockets of Japanese continued to fight on through November, and those holding out in hillside caves overlooking the airfield would occasionally make their presence known by directing

The airstrip on Peleliu, in the Palau Islands, where VMF(N)-541, nicknamed "Bat Eye Squadron," operated from September-October 1944 and January 1945 until the end of hostilities. In the lower left is a trio of the squadron's F6F-5Ns. (National Archives)

mortar and small arms fire on the American encampment, resulting in the death of one man and the wounding of five during October, while another was wounded in November. The squadron would fly 287 night-bombing strikes against targets in the Palua group and 461 NCAP between 25 September and 27 November, during which time one enemy aircraft was shot down. The single kill occurred the evening of 31 October, when GCI picked up a bogey 28 miles north of the airfield on an apparent mission to parachute supplies to remaining Japanese centered on Umurbrogol Mountain, north of the airfield. Maj. N.L. Mitchell was vectored and soon identified the aircraft as a Jake; he opened fire from a distance of 200 yards as the float plane's rear gunner returned fire. Both aircraft were in 15-degree dives and rapidly approaching the ground, so Mitchell made a second run at 7 o'clock, crossing from the Jake's port to starboard and pulling out only six feet from the aircraft's floats. Flames spread across the Jake's fuselage as it made its final journey to the ground. The squadron remained on Peleliu though the end of November.

TACLOBAN, PHILIPPINES

Lambrecht and his men received a reprieve as they languished on Peleliu when they were ordered to the Philippines. The primary reasoning behind the move was three-fold. First, Adm. Kincaid, of the Seventh Fleet, wanted additional air coverage due to kamikaze attacks on U.S. surface forces, which was understandable. Pilots of the "Divine Wind" had exacted a heavy toll on U.S. carrier forces. One escort carrier was sunk and five were damaged during The Battle for Leyte; afterward, kamikaze attacks damaged the *Intrepid*, *Franklin*, and *Belleau Wood* on 29 October, followed by *Lexington* on 5 November and *Cabot*, *Hancock*, and *Intrepid* (for the second time) on 25 November. All told, 40 ships were damaged between 24 October and 29 November by kamikaze attacks: five sunk and 35 damaged. Second, the magnitude of Japanese air attacks against the American landing forced Adm. Halsey of the Third Fleet to postpone his plan for striking the Japanese home islands. Third, General MacArthur was disappointed in the ability of the Navy and AAF to provide adequate air defense during dawn and dusk against Japanese fighters employed to bomb U.S. forces. On 26 November, MacArthur proposed a trade of night fighter units with Adm. Nimitz by sending a message to his counterpart: "Japs operating Oscars as night bombers, which are too fast for P-61s. In Palau, enemy employing bombers, which P-61 can effectively cope with. Would appreciate your considering a temporary swap of night fighter squadrons, the Marine squadron at Palau to operate from Leyte, and P-61s to go to Peleliu."[4]

As it turned out, MacArthur's request for a Marine night fighter squadron, along with Kincaid's desire for additional air support, opened the door for Halsey to suggest the use of MAG-12, which he considered underutilized by the Fifth Air Force. Lambrecht went to Tacloban to arrange for his squadron's movement to Leyte on 1 December, while the AAF's 421st Night Fighter Squadron prepared for the transfer to Peleliu. After a postponement of two days, 12 Hellcats of VMF (N)-541 landed at their new home after a 600-mile over-water flight for what was expected to be a two-week tour of duty. The hot, dry conditions of Peleliu, with its hard coral landing strip, were replaced by a rain-soaked muddy airfield without operative taxiways or parking areas. Rain scrubbed flight operations on the fourth, but a pre-dawn patrol on 5 December brought the Bat Eye Squadron its first aerial combat since Maj. Mitchell's downing of a Jake the last day of October. Second Lt. Rodney E. Montgomery, Jr., as part of a four-plane coverage of a convoy of minesweepers sailing off Southern Leyte, dove on a Ki-43 Oscar intent on attacking the ships and shot it down in flames. Thus began a successful two-month deployment that would net the Bat Eye squadron 21 aerial victories.

Two days later, Tech. Sgt. John W. Andre, a twenty-five-year-old native of Alabama and one of only two NAP (Enlisted Naval Aviation Pilots) pilots in the squadron, shot down a Kawasaki Ki-48 twin-engine light bomber (Lily) over Ormoc Bay at 0150 hours, after pumping over 1,000 rounds into it. It was Andre's first of four confirmed kills in the war and the first of only three successful GCI-vectored interceptions made by the squadron. Their primary mission for the night fighters was dawn and dusk defensive patrols

F6F-5N, F(N)-59 of VMF(N)-541 on Peleliu shortly after the squadron's arrival in September 1944. The aircraft is standard Glossy Sea Blue with white fuselage and tail markings. The white band around the radar pod is the bar of the U.S. national insignia. (Robert F. Dorr)

A ground crewman (left) inspecting the access panel on F(N)-59's radar pod on Peleliu. Land-based fighter squadrons based in the Central Pacific by late 1944 had few opportunities to engage Japanese aircraft. The "Bat Eye Squadron" scored only one kill while on Peleliu. (Emil Buehler Library, NMNA)

as requested by General MacArthur, since the Japanese often conducted raids during those hours. VMF(N)-541 frequently carried out the nocturnal missions it was trained to do, but of the 21 enemy aircraft destroyed in the air during their tour, only three occurred at night. For several weeks, Lambrecht's squadron did not operate as a true night fighter squadron, since local commanders did not believe in using such fighters to hunt, as they saw it, a few Japanese hecklers who posed little threat to operations.

When Bat Eye pilots flew night air defense, their lack of success was due to a combination of factors, consisting of poor communication between GCI and pilots, faulty airborne radar sets, and poor spotting of ground radar sites. Marine night fighter squadrons typically worked with their own GCI technicians, but in the Philippines, they were under the guidance of Army controllers who were unfamiliar with the procedures of the pilots they were handling. On one occasion, this unfamiliarity led Lt. O.K. Houston in the wrong direction when he was being vectored to a pair of bogies before dawn on 10 December. The inexperienced Army GCI led him away from the bogies and out to sea, where he became temporarily lost. His consternation over the radio, which included a series of vulgarities, was immortalized upon transcription and distribution in mimeograph form to the squadron.[5]

Maintaining airborne radar sets in the heat and humidity of the Philippines was another problem. Due to crowded conditions on Tacloban strip, where Marine, Navy, and Army aircraft of all types were based, VMF(N)-541 could not get permission to conduct test flights to check the functionality of the sets, and thus a considerable number of nocturnal interceptions failed because of problems that did not show up during ground tests. A third issue was the placement of two Army GCI sites that resulted in limited coverage. The "Blue Eye" station, located to the south of Tacloban field, had a 75-degree coverage to the northeast for only 40 miles, and it was partially blanked by a 4,000-foot mountain; coverage of the northwest by a second station was similarly inefficient. Army and Marine controllers assigned to VMF(N)-541 were successful in having the site moved, but not to the spot they recommended. Instead, it was moved near a site next to native huts with metal roofs that absorbed two-thirds of the radar energy. Consequently, it seriously limited the station's effectiveness, where it could not detect enemy aircraft flying below 10,000 feet and at a distance greater than 20 miles.[6]

Dawn and dusk patrols continued, with the Bat Eye Squadron providing convoy coverage, during which time the squadron conducted several daytime interceptions of enemy aircraft, including one on the morning of 12 December that resulted in the downing of 11 enemy aircraft. This particular mission began at 0615 hours, with

Tacloban Field, on the coast of Leyte, Philippines, was the temporary home for VMF(N)-541 between 3 December 1944 and 11 January 1945. The Philippines proved to be fertile hunting grounds, with the squadron shooting down 22 enemy aircraft. (Emil Buehler Library, NMNA)

VMF(N)-541 scoreboard at Tacloban Airfield, Leyte, January 1945. The "Bat Eye" Squadron scored 23 kills between 5 December 1944 and 3 January 1945. (Jeff Millstein via Thomas E. Doll)

Capt. David W. Thompson leading a three-plane division to protect a convoy in Ormoc Bay, while a second four-plane division, airborne at 0650 hours and led by Lt. Fletcher D. Miller, Jr., went to cover PT boats in Carigara Bay. GCI notified Thompson's group of a large formation of bogies to the northwest, heading for the convoy. The trio of Marine Hellcats nearing Ponson Island spotted 33 enemy aircraft composed of torpedo and dive bombers protected by Oscar and Zeke fighters. The Hellcats turned into the center of the enemy formation, despite 11-to-1 odds, forcing the enemy pilots to jettison their bombs too early and turn away from the convoy. Bat Eye pilots in the ensuing melee shot down five enemy aircraft and damaged one other in minutes. Lt. Miller's quartet arrived ten minutes later and joined the action, knocking down another six aircraft, during which

Photo 06-09BBB
A pair of VMF(N)-541 F6F-5N Hellcats escort TBM -3 torpedo bombers of Marine Torpedo Bombing Squadron 232 (VMTB-232) shortly after the former's return to Peleliu in January 1945. (Grumman Heritage)

time the Japanese pilots showed poor air discipline and seemed rather reluctant to tangle with the Americans.

American landings on Mindoro required the service of MAG-12 fighters at Tacloban on 15 December to protect the beachhead. Four Hellcats led by Capt. Harlan Morrison, providing cover for the assault forces, were vectored south to a pair of bogies heading toward a ship convoy. At 0805 hours, the four-plane division was flying at 8,000 feet when 1st Lt. Lyle R. Whitner spotted two D3AVal dive bombers 6,000 feet below. He dived on one of them, firing into its fuselage until it flipped over and crashed into the water. The other Val, seeing his partner go down, turned into the sun and managed to escape. Twenty minutes later, another alert sent them towards another group of unfriendlies flying low over the water 30 miles west of the Negros Islands. At 0840 hours, they made visual contact with two Vals and four B6N2 Jills. Capt. Morrison and 2nd Lt. Carl D. Williams went after the Jills, with Morrison's fire sawing off sections of one of the Jill's wings which spiraled into the sea, while Williams dispatched a second. Meanwhile, 2nd Lt. Robert F. Marr spotted a pair of Zekes approaching in an attempt to protect the torpedo bombers. The Japanese fighters peeled away from each other as Marr latched onto one of them, firing into the port wing of the Zeke until it exploded. The remaining enemy dive and torpedo bombers, along with the other Zekes, retreated and the convoy was left unharmed.[7]

During the waning daylight of 22 December, TSgt. Andre went aloft on a routine dusk mission. Over the northern end of Leyte, GCI vectored him towards three bogeys, but he lost them over the southeastern tip of Luzon. Light was fading as he began a disappointing return to base, when he spotted four burning smudge pots marking an enemy-held airfield at Bulan. He spotted a Jack fighter south of the field below him with its wing lights on, coming in for a landing. The Hellcat joined the landing circle behind the enemy aircraft, and as he did so, he saw another Jack approach ahead of him, turning on its wing lights. The two Japanese fighters, oblivious to the American trailing them, prepared to land. Andre made his move and fired a burst into the rear aircraft, sending it down in flames. He jumped on the second Jack and fired, sending it crashing onto the field. The fires from the two burning aircraft lit up the strip enough for Andre to torch three parked aircraft and two fuel trucks during four strafing runs.

The squadron's final two victories came on 3 January 1945, during convoy coverage off Mindanao. Capt. Morrison's four-plane division reached the convoy, but GCI vectored Morrison and another pilot to look for bogeys, leaving Lts. Harold T. Hayes and William J. Cook to protect the ships. Orbiting at 9,000 feet, Hayes spotted a Zeke flying low on the water to evade detection by radar heading for the convoy. He dove and began a three-mile chase, firing burst after burst before the fleeing Japanese fighter nosed over and crashed into the sea. The Hellcat pilot then climbed to 6,000 feet, spotted a Nick, and dispatched it with a well-placed burst into the aircraft's port engine.[8]

Three days later, MacArthur released VMF(N)-541 from operations in the Philippines. For their work, the Bat Eye Squadron received the Army's Distinguished Service Citation, the only Marine squadron to do so in WWII. Shortly before Lambrecht's squadron left the Philippines, MacArthur sent a message to Nimitz:

> With your concurrence plan to relieve 541 Marine Night Fighter Squadron from Operations at Leyte and recall the 421 Night Fighter Squadron from Palau on or about 9 January. If this plan has your concurrence, request you advise this headquarters with information to Commander, Allied Air Force and Commander Fifth Air Force. Your night fighter squadron has performed magnificently, repeat magnificently during its temporary duty in this area and your assistance in furnishing the squadron is appreciated.[9]

The squadron returned to Peleliu for the duration, where it resumed heckling Japanese garrisons that remained in the Palaus with detachments operating from Ulithi. Lambrecht turned over command to Maj. Norman L. Mitchell 21 June 1945, who in turn was replaced by Maj. Reynolds A. Moody 8 July.

VMF(N)-541 Hellcat F(N)-62 (on the right) parked at Falalop Island 14 July 1945. The squadron finished out the war conducting routine patrols and occasional harassing strikes against bypassed Japanese-held islands. (NMNA via Thomas E. Doll)

Chapter 7

U.S. Marine Corps Operations: Okinawa (April-August 1945)

He rides in the dark in a winged bolt of lightning that can carry him to destruction in the space of seconds.

- **Lt. Col. Marion** "Black Mac" **Magruder**

Defensive land-based tactical aviation on Okinawa fell under TG-99.2 (the Tenth Army's Tactical Air Force - TAF), but commanded by a Marine aviator, Maj. General F.P. Mulcahy. The trio of marine night fighter squadrons that operated from the island fell under the control of Air Defense Command (ADC) Task Unit 99.2.1. Units operating under ADC during the campaign were Hedron 43 and MAG-14, 22, 31, and 33, with Hedron 43 consisting of Army and Marine air warning units that handled GCI for MAG day and night fighter squadrons. TAF GCI operations began with AWS-8 establishing a radar station on Nagannu Shima, an islet in the Keise Shima group, eight miles off Naha, Okinawa, five days before the full-scale invasion. TAF established itself on Okinawa 2 April, when General Mulcahy and his staff went ashore to set up a command post. The afternoon of 7 April, MAG-31, VMF-224, 311, and 441, and VMF(N)-542 went into operation at Yontan, providing CAP and NCAP with MAG-33, VMF-312, 322, and 323, and VMF(N)-543 following suit a day later at Kadena. Army and Marine day fighter squadrons of TAF flew 12-plane dawn to dusk CAP over the invasion and picket fleet, while Marine night fighters maintained four-plane NCAP through the hours of darkness.[1]

VMF(N)-542, under the command of Maj. William C. Kellum, was the first Marine night fighter to arrive on Okinawa after six months training at Cherry Training, which was marred by the deaths of two pilots in aircraft crashes, including the executive officer. The squadron departed the U.S. aboard the aircraft transport USS *Kitty Hawk* (APV 1) and arrived at Los Negros Island 19 September. A week later, the air echelon ferried the Hellcats to Pityilu, Admiralty Islands, while ground personnel left for Falalop Island, Ulithi Atoll, to set up facilities. The next five months consisted of flying routine day and night CAP under the direction of Marine Base Defense Aircraft Group Forty-Five (MBDAG-45, later MAG-45).

The Nighthawks of VMF(N)-543 was formed 15 April 1944, with Maj. Claude J. Carlson assuming command 5 May. It too suffered two fatalities while at Cherry Point, including Carlson, who was killed 2 July when he crashed three miles east of Beaufort, North Carolina, apparently after falling unconscious due to oxygen equipment failure. Maj. Clair Chamberlain assumed command and training continued until late December 1944, when it transferred to Hawaii for an additional two months of training before heading out to Okinawa.

The Japanese command recognized the threat of American TAF aircraft to their ground forces on Okinawa and its air assets, and thus began bombing and strafing missions against Kadena and Yontan. The enemy launched a mass raid composed of conventional and suicide aircraft against Allied naval surface forces and the airfields 15 April, and thereafter attacks occurred almost every night during the month. It was in the evening that Capt. James A. Etheridge of VMF(N)-543 scored MAG-33's first night fighter kill when he shot down a Nakajima Ki-54 (Frank) at 1855 hours over Kadena, just as the Japanese fighter prepared to attack the field. VMF(N)-542's first scores occurred the following evening, when 2nd Lieutenants Arthur J. Arceneaux and William W. Campbell each splashed two fighters the following evening 45 miles west of Point Bolo at 1845 hours. Both pilots took off at dusk to

Aerial view of Yontan Field, Okinawa,, which was home to two Marine night fighter squadrons. VMF(N)-542 began operations from the field 7 April 1945 and -533 arrived 10 May. VMF(N)-533 operated under Marine Air Group 22 (MAG-22) and -542 under MAG-31. (Emil Buehler Library, NMNA)

Second Lt. Del W. Carlton of VMF(N)-542 and his F6F-5N during stopover in the Admiralty Islands, Fall 1944. The squadron flew on to their base at Ulithi Atoll, in the Caroline Islands. "Ramblin' Ruthie" was named for his fiancé. (Thomas E. Doll)

Pin-up art adorns F6F-5Ns of VMF(N)-542 on Falalop Island, Ulithi Atoll, where the squadron operated from 28 October 1944 to 6 April 1945. The aircraft in the foreground is named "1 o'clock jump." Routine patrols were flown from Ulithi until the squadron was called up to Okinawa. (Grumman Heritage)

Opposite:
Aerial view of Kadena Field, Okinawa, where VMF(N)-543 set up operations two days after VMF(N)-542 arrived at Yontan. The squadron operated under MAG-33. (Emil Buehler Library, NMNA)

relieve day fighters flying CAP and were approaching their assigned area when they spotted enemy fighters making a bombing run on a destroyer. Arceneaux recalled:

> I peeled off and attacked a Zeke who was pulling out of a bombing attack on the destroyer. I made a run on him and fired on him when I was within range. He began to smoke a little, but in the attack, due to my excess speed, I overran him. Looking back, I could plainly see the pilot in the cockpit. He could have easily dropped in on my tail, but he failed to do so and peeled off to the west, oscillating up and down, trailing a steady stream of grey smoke. I immediately caught up to him and fired a short burst with my six .50 cal guns. He exploded in a tremendous flash.[2]

Unknown to Arceneaux, whose focus was on the Zeke in front of him, the second enemy fighter, a Frank, was approaching from the rear in hopes of knocking the American fighter out of the sky. Campbell came to the rescue and dispatched Arceneaux's would-be executioner.[3]

The first victories by VMF(N)-543 and 542 were accomplished without the aid of radar or GCI control, but during the days and weeks to come, most aerial victories would be accomplished through the use of ground control night fighter teams. Second Lt. C. A. Engman scored VMF(N)-543's second kill on the 17th, destroying a Sally west of Naha at 2130 hours. The interception and destruction of the enemy aircraft occurred at very low level, and just after dispatching the Sally, the prop of Engman's Hellcat struck the water, stalling out the engine. Fortunately, the fighter had enough forward momentum to propel it 50 feet into the air, allowing the pilot to make a controlled water landing. He exited the sinking aircraft and tread water for the next four hours before a passing landing craft hauled him aboard.

Smaller-scale Japanese conventional and kamikaze air attacks continued approximately every five to seven days through the remainder of April and into late May. The two

Marine night squadrons claimed seven confirmed kills during April, five of which went to VMF(N)-542; in comparison, their daytime counterparts shot down 142 enemy aircraft.

On 3-4 May, the enemy launched a 125-plane attack (Japanese sources cite 159) against the airfields, supply dumps, and radar pickets to coincide with a ground effort by Japanese forces on Okinawa. Enemy aircraft appeared over the destroyer picket line just before sundown on the 3rd. The attack sank an American destroyer and an LSM, while two other ships were damaged. Night fighter involvement during the attacks was extremely ineffective, as early warning radar was disrupted by "window" dropped by enemy reconnaissance aircraft. The lone victory by a land-based night fighter occurred at 0345 hours on the 4th, when Capt. Paul. W. Mitchell of VMF(N)-543 was vectored 30 miles north of Okinawa, where he picked up a Zeke and shot it down.

At Engebi, the year-long wait for combat concluded when Lt. Col. Magruder's VMF(N)-533 were ordered to Okinawa. The squadron's order came as replacement pilots arrived to take over from those who had been overseas since May 1944. However, Lt. Gen Louis E. Woods, commander of the Fourth Marine Air Wing (4th MAW), stepped in and convinced them to stay, as veteran pilots were badly needed to help stem the fury of the kamikaze. Magruder was itching to get into action and waiting for a ship to ferry the squadron's pilots and aircraft from Engebi to Okinawa was out of the question. He therefore managed to secure permission for his Hellcats to make the 2,500-mile over-water journey with stops at Saipan and Iwo Jima to their new base of operations, arriving at Yontan 10 May. He therefore managed to secure permission for his Hellcats to make the 2,500-mile over-water journey with stops at Saipan and Iwo Jima to their new base of operations, arriving at Yontan 10 May. The arrival of the third Marine night fighter squadron coincided with another Japanese aerial assault. The first signs of trouble began when blips started appearing on the radarscopes of the early warning stations and picket ships. Air Defense Control Center (ADCC) plotted 19 raids between midnight and 0420 hours, each composed of one to nine aircraft. The aircraft orbited 40 miles northwest of Okinawa and waited until dawn before beginning their suicidal charge.

Only one Marine night fighter scored that day. At 0530 hours, Lt. Edgar F. Gaudette, Jr. of VMF(N)-543 was vectored by GCI to a bogey 60 miles northeast of Point Bolo. He picked up the enemy contact by radar at five miles at 0530, with a visual being made on a Tony at three-quarters of a mile. The Hellcat pilot approached from beneath and to the rear and fired a short burst. The Japanese fighter exploded with such force that the engine and still-turning propeller separated from the rest of the aircraft. Meanwhile, Marine day fighters destroyed eighteen additional enemy aircraft during the morning.

Night fighter defense during the first five weeks of operations was rather disappointing, with VMF(N)-542 and -543 averaging only two kills per week during that period. The ability of ground-based early warning stations to provide accurate information to patrolling night fighters was hindered by landmass interference. The picket ships, not hindered by such interference, fed accurate information to the night fighters, but in doing so bore the brunt of enemy air attacks. Adm. Spruance pointed out this problem and the urgency to correct it. "It is recommended that in planning all future

Unidentified men of VMF(N)-543 stand beside F(N)-7 "Queen Mike" at Kadena. Maj. Clair C. Chamberlain led the squadron from 3 July 1944 to 17 June 1945, during which time the squadron shot down 15 enemy aircraft. (Rich Dann)

A VMF(N)-543 pilot and ground crew pose before one of the squadron's Hellcats displaying the unit insignia at Kadena Airfield, Okinawa. The squadron shot down 15 enemy aircraft between 15 April and 7 August 1945. (USMC/Jeff Millstein via Thomas E. Doll)

An unknown pilot has the canopy open on "Wistful Wally" F(N)-89 of VMF(N)-542 while on patrol near Yontan Airfield, Okinawa, May 1945. (Thomas E. Doll)

operations much greater emphasis be placed on securing outlying land areas or islands at the earliest practicable date and installing adequate land-based radars and fighter direction units thereon in order that vulnerable shipping will have to remain on exposed stations no longer than is absolutely necessary."[4]

Air Warning Squadrons established additional radar sites on outlying islands by late June, but the threat of mass Japanese air attacks had since passed.

Between April and August, the three night fighter squadrons claimed 63 enemy aircraft destroyed, with VMF(N)-533 registering 30 of its 35 kills during May alone. The squadron would also produce the only Marine night fighter ace of the war. VMF(N)-542 would place second in the number of enemy aircraft destroyed with 17, followed by -543 with 11. In comparison, Navy and Marine night fighter pilots scored only 39 nocturnal kills between November 1943 and October 1944. The improved performance of shore-based night fighter squadrons was primarily due to better tactical training of pilots and communication with ground and ship-based director crews. Part of the success of VMF(N)-533 pilots has been attributed to a field modification made to the Mark VIII reflecting gunsight:

> The Mark VIII reflecting sight projected a ring of dots around the center pipper as a means of gauging range and deflection. But the luminescence from the dots caused excessive glare, and the rheostat could not be turned low enough to cure the problem. Therefore, 533 soldered over the dots, leaving only the pipper for sighting. It considerably enhanced a pilot's visual acuity.[5]

Lt. Col. Magruder's squadron became operational 36 hours after arriving on 10 May, and was assigned a search sector northwest of Okinawa, while -542 guarded the southwest search sectors for -542 and -543 covered the south, with each squadron responsible for sending up two shifts of four two-plane teams each night. Six days later, on the 16th, "Black Mac's Killers" ended a 360-day drought when ground control guided 22-year-old 1st Lt. Robert M. Wilhide to a Betty, who proceeded to shoot it down in flames at 0300 hours over Kume Shima Island. The following evening, while chasing after a pair of enemy bombers approaching Ie Shima, he was apparently shot down by friendly anti-aircraft fire. Three weeks later, his brother Wilfred, a pilot with VMF-311, based at Okinawa, was killed when his F4U-1D fighter crashed at sea while returning from a strike.[6]

Wilhide's destruction of the Betty was followed up an hour later by Lieutenants Arceneaux and Campbell of VMF(N)-542, both of whom recorded the squadron's first victories while on a pre-dawn night search and destroy mission to Amami O

Col. "Black Mac" Magruder, commanding officer of VMF(N)-533, on the wing of F6F-3N "LITTLE *Mac*," named after his fist-born son. The photograph was taken at Engebi Island, Eniwetok, prior to the squadron's move to Okinawa. (Col. Magruder Archives)

Shima, but only one of them would return to base. The Hellcat, upon reaching the target area, spotted a pair of enemy float planes with their running lights blazing, heading for a landing in a bay. Campbell went in and flamed one of the aircraft, but disappeared afterward. Arceneaux was unsuccessful in raising him on the radio and a subsequent search failed to locate the missing pilot.

"Black Mac's Killers" came into their own during the night of the 18th, when 1st Lt. Robert Wellwood shot down three Bettys and 1st Lt. Edward LeFaivre bagged a Mitsubishi A6M3 (Hamp) fighter along with a Betty in a span of less than two hours (between 2210 and 2353 hours). Wellwood, coached by controller Lt. Hugh Gallarneau, made a visual on the first Betty while patrolling at 10,000 feet, 30 miles from Point Bolo. Pulling up above the bomber, he fired a 20-round burst at the wing root. The Betty blew up and spun into the water. The second Betty was caught 20 miles from Point Bolo, 20 minutes after the first interception. Wellwood established a radar contact at a range of two miles flying at 15,500 feet and closed to make a diving attack. His first burst missed, as the bomber's top turret gunner fired in response while the Betty's pilot began taking evasive action. He missed it on a second pass, but his aim was true on a third and fourth. His third burst drew a puff of smoke, while the last run apparently wounded or killed the pilot, as the bomber went into an unrecoverable spin and crashed into the sea.

Over an hour elapsed before he latched onto his third and final kill of the evening at 2353 hours, but in doing so, he nearly joined his victim in a watery grave. He chased the Betty directly over friendly ships and their anti-aircraft batteries, which opened fire on the two aircraft. AA batteries missed the Betty, but two bursts hit the Hellcat, seriously damaging the fighter; the pilot managed to keep on the bomber's tail and sent it down into the water. Wellwood later counted 12 holes in his fighter, including an eight-inch hole in the left wing, an eight-inch gash in the right wing, seven inches torn from the right elevator, and a number of shrapnel holes in the engine cowling and belly.

Lt. LeFaivre was coached to his first interception 35 miles northeast of Point Tare by controller Lt. Jack Wilson. The Hellcat pilot made radar contact at three miles on a Hamp fighter flying 5,000 feet above him at 19,000 feet. The Hellcat climbed and began a 25-mile chase with a path that took them both over the American anti-aircraft fire zone, but unlike Wellwood, LeFaivre's aircraft was not hit. The night fighter gained on the unsuspecting Japanese fighter, dropping back 50 yards after making a positive identification. The first burst hit the Hamp's right wing root, and a second burst caused the engine to explode and the right wing to fall away. The Hellcat flew through the debris as the enemy aircraft spiraled into the sea. His second kill came 30 minutes later when he caught a Betty 20 miles northeast of Point Tare. Pulling up on his target, he fired a burst into the bomber's starboard engine, causing it to spark. The Betty nosed down, picking up speed as the night fighter followed, firing another burst and causing gasoline to begin streaming out of the right wing. Both aircraft continued downward before leveling off at 1,000 feet, with the Hellcat traveling at 220 knots (253mph). Dropping his landing gear to slow down, he pumped another burst into the Betty's right engine, causing it to explode in a brilliant flash of fire and debris. The night fighter followed down to 500 feet before leveling off to watch as the bomber crashed onto a small island.

Magruder's executive officer, Maj. R. Bruce Porter, received his orders 22 May to replace Maj. Bill Kellum as commander of VMF(N)-542. The 24-year-old pilot had three previous aerial victories from his tour in 1943, flying Corsairs with VMF-121 in the Solomons, and was one of the youngest majors in the Marine Corps. He attended night fighter training upon his return to the states, and upon completion was assigned initially to VMF(N)-544 and then VMF-511 before coming to -533 at the end of April 1945. His arrival sparked an impromptu party by -542 personnel, with heavy drinking of strong spirits; the celebration lasted way into the early hours. The morning of the 23rd found Porter hung over from a night of drinking in celebration of his arrival to the squadron as he drove by jeep to the flight line.[7]

Col. Marion "Black Mac" Magruder, flying the F6F-5N in the foreground, leading two other Hellcats of VMF(N)-533 over Okinawa, May 1945. His squadron became the most successful Marine night fighter squadron of the war with 35 kills. (Col. Magruder Archives)

Three non-commissioned officers of the squadron, who noticed the haggard appearance and a strong smell of alcohol coming from their new CO, greeted him upon his approach to the flight line. Porter wanted to see the Hellcat assigned to him and the trio took him over to Number 76. The fighter was Kellum's former bird and was the only F6F-5N in the squadron equipped with a battery of four .50-caliber machine guns and two 20mm cannon. He looked at the nose art painted on the engine cowling and scowled, "What in the hell is that?" There was a big red heart over-painted with the name *Millie Lou* painted in white. "Get that goddamned *Millie Lou* off my airplane. I want my own painting on the nacelle. Have a big fifth of Schenley's put on with the caption *Black Death*." Porter was referring to the disparaging nickname "Black Death" given to Schenley's Black Velvet Canadian whiskey, as it was held in low regard by Marine and naval personnel of the time. The men complied with the officer's request, pulled the engine cowling off, and sent it off to an artist serving with a nearby Air Force unit, where it was painted with the aforementioned motif.[8]

Col. Magruder (far right) briefing pilots before an NCAP over Okinawa. Front L to R: 1st Lt. Karl Witte, 1st Lt. Albert Dellamano, and 1st Lt. William Treynor. Back L to R: 1st Lt. Johnny Peacock and 2nd Lt. Ed Ryan. Behind them is the mission board with the in-squadron number for each aircraft in column 1, followed by the BuNo in the second column. (Col. Magruder Archives)

Porter barely had time to adjust to his new role as squadron commander when the enemy decided to conduct one of the most brazen cases of either extreme heroics or insanity of the Okinawa Campaign. American Army and Marine fighters based at Yontan, Kandena, and Ie Shima were highly successful in minimizing the effectiveness of Japanese suicide attacks. The Japanese high command, realizing the importance of neutralizing American air assets on Okinawa, made the decision to launch a two-prong attack 24-25 May, with commando-style attacks on the airfields while suicide planes targeted radar picket ships. The surprise ground attack was assigned to the Airborne Raiding Force known as the *Giretsu* (Act of Herosim), with the mission of destroying fuel depots and aircraft. Armed with grenades, demolition charges, and light weapons, the force of 120 men were loaded aboard

Sally medium bombers. The attack began at 2225 hours on the 24th; the bombers appeared over Yontan and attempted to land, but were met with withering anti-aircraft fire, and all but one of the aircraft were shot down. The one survivor belly landed on the airfield and a dozen commandos exited firing their weapons while tossing demolition charges and hand grenades at parked aircraft. The ensuing nighttime battle continued for several hours, resulting in nine aircraft destroyed, 29 damaged, and a 70,000-gallon fuel storage tank going up in flames. American casualties were comparatively light, with five killed and 18 wounded; one of the men mortally wounded was Lt. Maynard C. Kelly of VMF(N)-533, who was the tower duty officer that night; none of the attackers survived.

While American ground personnel at the airfield battled against the *Giretsu*, night fighters on station that night waged their own war in the air, downing six enemy aircraft that were acting as decoys to lure the American fighters away from Yontan. Pilots of VMF(N)-533 bagged five of the total, with Lt. Albert F. Dellamano bringing down three of them within 40 minutes. The first kill of the evening occurred with 1st Lt. James E. Smurr intercepting a Betty at 2105 hours that was in the process of dropping "window" in an apparent effort to disrupt American GCI for the pending strike. Ten minutes later, 1st Lt. T.B. Trammell encountered another Betty dropping "window" and dispatched it after firing a four-second burst into the bomber's port engine.

Dellamano lit up a Betty, Jake, and Sally between 2140 and 2230 hours northwest of Ie Shima, with his first contact, just as those of Smurr and Trammel, being a Betty dropping "window." The night fighter closed and fired a short burst without using the gunsight towards the bomber but missed. The bomber continued to orbit with its crew apparently oblivious to the Hellcat, since there was no return fire. He turned on his sight and fired again at the starboard wing root. Flame appeared from the right engine and the Betty started down in a slow spiral to the left. The night fighter fired again and the bomber flamed and continued on its downward plunge into the sea.

GCI vectored Dellamano towards another bogey ten minutes later a few miles northwest of his first victim. The night fighter picked up the target dead ahead a mile away with a visual confirmation made when the float plane became silhouetted against the bright moonlight. The Hellcat's speed rapidly closed the distance with the slower enemy aircraft and Dellamano had to drop his wheels to slow down. Pulling up behind and slightly below, he fired 15 rounds from each of the fighter's six guns, causing the Jake's right float to start burning. The float plane made a 60-degree diving turn with the Hellcat following, pumping more rounds into the enemy. The Jake began burning before diving straight down into the seat. His third victim was caught 20 minutes later, when GCI vectored the night fighter to a Sally located 15 miles northwest of Ie Shima; a 60-round burst from the Hellcat's machine guns sent it spiraling into the water. The sixth Japanese aircraft that fell to a Marine night fighter during that night was claimed by Lt. Carl M. Davis of VMF(N)-543, who flew through friendly antiaircraft fire to splash a Betty at 2345 hours. Most pilots on patrol that night were not allowed to land at Yontan, since thousands of rounds of ammunition were being fired into the air and across the field by both defenders and attackers. Smurr, Trammell, and Dellamano, after completing their patrols near midnight, landed at Kadena within minutes of each other.

The Japanese conducted 56 separate aerial strikes during 2-28 May against shipping beginning at 0730 hours, consisting of two to four aircraft each. Marine aircraft downed 32 – four by night fighters – during the next 25 hours, while the Army claimed another 17. Each of the night fighter squadrons scored, with -543 claiming a Jake and Hamp, while -542 bagged a Zeke and -533 a Jake. The interception of a Jake by 1st Lt. Smurr of -533 that night proved the effectiveness of a well-trained pilot and ground controller. On patrol northwest of Ie Shima, GCI directed Smurr to a bogey that was making a number of changes in altitude and direction. The erratic behavior of the enemy called for GCI to give the night fighter a number of course corrections before he was able to establish a head-on intercept and radar contact at a range of one-eighth of a mile. Bright moonlight allowed him to make a positive identification of the aircraft as Jake and he followed the float plane in a full circle and then cut inside with a starboard turn. He pressed

Japanese Mitsubishi Type 97-2 Ki-21 (Sally) bomber loaded with troops that crash landed at Yontan the evening of 24 May 1945. A dozen soldiers scrambled out and proceeded to destroy nine U.S. aircraft, damaged 29 others, and lit up 70,000 gallons of aviation fuel. One American died from wounds (Lt. Maynard C. Kelley of VMF(N)-533) and there were 18 wounded. None of the attackers survived, and sixty-nine Japanese bodies were found and buried. (National Archives)

the trigger, sending a short burst at the target less than 50 yards away, hitting the Jake between the floats and causing it to explode and fall into the water. The entire engagement took only 45 seconds and 62 rounds of ammunition – possibly the quickest and most efficient score by a Marine night fighter.

Col. Magruder's -533 continued to add to its score by claiming another three aircraft the following evening, giving the squadron 15 confirmed and one probable in just over two weeks of combat operations. First Lt. Foris M. Hollowell flamed a Betty at 0200 hours after the bomber tried to ram his fighter 50 miles from Drake Field. An hour later, 1st Lts. Robert S. Hemstad and Richard M. Moore each scored within five minutes of each other while on NCAP northwest of Ie Shima. Hemstad scored first at 0315 hours, when he was vectored from his cruising altitude of 11,000 feet to a bogey located 3,000 feet above and 25 miles northwest of Ie Shima. He climbed up to meet his target and established a radar contact and closed for the kill. He made a visual confirmation that it was an Irving and fired a short burst without effect when the Hellcat was 75 yards behind. The enemy fighter immediately took evasive action by diving to port, but it failed to shake off Hemstad, who followed, firing another burst that caught the aircraft in the starboard engine. The Irving rolled over and descended as another burst from the night fighter hit the starboard wing's fuel tank and it spiraled into the water, engulfed in a ball of flame. Five minutes later, Lt. Moore dispatched another Irving 30 miles northwest of Ie Shima in an encounter that took both hunted and hunter through American antiaircraft fire, but the -533 pilot pressed home his attack and brought the squadron its third victory of the evening.

Second Lt. Del W. Carlton of VMF(N)-542 at the controls of F(N)-86 "Ramblin' Ruthie," named after his fiancé. Carlton scored two victories while on Okinawa. (Emil Buehler Library, NMNA)

CLOSING THE RING (JUNE-AUGUST 1945)

Operations during the next several days came nearly to a standstill, as torrential rain fell (nearly 14 inches between 20 May and 5 June), limiting visibility in the air and turning the ground into oozing mud. The intense clashes of April and May gave way to sporadic engagements during early June, but it picked up during week two, and with the month ending in a spectacular fashion. Battling rain and poor visibility, night fighter operations continued, with Lt. William Smith of VMF(N)-542 claiming the first score of the month, getting an Irving on the third. Four days elapsed before another successful interception was made, with VMF(N)-543's 1st Lt. E.P. Pendrey bagging a Val on the seventh. Two days later it was -533's turn, with a Tony becoming the victim of 1st Lt. J.A. Stokes' guns during a predawn interception 60 miles north of Pt. Tare, followed that evening by Capt. Bob Baird's destruction of a Jake 30 miles off Pt. Mike at 2130. Baird's kill marked the beginning of his trek of becoming the highest Marine night fighter ace of the war. However, he would not be the first Marine Corps night fighter pilot to claim the ace title, as that distinction goes to Maj. Porter who, during the night of the 15th, downed a pair of aircraft giving him the necessary number to become an ace.

Porter was pulling the ten to midnight shift (2200-2400 hours) in his Hellcat *Black Death* at 10,000 feet when GCI gave him a vector to a bogey. Porter's call sign was Topaz 1, his controller that night was "Handyman," and he was 45 minutes into his patrol when the controller's voice sounded in his earphones:

> Suddenly, my GCI officer called excitedly, "Hello, Topaz One from Handyman. I have an unidentified bogey for you. Target range 30 miles at 10 o'clock. Angel 13 (13,000 feet). He's indicated 170 knots (200mph). Handyman out." Porter jettisoned his drop tank, increased speed, and began climbing to 13,000 as his controller watching on his screen on the ground rattled changes in range and direction. "Hello, Topaz One from Handyman. Target range three miles at 11 o'clock. Bearing one-one-owe (sic) 110 degrees. Target crossing your screen. Go!" Porter picked up the blip on his scope and called his controller, "Handyman from Topaz One. Contact!"

The night fighter closed from behind, and from 300 yards Porter unleashed his battery of four .50-caliber machine guns and two 20mm cannons, scoring hits on the enemy plane identified as a Nick twin-engine night fighter. He wanted to make sure of the kill:

> I wanted him to burn so that I would know beyond a doubt that I had scored a kill. Licks of flame showed up on the leading edge of the wing. Then a fiery orange tongue swept back over the fuselage. Suddenly, the twin-engine Nick stalled and lurched heavily to the right. My rounds poured into her vitals. I saw tracer strike the canopy. I doubt the pilot ever knew what hit him. It was over in about two seconds. When the Nick nosed over and fell away toward the sea, he was wrapped in flames from nose to tail.[9]

Maj. Porter returned to his assigned search sector and waited for another vector if it were to come, and it did. An hour later, Handyman's voice came on and directed him to another bogey. Handyman directed the fighter pilot as before, giving him closing distance and course corrections as *Black Death* gained on the unsuspecting Japanese plane. Porter picked it up on his scope and closed for the kill when he identified it as a G4M Betty, but this bomber was somewhat different:

> I saw it carrying an external load under its belly. Sure enough, it was carrying a Baka bomb, a manned, rocket-propelled suicide missile, typically hauled aloft by a "BETTY" (sic) bomber. [The Japanese called it the Yokosuka MXY7 *Ohka*, which meant cherry blossom; the Marines called it *Baka*, which meant stupid.] I closed carefully, opening up with .50 calibers and 20mm cannon. They ignited in a garish explosion. As I dived away, I wondered if the "BETTY" (sic) and "passenger" counted as two or not. Anyhow, this made me an ace, with my victories at Guadalcanal while flying with VMF-121.[10]

Bob Baird emulated Porter's double kill evening the following night with an interception of a Betty at 0351 hours, followed by a Mitsubishi G3M (Nell) medium bomber at 0501. Baird, with the call sign Scrapper 3, was orbiting at 10,000 feet when his controller "Arsenic" alerted him to a bogey at 23,000 feet. The 23-year-old Marine from South Gate, California, pushed the throttle and pulled on the control stick to reach the altitude of his quarry. Reaching the desired altitude, the hunt was on, as Arsenic guided him towards the target. At two and a half miles, Baird's scope showed the blip of the bogey 2,000 feet below him and the Hellcat descended, closing the distance to within a half-mile. The bogey at that point made a course change taking him over the American antiaircraft fire zone, and Arsenic told the pilot to break off the interception. The thought of getting hit by friendly fire did not deter him, and Baird requested his controller to ask for approval to continue the pursuit.[11]

Maj. R. Bruce Porter in F6F-5N F(N)-36 at MCAS Cherry Point, NC, 1944. Porter began training for night operations with VF-511 before a transfer sent him to VMF(N)-533, where he served as executive officer. On 22 May 1945, orders gave him the command of VMF(N)-542. (Thomas E. Doll)

Maj. R. Bruce Porter, commanding officer of VMF(N)-542, passes parked F6F-5N Hellcats. Porter had three kills from his previous duty with VMF-121 in 1943. He became an ace the evening of 15 June 1945 by downing a Kawasaki Ki-45 "Nick" fighter and G4M "Betty" bomber.

Arsenic's reluctance to allow Baird to enter the zone was understandable, since on a number of occasions night fighters had been subjected to friendly fire from shore and ship-based batteries while pursuing the enemy. It was impossible to tell friend from foe flying above them in the dark, and they therefore fired at anything moving. Five-Thirty-Three lost Lt. Wilhide in May, when he pursued two enemy bombers through a naval antiaircraft fire zone, while four pilots of -543 went missing in action between 14 May and 11 June due to unknown causes.[12]

Baird received word from Arsenic that AA gunners would hold their fire just as he spotted the contact he identified as a Betty. The Hellcat closed the distance to 300 feet and Baird fired from astern, but only three of his .50-caliber guns functioned and he had to fire three more bursts into the bomber before it exploded and the remains tumbled into the water. Baird's second kill came an hour later, with Arsenic guiding him to another bogey 35 miles from Point Bolo at 18,000 feet. He picked up the target at a range of one-and-a-half miles and began his descent from 21,000 feet, dropping his landing gear to reduce his speed from 220 to 160 knots (253/184mph) to match that of his target. Dawn was breaking, and Baird maneuvered his Hellcat to silhouette the target against the eastern horizon and saw that it was a Nell. He cut back and came up behind, firing from 100 yards. This time only two of his guns worked, and his initial burst failed to deliver the desired result, so he fired again. Rounds struck the starboard engine and wing root and the Nell nosed over, a massive sheet of flame engulfing it, and spun into the water.

A week later, during the early morning hours of the 22nd, "Black Mac's Killers" downed five enemy aircraft, two of them by Capt. Baird, giving him the double distinction of becoming the only pure Marine night fighter and only Marine Hellcat ace of the war. Baird, orbiting at 12,000 feet 35 miles northeast of Ie Shima during the midnight shift, was alerted by GCI "Ringtail" of a bogey at 23,000 feet. He increased RPM and began climbing to match the altitude of his prey while closely monitoring the blip on his screen that was less than a mile away. The bogey, a P1YS (Frances) night fighter, may have picked up the approaching American fighter on his Type 6 radarscope as it took evasive action. The Japanese pilot's actions failed to shake loose the pursuer, as Baird came up from behind and let loose his six .50 caliber machine guns at a range of 50 feet. The starboard engine of the Frances exploded and a second burst severed its tail from the fuselage. At 0045 hours, 35 miles northwest of Ie Shima, the Japanese had one less night fighter in service.

F(N)-16 of VMF(N)-533 off Ie Shima, Okinawa, 27 June 1945. Col. Magruder ordered all aircraft codes and markings painted black, changing from the standard white to better conceal the aircraft during night missions. (Robert F. Dorr)

Less than hours later, "Ringtail" called again, pointing Baird to another bogey located approximately 60 miles from Ie Shima at 20,000 feet making "S" turns in an attempt to locate Allied shipping. It was a Betty, and the Hellcat made a climbing attack from the rear and opened fire at 0233 hours from 100 yards, with rounds tearing into the bomber's belly and engines. It flamed and plummeted into the water. The destruction of the bomber made Baird the only Marine ace to reach that status by downing all five enemy aircraft by radar guidance. Two more Japanese aircraft and their crews met the same fate as Baird's Frances and Betty between the hours of 0057 and 0230 hours. Twelve minutes after Baird downed his first aircraft, 1st Lt. Karl W. Witte downed a Sally 15 miles northeast of Hedo-misaki, located off the northern tip of Okinawa. The squadron's fourth score of the evening was at 0230 hours, when 1st Lt. John R. Mahoney claimed another Sally 15 miles off Ie Shima. During lunch the following afternoon, Lt. Col. Magruder presented Capt. Baird with a trophy built from Japanese aircraft parts with a plaque bearing the inscription, "Captain Robert Baird, United States Marine Corps, Nightfighter Ace, Black Mac's Killers, VMF(N)-533, 22 June 1945."[13]

Lt. Col. Magruder was proud of his pilots, who were credited with 25 confirmed kills and one probable in six weeks of combat operations. Besides Capt. Baird earning ace status, his two victories on the 22nd made him one of only seven Marine night fighter pilots to score two or more kills on one mission. Members of -533 who scored similarly were Robert Wellwood and Albert Dellamano with three and two by Edward LeFaivre. Other Marine night fighter pilots with this distinction were Maj. Porter of VMF(N)-542 (2), T/Sgt John Andre of VMF(N)-541 (2), and 2nd Lt. Harold T. Hayes of VMF(N)-541 (2).

Photograph of Capt. Robert Baird of VMF(N)-533 taken in January 1945. He became the only "all-night" Marine ace to achieve all six of his kills at night, all occurring between 9 June and 14 July 1945. (Department of Defense, Official Portrait)

Magruder actively participated in Okinawa's defense by regularly participating in NCAP, but he had not scored himself; that changed while leading the second night shift. At 2220 hours, GCI "Ringtail" alerted Magruder of two bogies at 20,000 feet 15 miles from Ie Shima. He pointed his Hellcat "LITTLE *Mac*," named after his son, towards the enemy. The Colonel established radar contact at three miles and the night fighter descended to 15,000 feet, with the pilot dropping airspeed. One of the two blips on his screen turned away, while the other maintained a constant heading, making an easier target for the approaching Hellcat. He could tell from the aircraft's engine exhausts and outline that it was a Betty. The bomber began a slow right turn, with the night fighter following behind at five o'clock. The Hellcat's machine guns opened up, hitting the Betty in the right engine, wing root, and in the cockpit, but the bomber continued its gentle turn. He fired two more bursts before flaming both engines, but the Japanese bomber refused to die. "Black Mac" pulled alongside to check for any sign of life inside the cockpit. At that point the Betty, now engulfed in flames, suddenly veered towards "LITTLE *Mac*." He pulled away and watched as the stricken bomber flipped over and tumbled from the sky. Twenty-five minutes had elapsed since "Ringtail" had initially sent VMF(N)-533's CO on the hunt that resulted in his only aerial victory.

Other -533 pilots scoring during June were 1st Lt. Robert Hemstad, who bagged a Betty on the 19th and a Sally on the 24th, bringing his final score to three confirmed victories. First Lieutenant William T. Treynor destroyed a Betty on the 19th, while on the 26th, 1st Lt. Ralyn C Parkhill nailed a Rufe and 1st Lt. Johnny W. Peacock registered his only kill by bringing down a Jake. First Lieutenant Charles S. Stitt, Jr., closed out the month with an interception of a Jake float plane 35 miles from Point Bolo. In a span of three weeks, between 9-30 June, "Black Mac's Killers" destroyed 15 enemy aircraft in the air without a single loss to the squadron. In comparison, its sister squadron -542 brought down three aircraft, while -543 failed to score during the month.

Capt. Robert Baird (R) of VMF(N)-533 receives congratulations from Maj, Gen, Louis E. Woods, commanding officer of Second Marine Air Wing on Okinawa, July 1945. (USMC via Thomas E. Doll)

The end of June brought with it a major change to VMF(N)-533, with Lt. Col. Magruder receiving orders 30 June to ground himself and sixteen pilots who had been with him since May 1944. Replacements were on their way, and MAG headquarters saw no reason to subject the squadron's commanding officer or any of his experienced pilots to further danger. He stayed with the squadron another week before turning over command to Maj. Samuel B. Folsom, Jr. In recognition of his leadership, the Marine Corps awarded Lt. Col. Marion Magruder the Legion of Merit.

A two-week lull in successful interceptions developed, as -533 flight operations were reduced to one NCAP, and as veteran pilots left and new arrivals became accustomed to combat operations. The squadron would down another five aircraft between 14 and 30 July. Changes were happening with -542 and -543 as well, with the former moving operations from Yontan to Chimu airfield to the northeast, while the latter left Kadena for Awase, on the east coast. Maj. Porter remained CO of -542 through the end of August, while Maj. James B. Maguire, former skipper of VMF(N)-534, replaced Clair Chamberlain as CO of -543 on 18 June.

Baird's F6F-5N was one of two armed with 20mm cannons, the other being Bruce Porter's of VMF(N)-542. Most of VMF (N)-533's fuselage codes were black, while -542's were white, as was Porter's "F(N)-76." No fuselage code is visible on this Hellcat. (USMC via Thomas E. Doll)

Opposite:
Col. "Black Mac" Magruder illuminated by the instrument lights of his F6F-5N Hellcat prior to take-off from Charlie Field, Ie Shima, June 1945. He added to the squadron's scoreboard by downing a G4M (Betty) bomber off Ie Shima 22 June 1945. (Col. Magruder Archives)

F(N)-76 of VMF(N)-542 at Chimu Airfield, Okinawa, 1945. Maj. R. Bruce Porter flew an F6F-5N with the designation F(N)-76 and the name "*Black Death*" painted on the engine cowling, but this aircraft does not appear to have the artwork. (Bruce Porter via Thomas E. Doll)

Marine night fighters downed over a dozen enemy aircraft between 3 July and 8 August. In July, the Night Hawks of VMF(N)-543 claimed five kills, starting with 1st Lt. Gerald P. Anderson downing a Tony off Ie Shima at 0235 hours on the 3rd with only 80 rounds of ammunition. Nine days passed before Sky Hawk 2nd Lt. Louis McGowen found a G3M off Okinawa at 0420 hours and splashed it. VMF(N)-533 waited two weeks before making its first kill of the month, with Capt. Baird scoring his sixth and final victory. This time, his F6F-5N named "Fox-Nan-Four" carried an extra punch of two 20mm cannons along with four .50-caliber machine guns. On a predawn patrol Baird was vectored to Betty, overtaking it after a short chase. Closing to 100 yards to obtain confirmation that it was the enemy, he fired a short three-second burst with his battery of cannons and machine guns. The shells tore into both engines and the Betty became engulfed in a fiery inferno. It flew straight for a few seconds before flipping over and breaking in half as it plummeted. VMF(N)-533 raised its score three more times during the month, with 1st Lt. John R. Mahoney earned his second aerial victory by splashing a Jill 98 miles from Point Bolo at 2136 hours, and Capt. George A. Hanna claimed another Jill four minutes later, 20 miles northwest of Ie Shima. Approximately five hours later, 1st Lt. Karl B. Witte, who had downed a Sally 22 June, nailed a Zeke 110 miles from Point Tare.

Maj. R. Bruce Porter's VMF(N)-542 F6F-5N F(N)-76 "Black Death" with 20mm cannon at Chimu, Okinawa, 1945. The aircraft formally belonged to the squadron's previous commander, Maj. William Kellum, and was named "Millie Lou." (Bruce Porter via Thomas E. Doll)

Flight of Marine eight F6F-5N Hellcats with F(N)-78 named "LIT'TLa NANCE" in the foreground, followed by F(N)-80, F(N)-81 named "STINKY," F(N)-84, F(N)-77, and two unknowns. The aircraft appear to be from Okinawa-based squadrons, but have an unusual white horizontal stripe applied to the tails. (Tailhook Association)

July 1945 concluded with 2nd Lt. Tom Danaher of VMF(N)-543, a 21-year-old from Dallas, Texas, splashing a Betty at 0117 hours and damaging another at 0245 hours, while 2nd Lt. Paul Moser, Jr., bagged another one at 0205 hours. VMF(N)-533's last score occurred the following day, when 2nd Lt. Irving B. Handy bagged a Betty at 0206 hours 50 miles west of Zamba Misaki (Point Bolo). The squadron's tally of 35 enemy aircraft destroyed made it the most successful Marine night fighter squadron of WWII and earned it the Presidential Unit Citation.

The atomic bombings of Hiroshima and Nagasaki brought a quick close to the Pacific War. Okinawa Marine night fighters brought down a trio of snooping Japanese aircraft before combat operations ceased. Tom Danaher closed out the Sky Hawks' box score at 15 confirmed by downing two Bettys off Okinawa at 2331, 7 August. The last victory for a Marine night fighter pilot went to 2nd Lt. William E. Jennings of -542, who sent a Tony to a watery grave at 0308 hours on 8 August.

SUMMARY OF WORLD WAR II OPERATIONS

The success of Marine night fighter pilots on Okinawa would not have been possible without the exceptional work of ship-based fighter directors and ground controllers of the air warning squadrons located at 14 points on Okinawa and the outlying islands. The siting of radar stations, improved electronics, and tactics ultimately enabled fighter directors to bring a night fighter within 500 feet of enemy aircraft. Guiding those night fighters was Hedron 43, consisting of AWS-1, 6, 7, and 11, and four Army units (Company B, 568th Signal Air Warning Battalion; Detachment 1, 305th Fighter Control Squadron; 927th Signal Air

Warning Company; and the 5th Radar Calibration Detachment). The Marine and Army early warning units also performed other useful missions, including participating in air-sea rescues and guiding lost aircraft home.[14] During the Okinawa Campaign, carrier night fighters brought down 11 hostile aircraft in March, 27 in April, and six in May. In all, carrier-based VF(N) destroyed 60 enemy planes during the entire campaign, while VMF(N) accounted for 68 at a cost of four losses attributed to the enemy. Exact data concerning the effectiveness of USN and USMC night fighters is somewhat murkier, since a considerable number of conventional carrier-based squadrons utilized radar-equipped Hellcats in addition to designated night fighter units. What can be shown is that nine VF(N) squadrons claimed a total of 146 air-to-air victories, while six VMF(N) squadrons recorded 93 kills. However, the number of aerial victories attributed to the use of airborne radar interception is less certain, although an examination of after action reports shows a considerable number of kills were accomplished during the daylight hours, with VMF(N)-541 being the prime example: all but three of its 23 victories occurred during daylight hours or at dusk.

THE TIGERCAT'S LATE ARRIVAL

The Tigercat never conducted combat operations in WWII due to production delays setting it back until April 1944, and it took until January 1945 for the first Marine squadron to receive the first F7F-2Ns. VMF(N)-531, the oldest Marine night fighter squadron, reformed 9 October 1944 at MCAS Cherry Point. From there, -531 transferred to MCAS Eagle Mountain, Texas, on 29 November, as part of MAG-53 for advanced night fighter training; however, from its arrival to mid-January 1945, available aircraft for training consisted of seven SBD-5s and one J2F-6. Capt. R.E. Ballard arrived with the first F7F-2N on 17 January, and by the end of May it had 19 F7F-2Ns in its inventory. Pilots, radar operators, and support personnel (41 officers and 86 enlisted men) that completed training at the end of May 1945 were selected as the first Tigercat cadre for overseas deployment under the command of Maj. Robert P. Keller, while the remaining section of -531 remained at Eagle Mountain as a training and replacement squadron. Keller's group proceeded to MCAS El Centro, CA, in late June, where it received 18 F7F-2Ns and continued training before departing the U.S. with 16 Tigercats aboard USS *Attu* 24 July. The cadre arrived at Okinawa 14 August, via Guam and Iwo Jima, where it was absorbed into VMF(N)-533, with Keller assuming overall squadron command. Five-Thirty-Three flew patrols until until 2 September 1945, when the Japanese formally surrendered. It then moved to Nan Yuan Airfield, Peiping, China, on 6 October, to participate in the occupation of Northern China.

F7F-2N Tigercat F-N-20 of VMF(N)-531 at MCAS Eagle Mountain Lake, Texas, 23 May 1945, where advance night fighter training took place. (Bob Lawson via Tailhook Association)

Chapter 8

Postwar Night Fighter Development

Not to have an adequate air force in the present state of the world is to compromise the foundations of national freedom and independence.

-Winston Churchill

Peace brought a drastic reduction in U.S. defense spending, including a drawdown in naval aviation, forcing massive cuts to the NACTU night and all-weather program, which shrank from over 500 night fighters at the end of the war to only 70 by July 1946. The Marine Corps experienced considerable downsizing as well, with five of the eight designated night fighter squadrons active during the war disestablished between March 1946 and May 1947. VMF(N)-531, -533, and -542 remained, with the number of squadrons increasing to five with the establishment of VMF(N)-114 and -513 in August 1947. NACTU was reorganized into two units in November 1946 – VC(N)-1 and VC(N)-2 (Navy Composite Squadron One and Two) – and assigned the mission of maintaining night and instrument training of naval aviators, along with testing and development of aircraft and electronic systems. Less than two years later, VC(N)-1 and -2 were redesignated as Fleet All-Weather Training Units, Pacific and Atlantic (FAWTUPac/FAWTULant). Operationally, night and all-weather fighter defense of the fleet during the late 1940s through early 1950s became the primary responsibility of Composite Four (VC-4), established in September 1948, and VC-3 in May 1949.[1]

The Navy continued to rely on the F6F-5N for night operations until the late 1940s, as jet fighters for such work were either in the planning stages or under developmental testing, such as the Douglas F3D Skyknight, which became the service's first operational all-weather jet fighter in 1950. However, performance issues restricted the Skyknight's operational use primarily to land-based units, particularly with VMF(N)-513 in Korea. The Navy would find a suitable night/all-weather jet fighter in the McDonnell F2H-2N and F2H-3 Banshee, but neither participated in combat operations over Korea. The Navy did experiment with radar-equipped F8F Bearcats (the F8F-1N/2N between December 1947 and May 1948), but the APS-19 radar dome mounted under the starboard wing significantly reduced the aircraft's speed. FAWTUPac and FAWTULant tested all of the service's night fighters during the interim postwar years. FAWTUPac, formally VC(N)-1, participated in the sinking of the battleships *New York* and *Nevada*, which had survived the atomic bomb tests at Bikini Atoll. The battleships were towed from Pearl Harbor to a spot south of Oahu and were subjected to an unmerciful pounding by fleet air and surface units 7 and 30 July 1948. Capt. Paul H. Ramsey, CO of the all-weather training unit, led 26 aircraft consisting of two F7F-4N Tigercats, six F8F-1N Bearcats, twelve F6F-5N Hellcats, and six TBM-3N Avengers in strafing, bombing, and rocket attacks against the battlewagons. The first series of attacks sank the *New York*, while the *Nevada* rolled over and sank after three days of pounding from surface units and hits from Tiny Tim rockets and torpedoes carried by FAWTUPac aircraft.[2]

During the same time frame, VC(N)-2 tested the Vought F4U-5N Corsair for night operations, finding it to be an excellent carrier fighter, and by 1950, it had replaced the F6F-5N. The Marines went in a slightly different direction with night fighters beginning late 1944, by transitioning from the Hellcat to the Grumman F7F Tigercat, followed by the F4U-5N. The absence of a reliable jet all-weather fighter for operations in Korea led carrier and shore-based units to utilize the Corsair F4U-5N and F7F-3N Tigercat for close air support, CAP, and NCAP missions.

Grumman and the U.S. Navy looked at replacing the F6F-5N with a radar-equipped F8F Bearcat during the immediate postwar years. Two dozen F8F-1 and -2 Bearcats, designated as F8F-1N and F8F-2N and modified for nocturnal operations, carried APS-19 radar gear in a wing pod similar to the F6F-5N. The modification significantly reduced the aircraft's performance and the experiment was abandoned in favor of modifying the F4U-5 Corsair for night work. (Mark Aldrich Collection via Rich Dann)

The Navy continued to rely on the F6F-5N as the fleet's night fighter during the immediate postwar period. F6F-5N Hellcat L-30 of Carrier Air Service Unit One (CASU-1) on the ramp in September 1945 at Ford Island, Pearl Harbor. (Joe Gennz Collection courtesy of the Pacific Aviation Museum, Pearl Harbor HI via Tailhook Association)

F6F-5N (BuNo 79139), with a searchlight on the port wing, was tested by Antisubmarine Development Detachment, Atlantic Fleet (ASDEVLANT) at NAS Patuxent River, 29 August 1945. (Emil Buehler Library, NMNA via Rich Dann)

VMF(N)-513 F6F-5N WF-18 on board USS *Badoeng Strait* (CVE 116) circa 1947-48. The squadron was one of two postwar Marine night fighter squadrons established 1 August 1947. (North Island Collection via Mark Aldrich and Tailhook Association)

VMF(N)-513 F6F-5N WF-18 during carrier qualifications aboard *Badoeng Strait* circa 1947-48. The squadron would trade in its complement of Hellcats for the F4U-5N Corsair. The aircraft is overall Glossy Sea Blue with white code. (Emil Buehler Library, NMNA)

6F-5N WF-3 with VMF(N)-513 at MCAS El Toro, CA, with 20mm cannons with flash suppressors fitted to protect the pilot's night vision, June 1948. (Robert F. Dorr)

Navy F6F-5N TGV-417 (BuNo 80141), c. 1948-50, was converted to an F6F-5K drone, then transferred to the French Navy. (Thomas E. Doll collection via Rich Dann and Tailhook Association)

Navy and Marine 6F6-5Ns remained with reserve units until the early 1950s. This Navy Hellcat (BuNo 93679) is painted overall Glossy Sea Blue with an orange band and white markings. (Emil Buehler Library, NMNA)

F6F-5N Hellcat of Composite Squadron 21 (VC-21) landing aboard the USS *Badoeng Strait* (CVE-116) circa 1948. VC-21, formed in the fall of 1948, operated the radar-equipped Hellcat for a relatively short time before being reformed as an anti-submarine unit operating the TBM-3S and TBM-3W Avenger. (Robert L. Lawson Photographic Collection, Emil Buehler Library, NMNA)

F7F-3 AND F7F-3N

Grumman continued development of its Tigercat series with the F7F-3 and F7F-4. The next model of the Tigercat, a single-seat day fighter version of the -2, went into production 14 March 1945 as the F7F-3, with the last of 250 such aircraft rolling off Grumman's assembly line 20 June 1946, with a majority modified to operate as either the F7F-3N night fighter (106 units) or F7F-3P (61 units) photographic reconnaissance variant. The -3 retained the same armament and general performance characteristics as its predecessors, with a slightly faster top speed, increased range, and Pratt & Whitney R-2800-34W engines with better high blower performance replacing the R-2800-22Ws of the -1 and -2 models. All F7F-3s were built as single-seat versions at the Grumman plant, and those destined for conversion to a -3N or -3P configuration were then flown to the Navy Lockheed Service Center in Van Nuys, California. Engineers decided to increase the aircraft's stability by enlarging the vertical stabilizer, with the aircraft's height increasing from 13 feet 9 inches on the -1 and -2 to 14 feet 7 inches on early -3s (BuNos 80259-80364), and then to 15 feet 9 inches on subsequent units (BuNos 80365 onward). Grumman rated the -3's top speed at 460mph and the -3N at 447mph at altitude. The original specifications for the Tigercat called for the option for installing external wing-mounted fuel tanks to extend the aircraft's range. Pilots encountered buffeting with the installation of 150-gallon fuel tanks installed beneath the wings. This buffeting limited the speeds at which the aircraft could operate with tanks installed. The Navy requested wind tunnel testing on an F7F-3 at Ames Laboratory to obtain information on the sources of the buffeting and on means of alleviating the problem. The results of the study showed that buffeting was caused by airflow interference of the wing, engine nacelle, and the fuel tank's pylon fairing. Mounting the fuel tank to the fuselage's centerline eliminated the buffeting effects.[3]

The Tigercat was capable of entering a full-power 35-to-40-degree dive within 30 seconds, which proved quite useful while conducting close air support operations in Korea. Dives of up to 25 degrees under full high-speed level flight and full power were possible without running into any aerodynamic or compressibility effects. In dives beyond 25 degrees, however, pilots were cautioned to control speed and method of entry into the dive. At 30 degrees or above, the aircraft entered the aerodynamic compressibility range, quickly characterized by the loss of elevator tab effectiveness and sluggish elevator control, followed by the tendency for the aircraft to nose over into a steeper dive angle. Pilots were instructed to pull on the elevator control to get the aircraft into a shallower glide path before reaching the critical airspeed of 430 knots or 495mph.

462

Production of the F7F-3N night fighter configuration, starting with BuNo 80549 and ending with 80608, made it the most manufactured Tigercat variant, with deliveries beginning 15 May 1945. As with the F7F-2N, a radar operator's station behind the pilot's cockpit replaced the fuselage fuel tank. The major difference between the F7F-3N and the earlier F7F-1 and -2N night fighters was the replacement of the AN/APS-6 with the SCR-720 radar system. This change required modifying the nose to house the 720's larger antennae system; therefore, the sleek knife-like nose associated with earlier models was replaced with a radome nicknamed the "droopsnoot" nose, while the four .50-caliber machine guns were eliminated, leaving the four wing-mounted 20mm cannons for offensive and defensive armament. The installation of the droopsnoot extended the -3N's length by a foot-and-a-half, but overall performance remained unchanged, except the additional weight of the SCR-720 reduced the aircraft's range by 150 miles.

Five Marine night fighter squadrons operated the F7F-3N: VMF(N)-513, -531, -533, -534, and -542. The -3 series entered service with VMF(N)-531 at Eagle Mountain Lake, with the squadron receiving three -3 day fighters for evaluation in late June 1945. Training continued at Eagle Lake on a smaller scale due to postwar demobilization until February 1946, when -531 returned to Cherry Point. The squadron kept its Tigercats until 1952, when it transitioned to the Douglas F3D Skyknight. Meanwhile, a cadre from VMF(N)-533 transitioned to the -3N and deployed to Nan Yuan Airfield, China, in September 1946 for reconnaissance duty, remaining there until January 1947. The squadron retained the F7F-3N until 1949, when it transitioned to the F3D. VMF(N)-534, based at MCAS El Centro, CA, transitioned from the F6F-5N to the F7F-3N in late 1945, retaining the model until its deactivation 31 May 1947. VMF(N)-542, a veteran night fighter squadron of the Okinawa campaign, became the third squadron to transition to the F7F-3N, turning in its F6F-5Ns in 1947. The Tigercat would go to war in Korea with -542 in September 1950, remaining with it until March 1951, when it turned over its aircraft assets to VMF(N)-513, the last night fighter squadron to operate the model. The designation of -542, along with other Marine night fighter squadrons, was officially changed to VMF(AW) for Marine All Weather Fighter Squadron in 1948, yet the former -N designator is commonly used when referring to such units.

F7F-3N night fighter variant, possibly the first such aircraft modified for nocturnal work, at the Grumman plant with a tiger face painted on the nose. The "droop snoot" radome housed the SCR-720 radar system. Installation of the new radar system required deleting the nose-mounted machine guns. Grumman installed a pair of wing-mounted 20mm cannons in their place. (Grumman History Center via Roger Davis)

F7F-3N (BuNo 80549) was retained by Grumman for external stores testing. One series of tests included a 300-gallon auxiliary centerline fuel tank and duel wing tanks installed under the inner wing panels. (Author's Collection)

Opposite:
This F7F-3 (BuNo 80462) over New York in June 1945 was the third Tigercat single-seat day fighter produced by Grumman. Most of the -3s were converted to either the -3N night fighter or -3P photo-reconnaissance variant. (Robert F. Dorr)

Opposite:
Standard pilot instrument panel of the F7F-3N seen here in BuNo 80595, with the radar scope mounted in the center below the gun sight, 13 June 1946. One consequence of the streamlined fuselage was a somewhat tight and uncomfortable cockpit for the pilot. (Grumman Heritage via Tommy Thomason)

1. Radar Indicator Unit—SCR 720C.
2. Radar Indicator Control Unit—SCR 720C.
3. Left Instrument Panel.
4. Right Instrument Panel.
5. Chartboard.
6. Radar Antenna Control—SCR 720C.
7. Foot Operated Microphone Switch.
8. IFF Control Unit.
9. Communicating Control Unit.
10. Cockpit Heater Control.
11. Microphone Cord.

Radar operator's compartment of an F7F-3N shown in the pilot's manual. Attached to the radar scope is a viewing shroud. (Emil Buehler Library, NMNA)

F7F-3N LT-17 (BuNo 80590) of VMF(N)-531 over the North Carolina coast in April 1950, when the squadron was based at Cherry Point. Note the use of MARINES above the squadron designation below the tail. (Robert F. Dorr)

F7F-3N LT-1 (BuNo 80510) of VMF(N)-531 at MCAS Cherry Point during 1948. Coloring is overall Glossy Sea Blue with white codes and red propeller warning stripe. (Emil Buehler Library, NMNA)

VMF(N)-542 F7F-3Ns at MCAS El Toro, CA, 9 June 1948. The white horizontal stripe below "WH" on the tail appears to have been deleted from the aircraft within a year. (Emil Buehler Library, NMNA)

VMF(N)-542 F7F-3N (BuNo 80506) at Los Angeles Airport circa 1949, without the horizontal stripe seen on aircraft in the previous photograph. (Emil Buehler Library, NMNA)

F7F-4N

The last of the Grumman Tigercats produced in any quantity was the F7F-4N night fighter manufactured from 17 September to 7 November 1946. Grumman modified an F7F-3 (BuNo 80548) and delivered to the Navy 27 June 1945. The -4 was a two-seat night fighter with the AN/APS-19 radar system replacing the SCR-720 of the -3N. Structural modifications consisted of stronger inner wing panels and a heavier landing gear to improve carrier operations. Structural changes added additional weight and thus reduced the aircraft's speed, service ceiling, and rate of climb. Grumman produced 12 F7F-4Ns (BuNos 80609-80620), including the prototype, before the Navy canceled further production.

F7F-3N/4N CARRIER QUALIFICATIONS

Carrier qualifications of the Tigercat continued after WWII, with VMF(N)-534 participating aboard USS *Shangri-La* (CV 38) with the F7F-3N in February 1946, but after conducting several landings, the inner wing panel on one -3N collapsed on touchdown, which ended all further testing. In October 1946, carrier qualifications continued with the -4N variant aboard USS *Franklin D. Roosevelt* (CV 42). The -4 passed the carrier trials and it was approved for carrier operations, with Night Fighter Development Squadrons VC(N) successfully operating the aircraft for further evaluation aboard the *Roosevelt* and *Kearsarge* (CV-33).

Deprived of the chance to prove its fighting capability against the Japanese in WWII, the Tigercat's future looked grim with the arrival of jet-powered fighters. However, the start of the Korean War in June 1950 extended the aircraft's life and gave Marine aircrew of VMF(N)-513 and -542 the chance to prove the aircraft's capability to provide close air support for friendly ground forces and validate its role as a potent propeller-driven night fighter during the dawn of the jet age.

F7F-3N of VMF(N)-533 prepares to take-off from USS *Tarawa* (CV 40) for Guam 23 August 1946. Squadron aircraft were loaded aboard the carrier and then flown off, so this was not a carrier qualification exercise. (Emil Buehler Library, NMNA)

Another view of VMF(N)-533's N-2 as it heads into the sun after launching from USS *Tarawa*, heading for Guam and onward to duty in China with Marine Air Group Twenty-Four. (Emil Buehler Library, NMNA)

F7F-4N Tigercat Bureau Number 80620, the last such Tigercat variant produced, is shown on the deck of the carrier USS *Kearsarge* (CV-33) in September 1948, during carrier evaluations conducted by VC(N)-2/FAWTULANT. (Emil Buehler Library, NMNA)

VOUGHT F4U-5/F4U-5N/NL CORSAIR

The Corsair's superior performance in WWII extended the aircraft's service with the Navy and Marine Corps into the early 1950s. The aircraft underwent eight modifications during its production life, consisting of 435 major engineering changes and more than 12,000 production changes from the F4U-1 through the F4U-5. Postwar development continued with the F4U-5 series in 1945, an aircraft designed to serve as the next generation Corsair, and like its brethren, a high-speed, high-altitude interceptor. Since the Navy lacked a carrier-based night fighter, Vought would introduce the F4U-5N. The Korean War, a conflict unlike any other in American military history, changed the mission of the -5 series to that of close air support (CAS) and night interdiction: two roles the engineers at Vought never foresaw when developing the aircraft. The F4U-5, and its variants, which included a night and all-weather version, was an aircraft loved by some but hated by an equal number. The development of night and all-weather F4U-5 variants began with a concept to update the F4U-4B at a time when the Air Force and Navy began to realize that the future of aerial warfare lay with jet-powered fighters.

Vought's intention in developing the first postwar Corsair variant was to provide an aircraft with better overall performance than the F4U-4B. The vision for the next generation of the series was an aircraft that was faster, more maneuverable, had greater range, and one that would reduce pilot fatigue. Design modifications took shape at the company's facility in Stamford, Connecticut, with the selection of three F4U-4 Corsairs (BuNos 97296, 97364, and 97415) to serve as prototypes with the designation XF4U-5. The Navy approved Vought's latest design proposal and on 6 February 1946 gave the company a letter of intent to develop the aircraft.

Three-quarter front view showing the F4U-5's massive four-blade propeller. The -5 also featured redesigned cowl flaps, engine exhausts, and air intake gills, with a pair located at the lower leading edge of the cowling. (Vought Heritage)

This publicity photo shows examples of the 4,000 pounds of external ordnance the F4U-5 series was capable of carrying into combat, including rockets and bombs mounted on outer wing panel and centerline pylons. (Vought Heritage)

Improvements to overall performance consisted of a new power plant with automatic two-stage superchargers, spring and electric trim and rudder controls, automatic cowl flaps, and intercooler and oil cooler doors. To improve the aircraft's effectiveness at high altitude, the F4U-4's R-2800-42W "C" series engine was replaced with the more powerful 18-cylinder, 2,500-hp Pratt & Whitney R-2800-32W "E" series engine, with an automatic two-stage variable supercharger providing approximately 200 more horsepower than the F4U-4. The engine upgrade required lengthening the fuselage by five inches to increase longitudinal stability and angling down the engine three degrees to increase pilot visibility. The updated engine also maintained greater power at higher altitudes. This power plant enabled the -5 to become the fastest propeller-driven aircraft produced for the Navy with a top speed of 470mph at 26,800 feet and a rate of climb of 3,780 fpm (24 miles per hour faster, but a rate of climb 100 fpm slower than its predecessor).

According to the Navy, the F4U-5's trim, rudder, and elevator tabs increased the aircraft's maneuverability. The rudder and elevator tabs incorporated a spring mechanism that automatically deflected to assist in controlling the aircraft during high speeds, in a dive and in spin recovery while reducing the pilot's control forces by 40 percent. Vought replaced the mechanical rotating trim knob found on previous models with electrical trim tab controls consisting of two setting switches and an associated indicator, centralized in one location, near the pilot's left hand that offered quick, space saving, and accurate means of positioning the tabs. A center-left/right toggle switch controlled rudder trim, while a five-position switch located on the joystick with "nose up/down" and "wing left down/right down" positions controlled elevator and aileron trim.

From a head-on view, the only noticeable external difference between the -4 and -5 were the engine's air intake gills, called scoops. The -4 had one at the bottom of the engine cowling, while two were located at the lower leading edge of the -5's cowling due to the -42 engine's twin hydraulically driven and automatically controlled variable-speed auxiliary stage blowers. The size of the blowers required a two-piece engine mount, along with a redesigned induction system The airframe was of all-metal construction, with the last vestiges of fabric, an aspect of all earlier versions of the Corsair, removed from the outer wing panels and replaced with duralumin. This minimized the problem of fabric having the tendency to warp and reduce the aircraft's speed by a few miles per hour. The inclusion of a radio compartment door in the lower right side aft of the cockpit allowed for easier maintenance of avionics gear. For easier access to the cockpit, the manufacturer installed a telescoping step and hand grip on the right side of the fuselage, located below a folding step previously installed on the F4U-4. Additional changes also included a fully-retractable tail wheel and arresting hook.[4]

Understanding that sitting in a cramped space for extended periods often results in pilot fatigue, Vought redesigned the cockpit by seating the pilot more comfortably, installing automatic controls, and redesigning and placing controls in logical groupings and locations. New features included a heater located on the floor in front of the control stick, a power-actuated canopy, an adjustable pilot's seat with folding armrests, and brake pedals that could swing down, allowing the pilot to stretch his legs. Like many aircraft of the time, the F4U-5 also included a cigarette lighter.

The F4U-5's maximum armament package varied little from its predecessor, except in the total bomb load. Armament consisted of four wing-mounted M3 20mm cannons with a maximum ammunition load of 924 rounds (the same as the F4U-4). The aircraft could carry a maximum load of 3,000 pounds of bombs, compared to 2,000 on the -4 version, attached to Mark-51 bomb racks located on the wing center section and centerline of the aircraft. Additional firepower included carrying up to 12 three-inch and 11.75 rockets by installing a Mark 9 launcher on each outer wing panel. The day version of the F4U-5 utilized the Mk-6 fire control system with the Mk-8 gun sight. Actual operation of the sight showed it to be a cumbersome and difficult piece of equipment to use, requiring multi-tasking from a pilot hand flying an aircraft and trying to engage a target, all while fumbling with the gun sight controls. It took a great deal of training and skill to operate the sight successfully. By mid-1947, the Mk-8 gun sight, initially installed on both the day and night versions of the F4U-5, was replaced by the Mk-20 Mod 0 on the F4U-5N. Similar to the Mk-8, the new site provided the pilot with a selection of three reticles depending upon visibility. By turning a control knob mounted on the sight, a pilot could select any one of the reticle patterns depending on visibility. First, the reticle pattern provided a minimum amount of illumination and markings to reduce or eliminate pilot blindness. Second, the sight also operated during daytime, with reticle markings that furnished the pilot with reference points for use in fixed gun deflection firing, rocket firing, and glide and low altitude bombing. Third, the combination reticle provided the means of targeting under low or medium visibility conditions, such as dawn, twilight, or overcast.[5]

Two of the three F4U-5 prototypes took to the air 4 April 1946 at Vought's plant in Stamford, Connecticut, with test pilot Bill Horan flying the first production F4U-5 on 1 October 1947. The initial order was for 223, but subsequent interest for a night fighter version increased production. Four variants of the -5 series were produced between 1947 and 1952, consisting of the F4U-5 day fighter-bomber, the -5N night fighter, the -5NL all-weather fighter, and the F4U-5P photo-reconnaissance version. All four saw service in the Korean War with carrier and land-based Navy and Marine Corps units. The total production run consisted of 223 F4U-5 fighter-bombers, 214 F4U-5N, 101 -NL night and all weather, and 30 F4U-5P photographic reconnaissance aircraft. The Connecticut facility produced more than 250 of the series before the company packed up and moved to a new plant in Grand Prairie, Texas, near Dallas. In April 1949, delivery of F4U-5s from the Dallas plant began, with production terminating 22 October 1951.

F4U-5N NIGHT FIGHTER

The F4U-2N's success in WWII provided the basis for the development of a F4U-5N night fighter that served with distinction in the Korean War. The night fighter variant included all modifications included in the day version, except for a different gun sight; additional avionic and electronic components, including the installation of an airborne radar system; and noticeable exterior changes that enabled the aircraft to operate effectively at night. The added weight barely reduced overall performance, with the -5N's top speed only 10 mph slower than the day fighter and the rate-of-climb decreased by 500 fpm. Three production F4U-5 aircraft were pulled from the assembly line for conversion to the XF4U-5N prototype. Visible external changes included a radome mounted on the leading edge of the right wing, similar to that mounted on the F4U-2N. To aid in night gunnery practice, trihedral prism retroflectors were installed on each wing tip and the tail cone. Nicknamed "the aerial pinball device," the pilot would press the gun trigger and a light would shine on the target. If the pilot was on target, the light beam would be reflected from all three prisms at the target. If only one prism returned light, then the Corsair was off to one side, or too high or low. The results were recorded on the gun camera.[6] Armament was the same as the day version, but to minimize the F4U-5N's in-flight visibility to enemy ground forces, T-20 flash suppressors were mounted on the aircraft's four 20mm cannons, along with six exhaust flame dampeners located on the engine exhaust collectors.

Two major modifications allowing the aircraft to operate nocturnally consisted of the APS/APS-19 air intercept radar and the Mk-20 gun sight. In addition to the radar system and updated sight, the night variant included a second ARC-1 VHF radio transmitter and receiver used in conjunction with the ARC-28 relay system, the APX-2 IFF system, AN/APN-1 radio altimeter, and the P-1 Eclipse-Pioneer automatic pilot. Beginning in 1947, replacement of the APS-4 and APS-6 radar systems on Navy and Marine Corps night fighters began with the introduction of the AN/APS-19 search, intercept, and navigational radar, which consisted of nine major components.

F4U-4N (BuNo 97361) parked at the Vought facility with the AN/APS-6 radar. It was the sole aircraft of this type and was accepted by the Navy 3 March 1946. (Nicholas A. Veronico)

The F4U-4N served as the test bed for the F4U-5N and -5NL. In May 1947, the aircraft was transferred to NAS Patuxent for electronics testing and then to Cherry Point before being stricken from the Navy inventory in March 1948. (Nicholas A. Veronico)

Prototype for the F4U-5N (BuNo 122039) parked at the Vought factory. The night variant was the same aircraft as the F4U-5, except for the addition of specialized equipment for nocturnal operations. (Vought History)

View from below of the F4U-5N prototype with a different tail coloration of gull gray for the rudder. The forward portion of the wings appears to match the gray color seen on the bottom of the aft fuselage (Vought History)

F4U-5N in the foreground with an F4U-5P photographic reconnaissance variant in the background being towed. Note the difference in the engine exhaust system of both aircraft. The dash -5N featured flame dampeners. (Vought Heritage)

F4U-5N (BuNo 124493) with wing-mounted nacelle housing the AN/APS-19 radar. This aircraft has Glossy Sea Blue coloring on the upper fuselage and wings with gull gray stripes on the underside leading edges. (American Aviation Historical Society)

Photo 08-26BBB
F4U-5N prototype in flight. The F4U-5N's standard armament was the same as the daytime version with four 20mm cannons and hardpoints for external stores. (Robert F. Dorr)

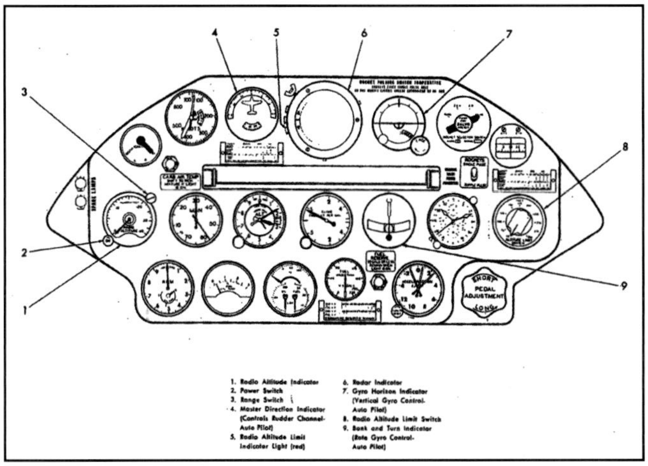

This cockpit view of the F4U-5N shows the locations of the air intercept radar gear. The Mark-20 gun sight is located directly above the radar scope. (Emil Buehler Library, NMNA)

This new system weighed less and offered better performance than the APS-4/6. Similar to the APS-4 used with the F4U-2N and F6F-5N of WWII, the system, constructed of aluminum with a removable plastic cone, housed the AS-238/APS-19 antenna, the RT-100/APS-19 transmitter-receiver, and the J-209/APS-19 test box. The rest of the equipment, located in either the cockpit or radio compartment, consisted of the C-282APS-19 control box, SN-35/APS-19 synchronizer-power, ID-158/APS-19 radar indicator, type 800-1D radar motor alternator, radar power junction box, and NAF-1221-1 capacitor box.

The lighter weight of the APS-19 was due to improved electronic circuitry and components coupled with the use of magnesium wherever possible. The enhanced ability to use both the intercept and search functions was the result of combining scanning abilities found in the AN/APS-4 and AN/APS-6. The result was a system with improved search coverage and mapping, with four operating modes consisting of search, intercept, aim, and beacon. Search operation could detect surface craft or land targets up to 100 miles away. In air-intercept operations, the system could detect aircraft at a distance of eight nautical miles. Aim operation allowed the pilot to shoot down a target without seeing it visually by looking at the radarscope. The maximum effective range in aim operation was 1,500 yards. Beacon operation provided a homing navigational aid with a maximum range of 150 miles.

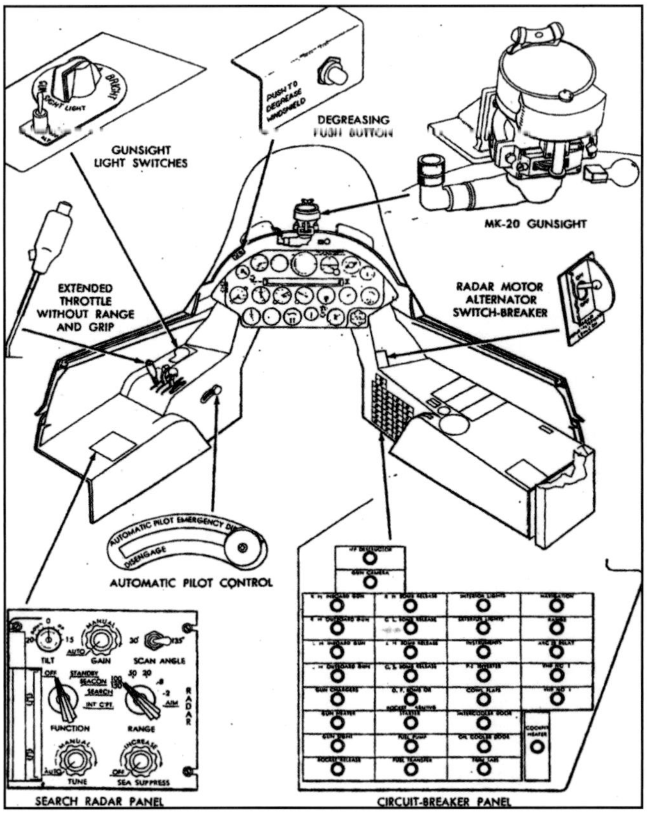

A reference diagram for the instrument panel for the F4U-5N with production modifications to the APS-19 radar system. The instrument panel for the night fighter variant was modified to house the radar scope. (Emil Buehler Library, NMNA)

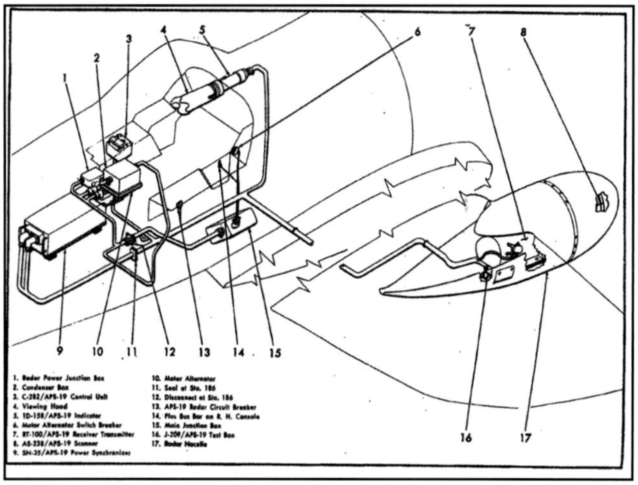

Reference diagram for AN/APS-19 radar equipment fitted on the -5N and -5NL variants. The nacelle was almost identical to that found on the WWII-era F4U-2N. (Emil Buehler Library, NMNA)

Side view of (BuNo 123190) of VC-4 with in-squadron number 97 reveals a modified VHF "football" loop antenna, probably added after the unit's return to the U.S., since the component hasn't been painted the standard blue to blend in with the aircraft's overall color scheme. (American Aviation Historical Association)

F4U-5N (BuNo 123187) with a Douglas Skyraider from VC-3 on a training mission near their home base of NAS Moffet Field, CA, prior to the Korean War. (U.S. Navy via Nicholas A. Veronico)

F4U-5N (BuNo 123195) of VC-4 based on the USS *Leyte* (CV-32), 8 January 1950, with five-inch HVAR rockets. VC-4 maintained night fighter elements of F4U-5Ns with the fleet, particularly in the Mediterranean, during the early 1950s. (Author's Collection)

The following three photographs were taken by John E. Adamic, a radio mechanic with VMF(N)-114, stationed at MCAS Cherry Point, NC, from 1948 to 1952. An F4U-5N of VMF(N)-114 (BuNo 123199) c. 1950 in all its splendor cruises somewhere over the Atlantic, possibly near the Florida Keys. The pilot is wearing a WWII-era flight suit, helmet, and goggles. (John E. Adamic via Mark Adamic)

F4U-5N aircraft with BuNo 121816 through 122206 were equipped with the AN/APS-19, while subsequent N-series beginning with BuNo 123144 were equipped with the AN/APS-19A. The A-model had adjustments not included with the earlier version that allowed the pilot to alter the focus and brilliance of the radarscope and the brilliance of the radio altimeter limit light.

Between 1947 and 1953, the Vought F4U-5N/L Corsair served as the last piston-driven front-line fighter with the Marine Corps, even as some of its air arm transitioned to jet-powered all weather fighters, such as the Douglas F3D-2 Skyknight in production at the time. Navy ship-borne units continued to operate the F4U-5N and -5L until the end of the Korean War, providing close air support for ground units and CAP for the U.S. Seventh Fleet, since an adequate replacement aircraft with the same versatility did not exist in quantity at the time. However, initially designed as a night and all-weather interceptor, the F4U-5N/L Corsair's speed and maneuverability, along with the ability to deliver a variety of ordinance on target, allowed it to remain in service with the Navy and Marine Corps as an essential asset for close air support of UN ground forces.

F4U-5N touches down on USS *Wright* (CVL-49) somewhere in the Atlantic. The squadron, formed 1 August 1947, remained active throughout the Korean War, but did not see action while deployed to that theater. (John E. Adamic via Mark Adamic)

Green Shirt arresting gear handler and a VMF(N)-114 F4U-5N (BuNo 123168) aboard *Wright*. The squadron operated in the Pacific during WWII. VMF-114 provided air support for Marine ground forces before moving on in the postwar years as an all-weather squadron. (John E. Adamic via Mark Adamic)

F4U-5NL ALL-WEATHER CORSAIR

The Marine pilots of VMF(N)-513 who participated in the early phases of the Korean War felt the strain caused by constant flying in terrible conditions, sometimes at tree-top level over mountainous terrain where the tops of the hills were often shrouded in fog. The arrival of extremely cold and icy weather conditions by late November did not help the situation for both F4U-5N pilots and F7F-3N pilots and radar operators, since both types of aircraft lacked deicing equipment. Flying an F4U-5N during the day with good visibility posed no serious problems, since pilots could easily see the mountainous terrain that characterizes much of Korea. Between August and October 1950, squadron aircraft could operate under adequate weather throughout day and nighttime hours with relatively few problems. However, problems with the aircraft quickly became apparent as Fall and Winter approached. Changing conditions made a significant impact on VMF(N)-513, with operations falling from 1,289 combat missions in September to only 714 in October. The land-based and carrier-based F4U-5N could not operate as an all-weather fighter in the extreme cold weather of Korea. Improved conditions in November 1950 allowed the squadron to fly a total of 1,351 hours in support of American and South Korean forces operating in North Korea, but the number of missions dropped to 633 missions in December.[7]

It was the period in Korea when friendly ground forces urgently needed close air support in the face of attacking Chinese and North Korean forces at the Chosen Reservoir. The squadron tried to provide as much support missions as possible under the terrible conditions, but the difficulty with operating the Corsair night variant in extremely cold temperatures sparked the commanding officer to submit a letter of complaint. Lt. Col. David C. Wolfe, commanding officer of VMF(N)-513, voiced his squadron's concerns about the aircraft's ability to conduct operations in snow and ice in a confidential letter submitted to the Chief of Naval Operations 4 January 1951. He identified three major defects found in the F4U-5N based upon information supplied by the pilots who operated the aircraft. They rated the aircraft's overall performance, ranging from fair to unsatisfactory during both normal and adverse weather conditions. Major deficiencies consisted of poor cockpit visibility, lack of deicing equipment, sensitivity of the electrical trim tab assembly, and a defective power system for electrically-driven instruments. The defects addressed by the squadron's commander possibly led to the losses of at least five aircraft and the death of one pilot.[8]

Corsair pilots also complained of restricted visibility during take-off and landing due to the aircraft's three-point attitude, length of the nose, and glow of the engine. Airfields in Korea were normally equipped with runway lights spaced between 350 to 400 foot intervals. The aircraft's nose-high takeoff and landing attitude reduced frontal visibility and pilots had nothing to line up with during takeoff, because only one light was observable out of each side of the cockpit. The same problem occurred during landing, when the tail wheel touched down and pilots lost all orientation on the runway. This condition caused pilots to attempt to raise the tail up on takeoff before gaining effective rudder control, necessitating applying the brakes to correct the aircraft's natural torque-induced tendency to swerve. VMF(N)-513 noted that this takeoff procedure caused one accident, three near misses, and one fatal accident. To aid in correcting the problem, airfield operations doubled the number of runway lights to intervals of 200 feet that allowed pilots to see two lights from either side. This helped the situation, but did not fully address the problem with the aircraft's three-point attitude. The issue of the Corsair's fuselage design and engine glow also caused consternation. The length and width of the nose hampered frontal visibility during night heckling and close air support, while engine glow interfered with night interception of enemy aircraft by reducing the pilot's night vision, thus making it difficult to see the instruments for proper flight orientation.

When VMF(N)-513 released the discrepancy report to the Chief of Naval Operations, while operations were being conducted from Wonsan and Yonpo, North Korea, barely days after the retreat of UN forces from the Chosen Reservoir. Typical weather conditions consisted of an average temperature of 15 degrees Fahrenheit, an average ceiling of approximately 2,500 to 5,000 feet, and icing occurring between 600 to 1,200 feet altitude. Those conditions resulted in frequent bouts of wing and propeller icing. Ice accumulation, compounded with the average ordnance load of aircraft, caused numerous aborted missions and, in extreme conditions, operations were entirely halted. Therefore, the squadron emphasized that winter conditions in North Korea rendered the F4U-5N unacceptable as an all-weather fighter. Poor cockpit visibility and/or the lack of deicing were probably the main contributors to the loss of some of the five aircraft that crashed during the period as noted by the commanding officer.

Col. Wolfe also identified problems with the electrical trim tabs, in that the aircraft was extremely sensitive to change in attitude, which required the pilot to constantly re-tab the rudder. "The electrical assembly does not have the 'feel' that the manual tab has in other aircraft...," such as the F4U-4 Corsair, Grumman F6F Hellcat, and Grumman F7F-3 Tigercat, "...and pilots often overcorrect. There is also no override for the rudder tab and failure of this control on takeoff means an almost certain fatal accident." A number of night variant Corsairs and pilots were lost in Korea in combat situations involving dive bombing during close air support strikes where enemy anti-aircraft fire may not have been involved. Was the electrical trim tab design at fault? Those losses could have been the result of a variety of reasons ranging from mechanical or trim tab failure, poor weather conditions, pilot disorientation, or even small

The winterized variant F4U-5NL, modified to operate in extreme cold temperatures. Too late to see combat during the Chosin Campaign in Korea during November-December 1950, the -5NL proved itself during the harsh Korean winters that followed. (Robert F. Dorr)

arms fire. Hence, without the testimony from those pilots who perished, the number of F4U-5s that may have been lost in Korea due to this control feature is speculative, since there is a lack of definitive proof that the electrical trim tab assembly was the cause, other than accounts by pilots who experienced the problem but survived to tell about it.

Lt. Col. Wolfe's report identified additional problems that were either critical to or would improve flight operations. First, the aircraft suffered from an unreliable power system for the electrically driven cockpit instrumentation. Pilots reported systems failure that resulted in the loss of power to instruments, except for the Needle and Ball. Second, the location of the radar control panel made it difficult for the pilot to reach and operate while wearing heavy (cold weather) clothing. Third, poor instrument lighting with bulbs burning out or shorting out and, when all worked, pilots rated visibility as only fair. The report ended with the following opinion:

> In addition to the above objections to the F4U-5, the primary belief, unanimously prevalent among the pilots…, is that an all-weather fighter should be a twin-engine fighter…It is highly recommended that the F4U-5N be returned as an all weather fighter (sic), at the earliest possible time. It is further recommended that satisfactory aircraft now in production (i.e., F3D and F2H-2N) be sent to the combat zone immediately…"[9]

Commander Air Force, Pacific Fleet officially endorsed the opinions expressed by VMF(N)-513 in a letter to the Chief of Naval Operations dated 27 February 1951. He concurred that all night configured aircraft be twin-engine and recommended that this configuration be incorporated in future designs. Furthermore, he explained that night fighter aircraft must have the performance equivalent to that of existing aircraft, it must have increased range, endurance, and a heavier load carrying capacity. In addition, he requested an upgrade of the aircraft's existing intercept radar, with one having a minimum air-to-air radar detection range of 30 miles.

He further elaborated by describing the aircraft's current performance and future prospects if the discrepancies were not corrected:

> The F4U-5N is adequate for night interception only under ideal conditions and within limits prescribed by the aircraft's performance and the capabilities of airborne and ground or shipborne radars. These limits are such that our night defense capability is far inferior to that during daylight hours. The interim use of the F4U-5N for night heckler, intruder, or air support is acceptable if the discrepancies said by 513 are corrected. VMF(N)-513 has flown a considerable number of night combat missions under the most difficult and varied operating conditions."[10]

Finally, in reference to the "Final Report on Tactical Evaluation of the F4U-5N, NATC Patuxent Restricted Report AC208 TT 35-34" dated 14 October 1949, Commander, Air Force, Pacific Fleet noted similar problems first mentioned by VMF(N)-513, plus those found during tests conducted by the Naval Air Test Center (NATC). Unknown to Col. Wolfe, the Navy and Vought Aircraft knew about potential problems operating the F4U-5 in cold conditions and were in the process of solving them. The issues regarding restricted visibility and the trim-tab assembly remained problematic.

THE F4U-5NL CRASH PROGRAM

Three months into the Korean War, it became obvious that the conflict would extend into the winter and beyond. Winter temperatures in the northern areas of Korea averaged 15 degrees Fahrenheit, with snow, ice, and poor visibility being typical operating conditions. This raised the question whether U.S. night fighter aircraft could operate successfully in such an environment. It appears the Navy was well aware of the F4U-5's shortcomings prior to Lt. Col. Wolfe's initial report; therefore, it seems the report reinforced the need to make modifications. In September 1950, Chance Vought in Dallas, Texas, received a request from the BuAer requesting detailed information on the feasibility of equipping the F4U-5N Corsair with de-icing equipment for the aircraft's wings, tail surfaces, propeller, and windshield. The proposal was a challenge, as rubber de-icing boots had never been applied to a high-speed Navy fighter. Boots were common on low-speed transports and bombers, but not for high performance aircraft. However, within 24 hours after receiving BuAer's challenge, Chance Vought accepted the request and announced a target delivery date for the first all-weather Corsair of 31 December 1950. Upon accepting the Navy's request, Henry Tereshkow, Chance Vought's project engineer, telephoned the B.F. Goodrich Rubber Company. Although unable to provide detailed information over the telephone, Mr. Tereshkow stated enough in general terms to ask what Goodrich could do in providing de-icing boots to meet his company's need. He then contacted Hamilton Standard concerning the propeller de-icing issue. Three days after the initial request, the project engineer flew to Akron, Ohio, to meet with Goodrich. Locations for the de-icing boots were explored and Goodrich said it could handle the rubber material requirement, but a driving mechanism for it would have to be provided by the Eclipse Pioneer Division of the Bendix Corporation in Teterboro, New Jersey.

After leaving the Goodrich people, he met with representatives of Hamilton Standard in Hartford, Connecticut, where he was told the propeller de-icing problem wouldn't present too much of a problem. Meeting with Eclipse the following day, Tereshkow ran into a major problem when he was told that, due to previous commitments by the company, delivery of a driving mechanism for the boots would take approximately four months. Tereshkow did not have that much time, so he went to Washington and met with John E. Sullivan of BuAer's Airborne Equipment section; J.J. Hopper, assistant general manager at Chance Vought; and Capt. Paul Ramsey.[11]

After a number of telephone calls, Eclipse reshuffled their orders and the company announced it would be able to deliver the necessary equipment in time to meet the first scheduled flight of the Corsair all-weather fighter, now called the F4U-5NL. Previously, in October, engineers at Chance Vought compiled enough material, components, engineering data, and reports to begin modifications on the F4U-5NL prototype.

To allow for extreme cold weather operations and wing and empennage de-icing, Vought engineers installed Goodrich-manufactured rubber deicing boots on the leading

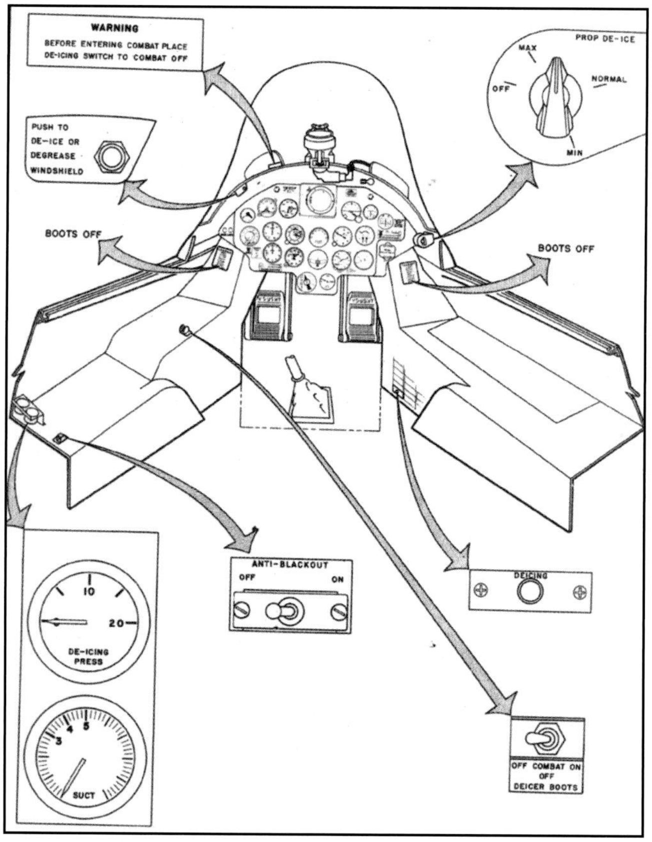

An interior view of the F4U-5NL cockpit with selector switches and gauges for the aircraft's deicing system. The system worked quite satisfactory during the winters 1951 through 1953 in Korea. (Emil Buehler Library, NMNA)

edges of the airfoil surfaces. By flexing the boots by means of pneumatic pressure and suction from an engine-driven air pump, ice buildup would be reduced or eliminated. Propeller and windshield deicing consisted of applying boots cemented along the blades' leading edges and an alcohol feeding system. For the propeller, alcohol pressure fed the fluid into a cup at each blade shank and forced it out centrifugally along troughs in the boots, resulting in a fairly even flow pattern along the entire length of the blades. Providing enough heat to keep the pilot warm inside the cockpit during freezing conditions also presented a challenge to the design team. A heating system already existed in the F4U-5 that allowed the pilot to stay warm in normal flying conditions, but in extreme cold, it could not provide enough heat to defog and defrost the canopy.

A new system with an external air scoop and a heater of 50,000 BTUs provided enough heat to defog and defrost the canopy, but it had the potential, at times, to overheat the cockpit, which could become almost unbearable for the pilot. Following delivery of the first aircraft, cold weather testing began at NAS Argentia, Newfoundland, with test flights beginning in mid-January and ending in mid-February 1951. Pilots conducting the tests reported two major problems with using alcohol for deicing the windshield: one that resulted in reduced visibility, and another that produced a potential deadly side effect inside the cockpit. To solve icing problems on the aircraft's windshield, a nozzle system allowed the pilot to spray alcohol when needed. The use of alcohol delivered by nozzles produced crazing of the canopy Plexiglass that reduced pilot visibility. The solution involved the application of a protective coating along the edges of the canopy in areas where the alcohol was likely to collect. During flight testing, pilots reported alcohol fumes in the cockpit that

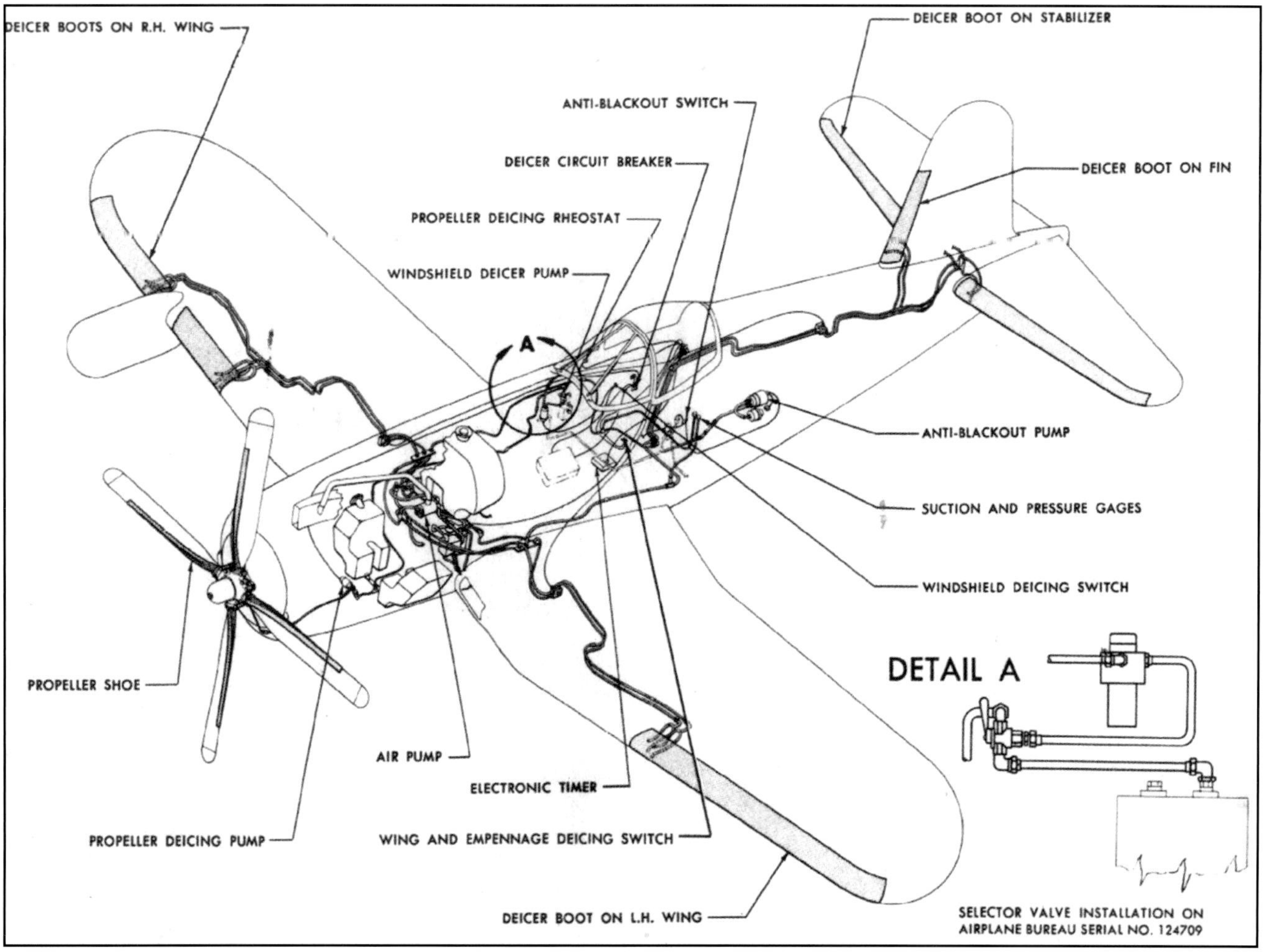

Illustration of the F4U-5NL showing the entire weatherization system that proved crucial for ground- and carrier-based units during the harsh winter months in Korea. (Emil Buehler Library, NMNA)

could possibly result in physiological toxic effects, as well as a fire hazard. Engineers investigating the problem, known as Operation Sniffer, soon found the cause when they substituted peppermint as a safe alternative for the alcohol during tests. They discovered that the aerodynamic shape of the windshield sent the alcohol into the air scoop, then into the ventilating system, producing the problem inside the cockpit. By being able to locate a heater scoop internally within the aircraft, the Vought engineers handily solved the problem.[12]

The winterization of the F4U-5N Corsair resulted in the Navy and Marine Corps having a night fighter ready to operate in any weather conditions. The external de-icing equipment was removable during spring and summer operations, but internal modifications remained permanent. By 2 March 1951, F4U-5NLs were in Japan, some seven months after Chance-Vought received the Navy's request for an all-weather Corsair. Although too late to see action over Korea during the winter of 1950-51, when the all-weather version would have allowed Navy and Marine units to conduct additional sorties against Chinese and North Korean forces during the breakout at the Chosen Reservoir, the F4U-5NL proved itself an excellent all-weather fighter during the two Korean winters that followed.

A pair of F4U-5NLs of VC-4, center and bottom left, prepare for launch off USS *Antietam* (CV 36) during a cruise of the North Atlantic, June-July 1953. VC-4 was one of two such squadrons that deployed detachments of pilots and men to carriers conducting combat operations in the Korean Conflict. (Vought Heritage)

Chapter 9

U.S. Marine Corps Night Fighters over Korea

Go in close, and when you think you are too close, go in closer

- Maj. Thomas B. McGuire

The end of the Pacific War in September 1945 brought with it the division of the Korean Peninsula, which Japan had annexed in 1910. Japan's surrender led to the division of Korea into two occupation zones in September of that year: the southern portion administered by the United States and the northern portion above the 38th Parallel by the Soviet Union. Negotiations between the Americans and Soviets concerning the future of Korea broke down within a year over who should become the peninsula's legitimate government. The American-aligned Republic of South Korea (ROK) was established 15 August 1948, proclaiming itself as the legal governing power of the peninsula with Seoul as its capital. Less than a month later, on 9 September, the North announced the creation of the Soviet-aligned Democratic People's Republic of Korea (DPRK) in North Korea, it too proclaiming itself as the legitimate government of Korea. On Sunday, 24 June 1950, at 0400 hours (25 June Korean Time), seven infantry divisions of the North Korean People's Army (NKPA), supported by one armored division equipped with Russian-built T-34 tanks, crossed the 38th Parallel into the Republic of South Korea. Within four days, NKPA forces captured Seoul and continued southward down the peninsula, sweeping aside ROK forces, which fell back southward to Suwon. A day later, the Security Council of the United Nations condemned the invasion and demanded North Korea withdraw its forces across the 38th Parallel.

On the 26th, President Truman committed U.S. forces to enforce the UN Security Council's demand and named General Douglas MacArthur as Commander-in-Chief, Far East (CINCFE) of all United Nation forces. The air component of FEC, responsible for providing defensive air cover, was the Far East Air Force (FEAF) under the command of Lt. General George E. Stratemeyer, with the Fifth Air Force based in Japan as its largest component commanded by Major General Earle E. Partridge. American forces quickly went into action, with the Seventh U.S. Fleet establishing a blockade of the Korean Coast, while FEAF struck North Korean targets affecting the safety of evacuating American nationals.

NKPA forces pushed American and ROK forces to an area around the South Korean port of Pusan, at the tip of the Korean Peninsula. The U.S. Eighth Army, supported by a U.S. Marine Corps Brigade and ROK forces, battled the NKPA through July and into September, finally crushing North Korean opposition in September 1950, with U.S. forces landing at Inchon, while the Eighth Army and supporting forces moved northward from Pusan. Afterward, UN forces went on the offensive after the Inchon landing and advanced into North Korea with the mission to destroy remaining NKPA forces and reunify Korea. However, Communist China's intervention on the side of North Korea in December 1950 ended any hope of reunification of the peninsula, as Chinese Communist forces (CHICOM) pushed UN forces into full retreat. This period of the conflict, known as the Chosin Reservoir Campaign, would be forever etched into the memories of those U.S. military personnel who fought in that bitter campaign that was characterized by extreme cold, hunger, and constant contact with overwhelming CHICOM forces.

UN forces retreated to the South, below the parallel, as NKPA and CHICOM forces advanced, retaking the South

Korean capital of Seoul. Thereafter, beginning in the spring of 1951, UN ground and air forces counterattacked, forcing the Communists back to the imaginary line that divided the country in half. Afterward, the conflict became a stalemate, with opposing sides attempting to gain better bargaining power during peace talks, with each side trading small parcels of real estate paid in blood by the men fighting on the ground and in the air. When the conflict ended in July 1953, the U.S. military had lost over 33,600 personnel killed in action, 103,000 wounded, and 8,196 missing in action.

NIGHT FIGHTERS OVER KOREA

The Korean War began while the U.S. Air Force and Navy were transitioning their fighter inventory from piston-driven to jet-powered aircraft, but both still relied heavily on WWII-era fighters like the Air Force's North American F-51 Mustang and the Navy's Vought F4U-4 Corsair. The early 1950s brought the development, production, and deployment of more advanced daytime jet fighters, the introduction of jet bombers, and the arrival of jet interceptors with the ability to operate throughout the day and night, and in adverse weather. However, such all-weather jet fighters were not available when hostilities began in Korea and piston-driven night fighters were pressed into service for day and night close-air support, interdiction work, and air interception.

U.S. Marine night fighter squadrons VMF(N)-513 operated the F4U-5N/NL and F7F-3N from airbases across Korea, while detachments from Navy Composite Squadrons Three (VC-3) and Four (VC-4) flew the F4U-5N(L) Corsair from aircraft carriers. Initially, F4U-5Ns of VC-3 and -4 assigned to Task Force 77 were assigned with the protection of the task force at night. However, it became apparent there was little threat from North Korean air or naval forces, and thus they were vectored to supply close-air support and interdiction missions. Pressed into service in the Korean War as a close air support platform due to necessity, the F4U-5N's AN/APS-19 airborne radar became practically worthless, except as a mapping and navigational aid. In search mode, the system could not locate the type of land targets engaged by the Corsair, such as troop concentrations, armor, and supply traffic, and when used for interception, the system often failed to lock on to enemy aircraft. Pilots often did not bother to turn the system on while conducting interdiction strikes as a precaution against enemy radar-guided anti-aircraft batteries.

Ground and carrier-based F4U-5N units began combat operations over Korea within weeks of hostilities, providing day and night interdiction strikes, night intercept, close air support, and CAP 24 hours a day, seven days a week. Postwar development of a night version of the -5 envisioned a ship-based fighter capable of intercepting enemy aircraft. Yet, the Korean War changed the role from an interceptor to a close air support fighter-bomber with the ability to operate at night and, as the war progressed, in adverse weather conditions, as shown with the development of the -5NL version. The Grumman F7F-3N made its combat debut with VMF(N)-542 in September 1950 and operated the aircraft until February 1951, when -542 transferred its assets over to -513 prior to the former's return to the U.S.

MAG-33 ARRIVES IN KOREA

In early July 1950, the United Nations supreme commander, General Douglas McArthur, requested the services of a Marine Regimental Combat Team (RCT) and supporting air units to provide air support for American and ROK forces attempting to hold on to the last bit of South Korean real estate called Pusan. The Marines responded by activating an air-ground team consisting of the Fifth Marine Regiment and the First Marine Aircraft Wing (MAW-1), Marine Air Group 33 (MAG-33), as the First Provisional Marine Brigade. Brigade strength as of 9 July 1950 was 266 officers and 4,503 men. Air support for the Brigade fell to Marine Air Group 33, under the command of Brig. Gen. Thomas H. Cushman, consisting of fighter squadrons VMF-214, VMF-323, All Weather Fighter Squadron VMF(N)-513, and observation squadron VMO-6. After leaving Marine Corps Air Station (MCAS) El Toro, California, 14 July 1950, the group set sail from San Diego as part of Task Group 53.7 aboard the transports USS *Anderson* and *Achernar* and escort carrier USS *Badoeng Strait* (CVE 116). The air arm arrived off Kobe, Japan, 31 July, and 44 Marine fighters from VMF-214 and 323 landed at Itami Airbase. The following day, VMF(N)-513, under the command of Maj. Joseph H. Reinburg, launched six of its 12 radar-equipped F4U-5N Corsairs from the Badoeng Strait for Itami Air Base, with the remaining six aircraft leaving the carrier the following day.

Between August and September 1950, VMF(N)-513, nicknamed "The Flying Nightmares," was the only Marine night fighter unit available to conduct night operations over Korea until the scheduled arrival of VMF(N)-542 in September. During the course of combat operations from August 1950 to July 1953, the squadron remained in constant operation, except for a brief period in January 1951, and during the course of its duty in Korea, the squadron's inventory included the F4U-5N, F7F-3N Tigercat, and F3D-2 Skyknight. Maj. Reinburg's squadron fell under the operational control of the USAF Fifth Air Force, which handled overall control of tactical air operations in Korea, while Marine Aircraft Wing 12 (MAW-12) held administrative control of the squadron until 21 September 1950, when -513 transferred to MAG-33. Since Reinburg's squadron fell under the operational control of the Fifth Air Force, the 49th Fighter Bomber Group conducted aircrew interrogations and briefings.

The Flying Nightmares of VMF(N)-513 operated the F4U-5N/NL Corsair, F7F-3N Tigercat, and the Douglas F3D-2 Skyknight during the Korean Conflict. F4U-5N WF-23 of VMF(N)-513 at an unknown location in Korea. The squadron began combat operations at the beginning of September 1950, flying heckling missions against North Korean forces around Pusan. (Author's Collection)

In general, the squadron's mission consisted of providing night heckler operations over Korea from its base at Itazuke Airfield, Japan. Specifically, the unit's primary mission was to provide both offensive and defensive support of amphibious operations during periods of minimum weather conditions, day or night. Its secondary mission was to augment or replace naval all-weather air units aboard carriers and to provide effective air defenses of advanced naval bases. Operations were carried out from 1900 to 0700 hours every day, with Corsairs staying on station over the Korean Peninsula for approximately two hours at a time. Marine and naval night fighter units in Korea relied on three methods for target acquisition at night that mirrored tactics utilized in WWII, except for the use of flare-dropping aircraft. Since the F4U-5N (and F7F-3N) radar system was incapable of locating vehicular or troop traffic, pilots had to rely on visual confirmation. Pilots could locate roads from the air on clear nights and it was easy to harass vehicle convoys once they were located. Typically, enemy convoys drove with their lights on, but quickly extinguished them after the first attack. Flares dropped where the convoy was last seen and attacks could continue. During cold weather, enemy drivers drove with their windows closed, making it difficult for them to hear approaching aircraft, so they came up with an early warning system. Upon hearing an approaching aircraft, North Korean troops would warn convoys to extinguish their lights by shooting tracer fire from surrounding hills, thereby making it extremely difficult to pinpoint the vehicles.

During August 1950, VMF(N)-513 flew 23 sorties against enemy troop concentrations, artillery positions, vehicles, and supply areas in and around the South Korean towns and villages of Kumch'on, Yonho-dong, Andong, Uiryong, Yongdok, Sonsan, Yongsan, Hakao, Pong Gong-Ni, Yosu Peninsula, and Pohang-Ni. On 6 August, the Eighth Army, with the First Provisional Marine Brigade, launched a counterattack to halt a Communist push through the southwest portion of the perimeter with the Marines' objective of seizing the towns of Sachon and Chinju. A day later, VMF(N)-513 began combat operations when the squadron sent four aircraft, pilots, and support personnel to Itazuke Air Base. The squadron's first combat sortie occurred at 1630 hours in support of the 25th Infantry Division, with Corsairs hitting the enemy near Kumch'on – an important road junction – where the aircraft destroyed two buildings and damaged another with 500-pound bombs.

During the next few days, additional Corsair night fighters, pilots, and support personnel arrived at Itazuke, bringing the total aircraft to eight, pilots to ten, and support personnel to 37. The following day, three more aircraft arrived at Itazuke and conducted a strike at 1400 hours against enemy tanks and troops hidden in a fruit orchard. Seven hours later, two more aircraft hit a truck convoy in the Kumch'on area, leaving a number of enemy troops dead and their vehicles burning. By the evening of 9 August, the American and ROK forces, with Navy and Marine air support, had broken enemy resistance, and the Eighth Army, along with the Marine Brigade, moved ahead rapidly.

Three days later, MAG-33 provided invaluable close-air support for the Marine Brigade and the Army's 24th Infantry in their effort to halt the NKPA Fourth Division, which was attempting to cross the Naktong River. During the day, VMF-214 and -323 bombed and strafed enemy positions, while at night, VMF(N)-513 Corsairs silenced enemy artillery and mortar positions by aiming at artillery muzzle flashes. One pilot dive-bombed with the aid of an "X" formed by tracer bullets from two widely displaced friendly machine guns that were sighted into the enemy-held position. By 4 September, Marine ground units were heavily engaged with the North Koreans and received air support from MAG-33, with Corsairs delivering their ordnance with deadly accuracy.

During the evening of the fifth, the Marines of the Third Battalion were shelled heavily throughout the night, killing one Marine and wounding two others. The Marines on the ground called in air support, and at 0230 hours VMF(N)-513 aircraft arrived over the target, bombing North Korean mortar positions, which reduced the shelling considerably. Completing this mission, the Marine pilots dumped general purpose and fragmentation bombs on enemy vehicles and troops in the area. Under the combined combat weight of Marine air and ground forces, the North Koreans withdrew across the Naktong.

VMF-214 and -323, in conjunction with VMF(N)-513, decimated NKPA forces during the six-week push out of Pusan. The three MAG-33 squadrons flew 1,511 sorties during the period, with -513 flying 343 sorties, of which 79 were close air support missions for Marine, Army, and ROK forces. Accurate damage assessment inflicted on enemy forces was often recorded as "undetermined," since the majority of missions flown by the squadron were conducted during the night and early morning when visibility was limited. The actual damage inflicted on the enemy by Marine and Navy night fighter units remains a touchy and controversial subject, as Lt. James Brown, a pilot with VC-3, later contends.

TIGERCATS OVER INCHON

While the Corsairs of VMF(N)-513 flew missions over the Pusan Perimeter, orders were issued 16 August 1950 for deployment of VMF(N)-542, commanded by Lt. Col. Max J. Volcansek, Jr., and its 24 F7F-3N Tigercats to Korea. A majority of the squadron consisted of reservists recently called to active duty, and for most of the pilots and radar operators, Korea would be their first combat assignment. At San Diego on 26 August 1950, VMF(N)-542 embarked on the USS *Cape Esperance* and the USS *General Morton* for Yokosuka, Japan, with a planned arrival of 11 September. Upon arrival in Japan, the squadron continued flight, navigational, and radar training while waiting for deployment to the war zone. Four days after VMF(N)-542 arrived at Yokosuka, Gen. McArthur planned and executed an amphibious landing at Inchon, 110 miles behind North Korean lines on South Korea's west coast. Named Operation Chromite, the Inchon Invasion began 15 September 1950, with the landing of the U.S. Navy's Joint Task Force Seven (JTF-7) of the First and Fifth Marine Regiment. Three days later, the Seventh Infantry Division, augmented by some 8,000 South Korean troops and the First Korean Marine Corps Regiment, arrived to block any threat from North Korean forces in the south. As a result, North Korean resistance quickly began to unravel.

The Army's X Corps captured Kimpo Airfield (K-14) 17 September, with combat engineers making the field operative within two days. Marine aircraft began arriving at the airfield two days later in preparation to provide support of the First Marine Division's drive to Seoul. VMF(N)-542

Corsairs and F7F-3Ns aboard USS *Cape Esperance* in September 1950, when VMF(N)-542 was deployed to Japan, eventually operating from bases on both sides of the 38th Parallel in Korea. (Author's Collection)

F7F-3N Tigercat WF-7 of VMF(N)-542 with a pair of F4U-5Ns of VMF(N)-513 at Itazuke Air Base, on the island of Kyushu, Japan, sometime in late 1950. (Author's Collection)

had the distinction of becoming the first fighter squadron to land at Kimpo when the squadron's commanding officer, Lt. Col. Max J. Volcansek, Jr., and five pilots arrived in their Tigercats the same day. The Tigercat squadron claimed the distinction of flying the first Marine combat mission from Kimpo at 0735 hours on the 20th, with four of the F7F-3N aircraft hitting NKPA transportation sites near Seoul, destroying two enemy locomotives after expending some 3,000 rounds of 20mm ammunition.

The Inchon landing coincided with the push out of Pusan. F4U-5N Corsairs of Maj. Reinburg's VMF(N)-513 ranging over the entire perimeter conducted 15 daytime close support missions for Army units from 17 to 19 September, hitting enemy troop concentrations, tanks, vehicles, and artillery positions. VMF(N)-513 pilots were very proficient in ferreting out the enemy, according to Maj. Reinburg, "We discovered that our mere presence over the hostile side of the lines did a great deal of good, even when we're not actively engaging. We got so proficient at uncovering him that the enemy thought we had a super electronic way of detecting his every move, so the North Koreans kept their lights out and stopped all movements and activities."[55]

Both Marine night fighter squadrons suffered no fatalities during the first two months of operations; however, this changed 22 September, when VMF(N)-513 sustained its first loss. 1st Lt. John P. McLaughlin was killed when his F4U-5N swerved off the runway and crashed and burned on takeoff for a night intruder mission. VMF(N)-542's Maj. J.J. Beebe and his radar operator were killed the following day when their Tigercat was shot down by ground fire on a close air support mission near Seoul. By 25 September 1950, the First Marine Division was on the threshold of taking Seoul, with Corsairs and Tigercats providing air support, but during the course of the day, the commanding officers of all three squadrons were shot down by enemy ground fire. The first to fall was VMF-214's skipper over the western portion of Seoul. Approximately two hours later, enemy ground fire shot down the Corsairs flown by the commanding officers of VMF-212 and -542; both survived, although each suffered wounds. Col. Volcansek's Tigercat sustained heavy damage from antiaircraft fire while leading a section of F7Fs against enemy positions in and around Seoul. Although wounded and with his fighter badly damaged by enemy fire, the squadron commander pressed on the attack, leading his flight on two more passes against the North Koreans.

Returning to Kimpo, he was forced to keep the battered F7F-3N's airspeed at almost 200 knots (230mph) – twice the aircraft's landing speed – to prevent it from stalling. He tried to jettison his right empty fuel tank, but it wedged itself between the right engine and fuselage. Air speed and control were lost and he had no other choice but to bail out from a height of only 1,000 feet. He pushed back the canopy and attempted to climb out, but the slipstream of the plunging aircraft pinned him inside the cockpit. He kicked violently on the joystick and as the F7F-3N pitched over, he was thrown clear, pulling the ripcord at 500 feet; the chute opened only seconds before he hit the ground a few miles northwest of Kimpo, and his aircraft crashed less than 100 feet away. Within 45 minutes he was picked up by a helicopter piloted by Lt. Gus Leuddecke, which delivered the squadron commander back to the airfield. Two days after Col. Volcansek's close call, ROK and U.S. forces eliminated the last pockets of North Korean resistance in the city of Seoul. During ten days of operations from Kimpo, VMF-542 flew 263 sorties in support of the Eighth U.S. Army and First Marine Division.

A group of pilots pose next to a VMF(N)-542 Tigercat with 48 mission symbols on the starboard nose at K-14 (Kimpo). Howard Bollman and Frank Lang, standing second and third from left, served with VMF(N)-532 during WWII flying F4U-2s. (MGen Frank C. Lang via Thomas E. Doll)

A VMF(N)-542 (WH-4) lands at Kimpo Airfield after a night close air support mission in September 1950. The squadron's Tigercats, along with VMF(N)-513 F4U-5N Corsairs, provided air support to embattled United Nations forces during the war's first crucial months. (USMC/ Dave Steinbacher via Thomas E. Doll)

F7F-3N Tigercats at Kimpo circa September 1950. Note the unusual "Navy" marking on the Tigercat to the left, possibly a replacement aircraft, as the Navy operated only a few F7F-3Ns for night fighter training and utility duties. (MGen Frank C. Lang via Thomas E. Doll)

A pair of F7F-3Ns (with BuNo 80466 in the foreground) over Korea during September 1950. It was hit by AA fire near Seoul, South Korea, 24 September 1950, with the loss of pilot Maj. John W. Beebe and radar operator T/Sgt. Karl V. Kludt. (Author's Collection)

SERVICING THE TIGERCAT

Garry Cleveland, with VMF(N)-513 based at K-18 at Kangnung, Korea, served as a member of a F7F-3N check crew that conducted most of the mechanical work on the Tigercat. He remembers, "On the check crew, we did almost any mechanical thing that needed to be done in order to keep the planes in the air. We frequently had to remove parts from a severely damaged plane in order to restore another." The most difficult task for the check crew was maintaining the Pratt & Whitney R-2800-34W engines, and in this case, removing the engines from a damaged aircraft to make another Tigercat airworthy. "Exchanging engines always took the most time, because all the cowling, hoses, cables, etc. had to be removed on both planes and replaced again on the serviceable aircraft. Also, removing and mounting the heavy engines via a cherry picker was a little tricky."

Cleveland was assigned to the flight line crew, which operated on two 12-hour shifts from 0700 to 1900 and 1900 to 0700 hours, seven days a week. Every two weeks or so, the crews would switch the rotation. A flight line crew consisted of a plane captain assigned to a particular aircraft, electronic technicians, and an ordnance crew. The plane captain's overall responsibility was to insure the aircraft was ready for its next mission. His job, according to Cleveland, began with "a thorough visual inspection of the aircraft. This started with a complete walk around at ground level, looking for oil leaks, bullet holes, shrapnel damage, tree limbs or cables entangled on the plane, and any other thing out of the ordinary. On cold days, it was necessary to check for water condensation in the gas and remove it via the bleeder tube. At ground level, the hydraulic fluid level was checked and topped off, if necessary."

After visually inspecting the aircraft from the ground, the plane captain would ascend the aircraft and perform a visual inspection of the upper part of the plane. After completing the visual inspection, he would climb into the pilot's cockpit and follow a written set of procedures, which included running both engines and checking the functioning of gauges. If anything out of the ordinary was detected during the overall inspection, a specialist might have to be brought in to make a repair or change a part. After completing all tests and any repairs, both the oil and gas tanks (including the belly drop tank) were topped off.

During the day, electronic technicians would go to each fighter to check out the radio, radar, and IFF systems, with the latter having to be re-coded on a daily basis. If any of the major electronics gear was inoperable, the aircraft would remain grounded until the deficiency was corrected. Next came the ordnance crew, who cleaned and replaced the guns after each mission and then rearmed the aircraft with 20mm ammunition and external ordnance in the late afternoon.[2]

WONSAN OPERATIONS

Having defeated North Korean forces south of the parallel. on 1 October 1950, General MacArthur called for the surrender of all NKPA forces. A reply from North Korea was not forthcoming and "United Nations Command Operations Order 2" was issued 2 October 1950, with the objective of destroying the North Korean military by crossing the 38th parallel and reunifying the Korean Peninsula. On 11 October, the ROK I Corps took the North Korean port of Wonsan and the Marines landed unopposed on the 26th. The Marines, after a period of clearing operations around Wonsan, headed north to relieve ROK forces and to establish a new base at Hungnam before striking inland toward the Manchurian border. The North Korean capital fell on 21 October, and the U.S. Navy opened a resupply port nearby at Chinampo, while the Eighth Army and X Corps moved up toward the Yalu River. With the conclusion of the Inchon operation 8 October, VMF(N)-542 remained at Kimpo, while VMF(N)-513 flew to Itazuke from Itami Air Base in preparation for the Wonsan Operation. Maj. Reinburg's squadron aircraft and material was boxed and loaded aboard an LST, and personnel were issued cold weather clothing and other essential equipment; such forethought for the clothing would make life somewhat tolerable for the men during the frigid winter months in North Korea. Within the next three days 22 aircraft, 42 officers, and 146 enlisted men making up the forward echelon left Itami for Wonsan, while two officers and 150 enlisted men remained behind as the rear echelon. At Kimpo, the aircraft started to ferry bombs and ammunition to Wonsan while support personnel and equipment were flown to the new base.

Living conditions at Wonsan (K-25) were primitive, with -513's personnel having to live at an abandoned hotel at the airfield. A majority of the windows had been broken and they were boarded up to keep the cold out, as the outside temperature would plunge below zero by late November. Portable generators supplied electricity for the hotel and portable heaters kept the men somewhat warm, but sanitary facilities were lacking and water had to be carried from the mess hall. There never was a serious shortage of parts due to the efforts of the materiel section and the removal of parts from damaged aircraft. Ground personnel conducted maintenance of aircraft during daylight hours, which were rather difficult due to the intense cold weather. Fuel was pumped by hand from 55-gallon drums that had been rolled along the ground about a mile from the dump to the flight line. Muscle also had to substitute for machinery in ordnance sections which had only one jeep and eight bomb trailers for moving ammunition.

Direction of air operations in support of X Corps was exercised by MAG–12, 1st MAW, from 15 October to 9 November. Night operations did not begin until late October due to a lack of runway lights at Wonsan, so VMF(N)-513

A member of the ground crew gives a "thumbs up" as an F7F-3N prepares for a night intruder mission somewhere in Korea. VMF(N)-542 and later -513 Tigercats provided round-the-clock support for UN forces beginning mid-September 1950. (National Archives)

A Flying Nightmare F4U-5N waits for its pilot to climb in and fly a close air support mission from Wonsan, 2 November 1950. The squadron operated from this captured North Korean airfield from late October to late December 1950 in support of the 1st Marine Division. The wing pod housing the radar system was useless in close air support missions and pilots typically only used it for navigational purposes. (DOD)

Opposite:
A ground observer in the bottom of this photograph watches as an F7F-3N Tigercat conducts a low-level attack against enemy positions in Korea circa 1950-51. An explosion rocks the hillside from an attack by another Tigercat just seconds before. (Robert F. Dorr)

flew daytime missions along with VMF-312. Reinburg's men began flight operations 17 October with eight aircraft sent to locate an F4U-5N from the squadron that went missing on a flight from Kimpo to Wonsan, but no trace of the pilot or the aircraft were found. One day later, combat sorties began with a four-plane strike led by Maj. Reinburg, which only resulted in the destruction of one enemy truck. Sorties between 19-21 October were negative due to poor weather conditions or for a lack of targets. Contact with the enemy picked up again on the 22nd and continued to increase, as the squadron provided almost constant close air support missions for the duration of UN operations in North Korea between October and December 1950.

After landing at Wonsan, Marine ground units began moving out to assist ROK forces in the northeast, with the Fifth Marines taking control of a 50-mile area around Wonsan and the port of Hungnam, while the Seventh Marines moved north to relieve ROK forces at Sudong, 30 miles northwest of Hungnam. Supporting the Marines' advance, a four-plane section from VMF(N)-513 hit enemy troop concentrations, killing an estimated 150 North Koreans with fragmentation bombs and 20mm fire. Three hours later, a four-plane section consisting entirely of enlisted pilots came upon oxcarts carrying men and supplies, destroying 30 and damaging some fourteen.

On the morning of the 28th, three battalions of North Koreans attacked the First Regiment, First Marines at the coastal town of Kojo, 25 miles south of Wonsan. The enemy staged well-coordinated night attacks, outflanking the Marines, who called for close air support. The Flying Nightmares launched a dozen sorties beginning at 0630 hours on the 28th, with Capt. F.K. Fulton leading three aircraft on a strafing and bombing mission that resulted in 20 enemy casualties and the destruction of 25 buildings. The night fighter squadron, along with VMF-312, remained over the battle throughout the day and night, with VMF(N)-513 alone flying continuous sorties from 0630 to 2210 hours. Close air support inflicted heavy damage to vehicles, buildings, artillery pieces, and troop positions, which turned the tide against the North Koreans and saved the Marines from being overwhelmed.

The morning after the night interdiction strikes, Marines counted several hundred North Korean casualties. The first night intruder mission from Wonsan occurred at 1800 hours, with Capt. Pendrey and 1st Lt. T. Clark strafing and rocketing enemy positions. Four additional night missions flown from 2200 through 0210 hours destroyed an enemy-held village and a bridge. Squadron totals for October were 397 combat missions flown in support of the Seventh Marines. That number was substantially surpassed during November, when Communist China intervened in the war just as the U.S. military was about to declare victory over North Korea. The squadron also had a change in command, with Lt. Col. David C. Wolfe relieving Maj, Reinberg, who returned to the U.S. for assignment with Marine Corps Headquarters as a consultant on night fighter operations.

THE FROZEN CHOSIN

The quick successes by American and ROK forces precipitated the intervention of the Communists, which would turn UN forces back towards the parallel. Chinese troops began crossing the Yalu River over a bridge at Antung, Manchuria, 14 October, with their movements concealed from American aircraft by the rugged terrain, weather, and smoke from forest fires. Warnings about elements of CCF (Chinese Communist Forces) entering North Korea began to filter in when the ROK 26th Regiment took 16 Chinese prisoners belonging to the 124th CCF. Evidence of CCF presence in North Korea was further corroborated by eyewitness accounts of pilots of VMF(N)-542, who provided G-2 officers with that information in early November. The Marine airmen made nightly strikes from the 1st to the 9th against Sinuiju, at the mouth of the Yalu, and they repeatedly reported a steady stream of trucks moving into northwest Korea from Antung, Manchuria. Time after time, they blasted Sinuiju with bombs, rockets, and 20mm shells, and though parts of the city were continuously aflame, it still seethed with enemy activity. They described southward bound traffic as "heavy," "very heavy," and even "tremendous," and at least one convoy was reported to be "gigantic."[3] 1st Lt. W.P. Garton, an F7F-3N pilot with VMF(N)-542, was one of the eyewitnesses that saw the beginning of Chinese intervention in the war:

> November 1st, I flew my first night sortie to Sinuiju, on the west coast of Korea, just across the Yalu River from Antung, Manchuria. I was forbidden to attack targets north of the river (inside Manchuria). For one hour, I orbited the Korean side of the river and counted the trucks coming across the bridge. The trucks left Antung with their headlights on; halfway across the bridge, they would switch to black-out lights and grope their way through dimly lit Sinuiju to assembly areas... The traffic appeared to be almost entirely one-way, and I believe my count was over 150 trucks for the one hour period.[4]

The sighting of Chinese forces and strong resistance from remnants of the NKPA created a very busy schedule for Marine night fighters, with 24-hour coverage beginning in late October and lasting through the second week of December. A foreshadowing of what -513 and -542 would experience during the next two months began on 3 November at 0030 hours, when -513's Capt. L.R. Denham and Capt. Marvin L. Berg surprised a 39-truck convoy heading south, and during the ensuing attack destroyed 23 of the vehicles with fragmentation bombs and 20mm fire. The NKPA came under intense fire from a flight of four night fighters the following morning at Sudong village at 0910 hours under Maj. Robert

F4U-5Ns of VMF(N)513 (BuNo 121974 in the foreground) at Wonsan, North Korea, 2 November 1950, when UN forces were attempting to defeat remaining elements of the North Korean Army. The Marine squadron initially conducted daytime missions only, as there were no field lights at the airbase. This aircraft experienced engine trouble and crashed 30 November 1950 near the Chosin Reservoir, and its pilot, Capt. Marvin L. Berg, is presumed to have been killed. (DOD)

L. Cochran. After raking enemy troops with 1,500 rounds from their 20mm cannons, Cochran and his three pilots unloaded three general purpose and fragmentation bombs along with 15 high-velocity rockets, killing approximately 40 of the enemy troops.[5]

Throughout the morning of 5 November, -513 struck at the enemy between Chinhung-ni and the Chosin Reservoir. Pilots reported that "the surrounding ridges were filled with enemy troops," and that their strikes against these Chinese were "extremely effective." Eight separate flights comprised of two to four Corsairs blasted troops, buildings, supply vehicles, and gun emplacements scattered along an area from the village of Koto-ri to the top of Funchilin Pass and Hagaru, at the reservoir. Gen. Smith, during a helicopter visit over the area, remarked on VMF(N)-513's handiwork, commenting that a "considerable number of planes... really worked the place over."

The Marine night fighters continued to stage strikes against NKPA positions through the 21st, but something strange occurred for the next seven days, when pilots reported very little enemy activity 22 through 28 November. The brief respite from heavy combat would not last long, as CHICOM forces prepared for a full assault on UN positions. The full commitment by Communist China to save its North Korean comrades began 25 November, with the Chinese launching massive attacks in depth across the UN front. The Chinese offensive came as a surprise to Gen. MacArthur and his field commanders, although there had been strong indications of impending intervention due to previous clashes resulting in the capture of Chinese prisoners and visual sightings by friendly aircraft. The surprise attack and fighting tenacity of nearly a quarter of a million Chinese troops completely overwhelmed American and ROK forces, causing the entire UN front to fall back towards the south.

By the 29th, Corsairs and Tigercats were in the thick of the battle, as they tried to slow the Chinese advance. During the last few days of November 1950 and into December, VMF(N)-513 and -542 conducted around-the-clock close air support and interdiction missions for Army and Marine units attempting a breakout from the Chosen. The aircraft were relentless in attacking Communist forces with bombs, rockets, napalm, and cannon fire in an effort to protect the retreating Seventh Army Division and elements of the First Marine Division trapped at the Chosen Reservoir who were desperately trying to retreat towards Hungnam for evacuation by ship. On 30 November, a joint strike force composed of VMF(N)-513 F4U-5Ns and F4U-4s of VMF-214 and -312 devastated Chinese troops massing near the Chosen. A flight of three -513 aircraft piloted by Captain F.K. Fulton, Jr., and T/Sgts. G.H. Pennell and L.J. Keegan with five F4UBs from -214 and -312 took off from Wonsan at 0830 hours for a close air support mission. In the ensuing strike against the enemy, the aircraft delivered a withering attack, dropping napalm, fifteen 265-pound fragmentation bombs, seven 500-pound bombs, and expending 1,100 rounds of 20mm cannon and 9,500 rounds of .50-caliber machine gun ammunition. Three additional sorties conducted that day by the Flying Nightmares against enemy troops caused an undetermined number of enemy dead and wounded.

Advancing Chinese and NKPA forces forced the evacuation of -513 from Wonsan, with the first squadron elements leaving the evening of 30 November. On 1 December, the forward echelon of Marine VMF(N)-513 completed the move from Wonsan to Yonpo Air Field without any interruption in combat sorties. For the first two weeks in December, the squadron continued to operate against enemy forces in northeast Korea. Survivors of the "Frozen Chosen" began arriving at Hungnam 11 December, and by Christmas Eve, 100,000 troops, their equipment, and 90,000 Korean civilians had been evacuated. Orders for ground-based Marine units to evacuate Yonpo Airfield (K-27) was issued 13 December, and within two days VMF(N)-513 personnel and aircraft were at Itami Air Base, Japan, eating hot food and sleeping in warm beds. By the end of December, UN forces had withdrawn south of the parallel.

The last pilot to fly over Hungnam was Lt. R.B. Mack, a USS *Princeton* F4U-5N carrier pilot from VC-3. He described the night skies over North Korea as "... cloudless, cold, and unfriendly. Haze was everywhere," said Mack. "The artificial haze of war, one part hate, one part frustration, stirred to an even pall by high explosives." His orders before his night fighter launching off the carrier were to serve as target combat air patrol over Hungnam as UN forces evacuated. He arrived over the harbor area on Christmas Eve, orbiting at 15,000 feet, and remembered, "I had a grandstand seat for the most dismal and distressing sight I had ever witnessed." He watched as tired American and South Korean troops dressed in tattered uniforms, along with their supplies and equipment, were loaded aboard landing craft and other rescue vessels and pulled away from the docks. "There were fires everywhere throughout the area, and as I watched, flames broke out around the docks, growing and spreading until the whole waterfront seemed ablaze. Whatever had been left behind was being made useless for the Reds." After the ships had pulled away from the docks, several U.S. destroyers began shelling to insure that nothing useful remained for the Communists. Lt. Mack remained overhead until the ships were out to sea, and to him, "The ships below formed up single file, nose-and-tail like circus elephants, and headed seaward and then south to Pusan."[6]

Close coordination of Marine air and ground units during fighting at the Chosin Reservoir against Chinese Communist (CHICOM) forces in Korea. U.S. Marines drive forward after effective close air support from F4U-4 and F4U-5 Corsairs. (National Archives)

Marine Corps Staff Sergeant Ed Barnum photographed this overall glossy blue F4U-5N with white markings at Wonsan Airfield, North Korea, circa November 1950. VMF(N)-513, led by Major Hunter Reinburg, inflicted heavy casualties on North Korean and Chinese communist forces, stopping most enemy movement at night, and silencing enemy artillery. (Robert L. Lawson Photographic Collection, Emil Buehler Library, NMNA)

Photographed by Marine Corps Technical Sergeant J.W. Helms, Jr., 2 November 1950, personnel load an F4U-5N of VMF(N)-513 at Wonsan Airfield, Korea, with napalm tanks, rockets, fragmentation bombs, 20mm ammunition, and two high-intensity parachute flares. The flares were used to illuminate targets at night during close air support sorties. (Robert L. Lawson Photographic Collection, Emil Buehler Library, NMNA)

The wreckage of an unidentified F4U-5N Corsair of VMF(N)-513 at Wonsan became the source of spare parts during the squadron's tumultuous days supporting UN forces during the Chosen Reservoir campaign. (Robert L. Lawson Photographic Collection, Emil Buehler Library, NMNA)

VMF(N)-542 Tigercats during Fall 1950, when the squadron was engaged in providing around-the-clock air support for UN forces fighting Chinese Communist forces in North Korea. (Thomas E. Doll)

A group of Marines from VMF(N)-542 with a Christmas greeting painted on drop tanks in December 1950 during the Chosen Reservoir Campaign in North Korea. Left to right are: MSgt. Robert T. Hunt, 1st Lt. David W. Bowman, MSgt. Thomas H. Allom, Lt. Arnold J. Hammons, Lt. Walter J. Waldo, Capt. Leland A. Gaug, Capt. William G. Diar Jr., MSgt. William R. Goodall III, and Maj. George A. Hanna. (DOD)

The radar operator (R/O) in the rear seat of F7F-3N and the pilot in front prepare for departure at an undisclosed location in 1950. The viewing shroud for the SCR-720 radar protruded from the instrument panel to reduce ambient light (USMC via Thomas E. Doll)

An unknown member of VMF(N)-542 standing beside an F7F-3N at Pusan-West Airfield sometime between December 1950 and February 1951. Behind him is a bomb mounted under the inner wing panel. (Emil Buehler Library, NMNA)

UN forces retreated as CHICOM and NKPA forces drove south 50 miles beyond the 38th, capturing Seoul 4 January 1951 before finally being stopped. UN forces counterattacked in Operation Ripper, driving back enemy forces back to the parallel and recapturing Seoul.

January 1951 marked a period of regrouping and retraining for VMF(N)-513, with a section of four aircraft, pilots, and support personnel joining -542 at Itazuke Air Base for CAP missions. On 20 January, VMF(N)-513 arrived at Pusan East (K-9) to relieve VMF-311, while -542 left Itazuke to start operations from Pusan West (K-1) in support of ground operations, primarily for the U.S. Eighth Army. The Flying Nightmares flew 1,341 combat hours and 1,184 sorties in support of the UN offensive and defensive operations in North Korea during December, with the squadron losing three aircraft and two pilots during that time. On the 20th, during a predawn interdiction strike north of the Chosen, Maj. Jack L. Brushert became separated from his wingman and disappeared. Ten days later, Capt. Marvin L. Berg, returning from a close air support mission to the Chosen Reservoir, radioed his wingman that his engine was running rough and he too went missing in action.

Chapter 10

Stalemate in Korea (May 1951-July 1953)

No aircraft ever took and held ground

- U.S. Marine Corps Manual

As the opposing sides battled on the ground in early 1951, VMF(N)-513 and -542 exchanged some personnel and the latter returned to El Toro, California, for operational training in the new Douglas F3D Skyknight all-weather jet fighter. The transfer of 542 left 513 as the only Marine All-Weather Squadron in the Far East for more than a year. Personnel transfers began 20 February, with 24 officers and 43 enlisted men transferring to -542. Two days later, ten additional men were transferred along with 513's commanding officer, Lt. Col. David C. Wolfe, while Lt. Col. James R. Anderson, commanding officer of 542, assumed command of 513. On the 23rd, 15 of 542's F7F-3N aircraft were transferred, giving the newly-formed composite squadron 15 F7F and 15 F4U-5 fighters. For the next two years, the Flying Nightmares continued flying close air support missions for UN ground forces and interdiction missions against NKPA and CHICOM forces positioned near the 38th Parallel. During this time, VMF(N)-513 participated in operations with such names as Killer, Punchbowl, Hook, Bunker Hill, Vegas, and others – battles remembered only by the veterans who participated in them and by historians who read or write about them.

By the end of May 1951, the opposing forces established battle lines less than 30 miles from Seoul, where they remained. For the remainder of the conflict, a frustrating stalemate ensued, with neither side exchanging much territory. Marine and Navy night fighter units continued to provide close-air support and fly night interdiction missions, with an occasional intercept of enemy aircraft. May 1951 proved costly to CHICOM forces during their spring offensive, which began in late April. Combined UN air and ground forces annihilated the enemy ranks, with CHICOM forces suffering approximately 100,000 casualties. To better support Army and Marine ground forces, the Fifth Air Force and 1st MAW moved MAG-12 day squadrons VMF-212, -323, and a forward echelon of VMF(N)-513 to K-46 at Hoengsong. This new field was only forty miles (10-15 minutes flying time) from the MLR (Main Line of Resistance), allowing Marine fighter aircraft to quickly support the First Marine Division. The lone Marine night fighter squadron in Korea adopted a new tactic for night interdiction by teaming up with Douglas R4D (C-47) transports, and later Navy Consolidated P4Y-2 Privateer patrol bombers equipped to drop high-intensity flares. These "firefly" missions, as they were called, involved a flare plane to illuminate enemy positions or vehicular traffic for orbiting F4U-5Ns and F7F-3Ns to attack with cannon fire, bombs, rockets, and napalm. It was quite effective on one particular strike 23 May 1951, when Capt. Walter L. Redmond, flying a Tigercat, made a low-level strafing run from 600 feet on five trucks in a village. Upon completion of the run, the village, which was probably being used by the Chinese as an ammunition dump, blew up. In the conflagration that followed 15 buildings were destroyed, but flying through the debris, Redmond's aircraft was considerably damaged: the Tigercat suffered a large hole near the left wing oil cooler, the inboard wings were dented, the wing flaps were perforated, and the radar antenna was destroyed. Neither Redmond nor his radar operator were injured, and the rugged aircraft flew on and arrived safely back at base. Two days later, at 1830 hours, squadron aircraft

VMF(N)-513 F4U-5N after making a wheels-up landing at Pusan West Airbase (K-1) in 1951. Two of the four propeller blades were bent and the nose cone from the radar pod was knocked off from the impact. (Emil Buehler Library, NMNA)

VMF(N)-513 F4U-5NL WF-5 (BuNo 124525), possibly at Pusan in early 1951, since VMF(N)-542 Tigercats can be seen in the background. The squadron repainted its aircraft from the standard blue with white codes to an overall flat black finish and red codes for better concealment during night operations. This aircraft was destroyed when Capt. John P. Roden was forced to bail out after losing oil pressure during a mission 17 December 1951. He was rescued by friendly forces. (Emil Buehler Library, NMNA)

F7F-3N WF-20, assigned to VMF(N)-513, undergoing maintenance between missions. Most of the squadron's Tigercats came from VMF(N)-542, which turned over its complement of aircraft prior to its departure for the U.S. in early 1951. (NMNA via Thomas E. Doll)

conducted close air support and night interdiction missions against an estimated 60,000 Chinese troops trapped in a valley by the First Marine Division, attacking enemy trucks, gun emplacements, and troops. One mission alone devastated a concentration of CHICOM troops, resulting in more than 400 enemy casualties. However, these hazardous missions claimed three aircraft and one pilot from enemy ground fire.

During 26-27 May 1951, the squadron launched an all-out effort beginning at 0950 hours, when ten F4U-5Ns from Chunghon (K-46) and eight F7F-3N aircraft from Pusan West (K-1) conducted multiple strikes against the enemy from an altitude of less than 1,000 feet above the terrain due to low ceilings, heavy cloud cover, and low visibility. While hitting enemy antiaircraft and troop positions during a mid-morning mission, 1st Lt. H. E. Roland's Corsair received hits from enemy fire. On approach for landing at K-46, he realized he couldn't lower his landing gear and was forced to make a wheels-up landing, demolishing the aircraft in the process. In the afternoon, Maj. E. C. Carlson led a three-plane strike with Capt. Arthur Wagner and 1st Lt. Howard Wolf. Wagner ran into trouble when the napalm tank on his aircraft caught fire during a shallow dive in preparation to drop it on an enemy position located on a 7,000-foot mountain peak. Lt. Wolf called to Wagner, "Drop your napalm, Wag, you're on fire!" Wagner bailed out with his parachute trailing behind him at an altitude of only 200 feet as his aircraft hit the north slope of the mountain. Somehow, Wagner survived the low-level bail out and became a POW; he was repatriated in Operation Big Switch.[1]

Another pilot nearly became captive when his aircraft was hit by ground fire during a strafing run. Capt. Herbert E. Roser bombed an enemy-held bridge, destroyed two trucks, and dispatched 15 Chinese troops before his luck ran out while making a strafing run on a ferry boat. Ground fire hit the Corsair's belly tank and it burst into flames. Failing to jettison the tank, he bailed out at only 500 feet. He landed safely and a helicopter picked him up one hour and twenty-five minutes later. The Flying Nightmares ended the day with six additional Corsairs and Tigercats damaged from enemy ground fire, but they all managed to return to base.

BLOODY OCTOBER

Engagements with hostile aircraft were quite a rarity for night fighters over Korea, so the main effort continued with close air support combined with interdiction missions. Providing such support resulted in the costliest month for the Flying Nightmares (October 1951) for the entire war for VMF(N)-513, during which time the squadron lost two Corsairs and five Tigercats, along with four pilots and four radar operators while conducting 680 combat missions. Operating from Pusan West, the squadron launched a maximum effort against the main road routes of supply in North Korea to interfere with the enemy's ability to reinforce and resupply their forward positions.

The first human casualty was not a result of enemy action, but an in-flight engine fire of a Tigercat and a malfunctioning parachute that occurred on the 4th. Maj. Leo F. Tatro, Jr. and Warrant Officer Florenz M. Banjavcic were outbound for an interdiction sortie when the aircraft's starboard engine burst into flames. The aircraft began losing altitude and Maj. Tatro called for Banjavcic to bail out. The Major successfully bailed, but suffered a broken leg, while Banjavcic's parachute failed to open and he was killed upon impact with the ground, his body being recovered a day later by friendly forces. The squadron lost a second aircraft and another radar operator a week later on the 12th, when enemy ground fire shot down an F7F-3N piloted by 1st Lt. Robert J. Gillette during an interdiction strike. Gillette successfully bailed out and became a POW, while his radar operator, MSgt. Julius G. Harrington, for some unknown reason, stayed with the plummeting aircraft and died in the crash.

Night interdiction strikes continued taking a toll on the squadron, with a third loss in as many weeks, this time taking the lives of an enlisted NAP and his RO. Unlike the Air Force, the Marines allowed senior enlisted men to operate various types and models of aircraft during WWII and Korea. Many of the NAPs in Korea had served in WWII as commissioned officers, resigned their commissions at the end of the war, and left the service. Many of them regretted their decision, and when the Marines offered them the chance to return to flying status, this time as a Master Sgt. E-7 (MSgt) – the highest enlisted rank at the time – they jumped at the chance. VMF(N)-513 was no exception, having a number of such pilots on hand operating the Corsair and Tigercat. During the evening of 18 October, MSgt. H.F. Heyliger and his RO, MSgt. A.J. Morton, spotted enemy trucks, dropped a flare, and requested a P4Y-2 Privateer belonging to Navy patrol Squadron 28 (VP-28) to do the same in the general area. Heyliger pointed his F7F-3N towards the enemy and prepared to attack when the patrol aircraft illuminated the area. The P4Y-2 dropped three flares and started a 180-degree turn when the aircraft's crew saw a large orange fire on the side of the hill in the general direction of where MSgt. Heyliger was heading. The Privateer's crew reported no enemy antiaircraft firing towards the Tigercat; therefore, either the F7F was shot down and the patrol aircraft's crew did not see it happen, or, in the dangerous business of flying night interdiction strikes, Heyliger possibly misjudged his altitude and crashed into the hillside. Three days later, on the 21st, the squadron nearly lost another pilot to the enemy, but he was rescued by helicopter while aircraft from his squadron aided by Air Force F-51 Mustangs orbited above, suppressing all enemy attempts to capture the downed pilot.

VMF(N)-513 pilots and radar operators between an F4U-5N and F7F-3N - photograph at an unknown location circa 1951-52, although the sign designation is Marine All Weather Fighter Squadron 513. What is peculiar about this photograph are some of the bomber jacket patches. Some of the officers have the VMF(N)-513 patch (back row, second left); one has a patch of VMF(N)-531 (back row, fourth left); several of the enlisted men have a circular patch with a divided white and black background with a pair of red lightning bolts shaped in a V; and a full Colonel (front row, third left) sports another unknown patch. (Emil Buehler Library, NMNA)

VMF(N)-513 Bar at K-1 Pusan, displaying the squadron insignia above the porch. The small square sign, painted overall red with yellow lettering, reads, "NIGHTMARE ALLEY 'QUITE PLEASE' NIGHTFIGHTERS AT REST!!." (Lt. Col. John E. Shields Collection via Mark Leonard)

Capt. LeFavre lifted his Tigercat off the strip at Pusan West on a similar Firefly, with Air Force Capt. Bruce Nims riding in the radar operator's station as an observer. One hour into the flight, LeFavre spotted six to ten enemy trucks illuminated in the dark by the flares from a P4Y-2. The F7F pilot descended and began strafing the vehicles with 20mm ammunition, but all four of his guns jammed after damaging only two of the trucks. LeFavre, his aircraft still armed with napalm and bombs, decided to head north with the Privateer. The P4Y-2 spotted a large enemy convoy heading south and the flare plane lit up the area for the Marine night fighter. The Tigercat's pilot spotted ten illuminated trucks parked next to freight cars on railroad tracks, seemingly waiting to load supplies onto the vehicles. According to Capt. LeFavre, "I dropped the napalm and felt the aircraft receive two hits in the starboard wing area, presumably from small arms fire."

He turned the aircraft around and saw six trucks and two tankers on fire before making another bombing run. "I climbed to 3,000 feet and made a shallow bombing run, releasing at 1,000 feet. His bombs hit ten yards from the vehicles," he said. As LeFavre climbed to port, he saw a stream of sparks coming from his starboard engine. A few seconds later, Capt. Nims, in the backseat, called the pilot and reported the engine was on fire. The pilot feathered the engine and switched the fuel to the other one.

"About three seconds later, there was a muffled roar and sheets of flame started pouring out of the accessory section," LaFavre reported. He told Nims to bail out and radioed the P4Y-2 flare aircraft about his predicament. The Tigercat was at 2,500 feet when LaFavre unbuckled his safety belt, took off his helmet, pulled back his canopy, stood up, and prepared to bail out, or so he thought. "When I released the stick, the plane commenced to dive to the right. I sat back down in the cockpit, cut the left engine, and rolled on full elevator tab," he said.

The aircraft was now dangerously close to the ground at 1,500 feet, nearly too low to conduct a safe egress. LaFavre then made a second attempt to jump out of the dying Tigercat, diving out of the aircraft's left side and rolling into a ball. When he jumped, he noticed the rear cockpit's canopy was still closed, evidence that Capt. Nims was unable to get out for some unknown reason. Capt. LeFavre made it to the ground uninjured, but as he landed, he came under enemy rifle fire. He ran through several rice paddies before hiding in an irrigation ditch, with the enemy continuously searching for him, sending up flares and firing rifles in hopes of flushing the American out of hiding. He did not sleep during that night, as he could still hear the enemy searching for him, although they were a considerable distance away. At approximately 0930 hours, he sighted a Corsair and a Tigercat, soon joined by a pair of F-51 Mustangs and two more F4Us. He pulled out his mirror and began flashing it to attract their attention, which apparently worked, as the Corsairs came in low, wagging their wings in confirmation that the downed pilot had been spotted.

Two hours later, a rescue helicopter arrived and LaFavre lit a smoke grenade, which also attracted the attention of some hostiles. "Immediately after lighting it, several people on a hill began firing in my vicinity, with three or four bullets hitting the dirt behind where I was hiding," LaFavre said. The helicopter continued its descent, which drew additional enemy fire, but an orbiting Tigercat, flown by Capt. W.A. Dougherty, came in low and fired a burst of 20mm ammunition at the enemy troops approaching LaFavre's position, which dissuaded them from further action, while Capt. R.P. St. John, in an F4U-5N, unleashed cannon and napalm on enemy antiaircraft positions attempting to bring down the helicopter. Meanwhile, the downed pilot climbed into a sling lowered by the rescue ship, which hauled him aboard to safety.[2]

The following evening, Capt. St. John, who participated in the rescue of Capt. LaFavre, found himself in a similar predicament after bailing out of his stricken aircraft. He did not have to wait for a rescue, as he walked out and safely rejoined his unit with the help of friendly Koreans. The bloodletting of the Flying Nightmares continued through the end of the month, with the loss of two more aircraft and crews. Enemy ground fire claimed the life of 1st Lt. Donald W. Dorn when his Corsair was shot down while attacking enemy vehicles on the 29th. Bloody October ended with the loss of an F7F-3N on the 30th flown by Maj. William Hughes, with Capt. Joseph Babin, Jr. as the R/O. This loss was a result of the squadron's continued need to fly precision, low-level close-air support, and such accuracy depended on the skill and bravery of the attacking pilot. Such a mission cost the lives of Hughes and Babin when their aircraft was damaged by its own bomb blast. The crew managed to bail out, according to a radio transmission, but nothing was ever heard from them again.

THE FLYING COFFIN

Garry Cleveland remembered some individuals who referred to the F7F-3N as the "flying coffin," because the aircraft was not originally designed for a crew of two and, therefore, a number of radar operators were either unable or incapable of bailing out of a mortally-damaged Tigercat. At least three radar operators and one rear passenger (Capt. Nims) went down with their aircraft in Korea while the pilots successfully escaped. The F7F's small cockpit configuration might have led to some of the deaths according to Cleveland, who witnessed the crash of a Tigercat piloted by Capt. "Pat" Flynn, Jr. shortly after take-off 22 April 1952. The loss occurred moments after the Tigercat lifted off the ground, when the aircraft's center of gravity shifted due to an improperly secured box of flares stored in the aircraft's inspection compartment sliding back

VMF(N)-513 personnel pictured next to the wreckage of one of the squadron's F7F-3N Tigercats at K-8 airfield in Kunsan, South Korea. The squadron operated from that base from April 1952 to May 1953. (Emil Buehler Library, NMNA)

into the tail section. When the aircraft was approximately 150 feet over the runway, according to Cleveland, the aircraft's tail suddenly dropped to a dangerous level relative to its airspeed. The squadron found out later the flares either severely unbalanced the aircraft in pitch axis or jammed the elevator control cable into the tail down position. "Capt. Flynn was a very experienced pilot and had quick reactions. Consequently, when the tail dropped, he almost instantaneously applied full power to both engines and the plane accelerated at a rapid rate. However, as the aircraft gained altitude, its climb angle appeared to increase, which caused the plane's air speed to decrease until the aircraft stalled at an altitude of approximately 800 feet," Cleveland said. Approximately eight seconds had elapsed. Capt. Flynn knew he was in some serious trouble and slid his canopy open, stood up, and pulled the ripcord of his parachute before jumping out.

The rushing air partially deployed the chute and the pilot was yanked out and away from the aircraft. He watched as the pilot and his partially opened chute fell towards earth. His parachute did not completely open until he was at less than 200 feet, but he safely landed in mud. MSgt. John McAvoy was not as fortunate. He was, according to Cleveland, not only in a cockpit that made safe bailouts difficult, but he probably had trouble escaping because of two rolled-up sleeping bags laying on his lap, since the crew planned on sleeping when they arrived at another airbase, which could have impeded the radar operator's ability to unlock and push out his canopy:

> The aircraft was at about 150 feet and in a near-stalling altitude when McAvoy jettisoned the canopy and threw out the two sleeping bags. He then struggled to get out of his cockpit. However, the positive G forces seemed to pin him back. When the plane finally stalled, it rolled off into a sharp left bank and went into a steep dive.

The radio operator apparently was thrown down inside the aircraft, since nobody on the ground could see him standing. "The aircraft then mysteriously pulled out of its dive at about 150 feet from the ground and flew level for about four seconds, after which it again rolled off to the left, dove into the ground, and exploded." MSgt. McAvoy's remains were found at the crash site. Afterward, Cleveland was instructed on the proper bailout procedure after the death of McAvoy. "Sometime later, I flew in the back seat of the F7F during a test ride after we replaced a fuel pump," Cleveland said. Before departure, the pilot instructed him on emergency egress procedures. The pilot said before take-off, "If we run into trouble and have to bail out, I will give you two negative Gs. On the first G, pull the two canopy lock tabs and push the canopy up to jettison it. On the second negative G, dive out straight down with legs tucked in to avoid the horizontal stabilizer."[3]

SURGICAL AIR STRIKES

The stresses of flying daily missions eventually wore down the men of 513, with morale among flight personnel dropping to an all-time low as the squadron lost additional men, especially after the disastrous month of October 1951. However, the appearance of a new bombing apparatus installed on a few Corsairs and Tigercats the month before brought new hope to the flight crews, since it held the promise of reduced risk and better accuracy when delivering conventional bomb loads. The advent of night and all-weather fighters in Korea increased the ability of U.S. forces to provide around-the-clock coverage at night and in adverse weather. However, engaging in close air support and night interdiction missions was still a deadly business due to the presence of enemy antiaircraft positions, limited visibility, and the rugged terrain in which enemy positions were often located. Limited visibility forced pilots to conduct such missions at low altitudes, and bombing accuracy depended upon the experience and expertise of the pilot, who had to contend with the hurdles facing them. The ability to conduct precise close air strikes at any time, especially in adverse conditions, simply did not exist before 1951, but that changed during the Korean War with the development of the AN/AMQ-14 radar and the Automatic Bombing Control (ABC) unit. The ABC unit, first installed on the F4U-5(N) and later the F7F-3N in 1952, worked in conjunction with AN/MPQ-14 ground control radar. Together, these systems revolutionized close air support tactics and became the genesis that paved the way for conducting surgical air strikes during subsequent conflicts involving American air forces.

The AN/MPQ-14 was the ground control station of the Marine Guidance System for close air support in all weather conditions. Its purpose was to track an aircraft's course, then take control of the aircraft, guide it to a target, and automatically release the bomb load at the proper time in support of friendly forces in daytime close air support and in night close air support, referred to as MPX-CAS and MPX-NCAS. After the fighter left the airfield, the pilot reported to a GCI squadron, which guided him to a predetermined orbit point. Upon arriving over the orbit point, the pilot contacted the AN/MPQ-14 ground control station. As soon as the ground control station acquired the aircraft on its radar, the pilot received a vector. Approaching the target location, the pilot switched on the ABC equipment, and it began receiving commands from the ground control station. These commands guided the aircraft to the target and released the bombs. The length of the run lasted approximately three minutes. At the conclusion of the run, the pilot was directed to take control of the aircraft and either return for another run or return to base.

The ABC unit controlled the aircraft by receiving a frequency-modulated tone from the AN/MPQ-14, which activated the unit. Night fighters carrying the equipment typically operated from an altitude of approximately 18,000 to 20,000 feet. The aircraft was guided to the target area by the MPQ-14 and, when the aircraft arrived over the target area's center, bombs were released by a signal from the ground. To prevent the aircraft from receiving erroneous signals from a source other than the ground control stations, a code selector switch was installed on the F4U-5N and F7F-3N. The coding arrangement was made by selecting a combination of two or more relays in the receiver that had to be actuated simultaneously before a signal could reach the gyro or armament relay.

Combat evaluation of this system first began 4 August 1951, when the First Marine Air Support Radar Team arrived at First Marine Air Wing Headquarters with an MPQ-14 and 24 ABC units attached to MTACS2 (Marine Tactical Air Control Squadron Two). Installation of the ABC units began the following day on VMF(N)-513 aircraft stationed at Pusan West Airbase and was completed 16 August, with eleven F4U-5Ns and two F7F-3Ns receiving the equipment. The squadron conducted demonstration runs between 16 and 18 August with 100-pound general purpose bombs dropped on an island located six miles from the airfield. Satisfactory results were achieved and the radar team moved to the 1st Marine Division to begin operations in conjunction with VMF(N)-513. The ABC units were installed on the F4U-5N in place of the baggage rack originally provided for the aircraft. The unit consisted of a five-tone channel frequency-modulated receiver (ARW-61); a gyroscopic compass; a junction box; and a dynomometer.

The unit increased the aircraft's weight by 50 pounds, but caused no noticeable adverse effect on the aircraft's center of gravity. The installed receiver antenna took the place of the ARR-1 antenna, while the cockpit installation consisted of a standard ILS indicator, ABC control switches, code selector switch, and a modified P-1 autopilot controller. On 2 September, four F4U-5N aircraft conducted the first combat use of the system against enemy positions. The equipment proved a more effective and efficient means of providing night and foul weather close air support against enemy positions that previously were inaccessible to ground troops or too difficult to attack by standard close air support tactics. The MPQ also improved VMF(N)-513's morale, because it reduced the danger posed by antiaircraft fire and the possibility of a pilot becoming disorientated while flying in low visibility and striking the rugged terrain, which happened a number of times.

From beginning to end, a typical MPQ mission began with a departure from Kunsan airfield (K-8) carrying two 1,000-pound and eight one-hundred pound bombs. After departing, he checked his IFF, then continued on course to a homing signal located at K-14 (Kimpo). Twenty miles south of K-14, the pilot checked in with the TDAC located in that area and stated his mission, altitude, position, and destination. Afterward, he called in and requested bearings for the MPQ site situated near the vicinity of the First Marine Headquarters. Heading for the target area, the pilot began climbing from his pre-briefed altitude to 13,000 feet; aircraft typically made the bombing runs at 160 knots (184mph) from 13,000 to 16,000 feet. Once the pilot was given his vector, he remained steady on course while maintaining speed, altitude, and making course corrections provided by MPQ. At the command of the ground controller, ordnance was armed and at a pre-calculated moment, the pilot dropped the bombs manually. The command for arming the bombs was "Armstrong," which was given at a ten-second interval prior to the drop. The command for releasing the bombs was "Standby," "Standby," "Mark." The bombs were pickled off at "Mark." With the completion of the last run, the results and target coordinates were transmitted to the pilot by a ground observer connected with MPQ.[4]

Award ceremony for five VMF(N)-513 radar operators circa 1952, with Sgt. Noel Hales receiving the Air Medal. (Garry Cleveland)

MARINE F4U-5N AND F7F-3N AIR-TO-AIR COMBAT

Typical support missions for those flying Marine Corps night fighters were supplemented with action against hostile aircraft that occasionally conducted harassing raids in and around Seoul. Night fighter pilots with Navy squadron VC-3 and VMF(N)-513 brought down 15 enemy aircraft during aerial engagements, with VMF(N)-513 claiming ten while operating the F4U-5N, F7F-3N, and F3D. Four of the kills came from pilots flying the night variant Corsair and Tigercat, with each type claiming two enemy aircraft, while the other six went to the F3D-2. There are two primary reasons for the low number of kills attributed to the squadron's two prop-driven aircraft in comparison to the record of air-to-air kills claimed by fighters operating during the day. First, there were few enemy aircraft within the operational areas of VMF(N)-513 both during the day and night time. Second, the night fighter's primary role was close air support and interdiction against enemy troop concentrations, supply depots, and vehicles.Night fighter squadrons, as with all other day or night air units, adhered to a set of strict operational rules. Garry Cleveland recalled how a typical night fighter NCAP mission began:

> The mission departure times were staggered at about half-hour increments. The first mission departure normally started after 8:00 PM, while the last mission went out before 3:00 AM. One plane and its two-man flight crew were always on standby status if needed to intercept any incoming unidentified aircraft. Two members of the ground crew were normally at an aircraft when the pilot and RO arrived in the jeep.

Before the crew arrived at the flight line, they spent an hour in a darkened Quonset hut to acquire their night vision. Driving a jeep to the aircraft, the crew climbed out, grabbed their parachutes, and placed them in the cockpits while the ground crew completed a walk-around inspection of the Tigercat using small flashlights with red light filters. "The ground crew was not allowed to have any light sources when they arrived. The field was also kept dark to protect the men and aircraft from insurgent activity. The only lighting used to guide the pilot on the taxi and landing strips was by way of small canisters filled with napalm burning at a slow rate, emitting a dim light source," Cleveland said. Meanwhile, the pilot and radar operator climbed into their cockpits, where two other members of the ground crew helped them into their chutes and seat restraints. When the flight crew was secured in the aircraft, the ground crew descended and the control member would guide the pilot for engine start up, while the other member would plug in and start the auxiliary power unit (APU) if needed for engine starts on a cold night.

While the engines were warming up, the flight crew would check their instruments and controls for anomalies. The pilot would give the "thumbs up" sign when he was ready to go and the control member of the ground crew would give his partner the sign to pull the wheel restraints (chocks). This was a dangerous task in a dark environment because of the close

Cadre of VMF(N)-513 F4U-5N pilots circa mid-1952. Two of the squadron's Corsair pilots (Capt. Donald L. Fenton and 1st Lt. John W. Andre) scored aerial victories against North Korean aircraft. (Garry Cleveland)

proximity of the chocks to the two spinning propeller blades. The control member would then guide the aircraft out of its enclosure and onto the taxiway, where the pilot was on his own. When the aircraft returned from its mission, the control member would guide it in from the taxiway onto its reserved enclosure parking space by the use two dim light sticks called wands.[5]

The first aerial victory for -513 came 30 June 1951, when a Tigercat piloted by Capt. Edwin B. Long, along with his R/O Chief Warrant Officer (CWO) Robert C. Buckingham, intercepted a North Korean Polikarpov PO-2, a Soviet-built biplane. Their night armed recon mission started at 2240 hours with the aircraft orbiting the skies over the Seoul area, directed by Fifth Air Force TADC at Kimpo (codename Dentist). CWO Buckingham picked up a bogey at a range of 5,000 feet and at the same altitude (3,500 feet) 12 miles north of Kimpo. The PO-2 was flying at 80 knots (92mph), compared to the Tigercat's 200 knots (230mph), and the night fighter soon overran the bogey. Capt. Long dropped his flaps and landing gear, then conducted a 360-degree turn, which slowed the night fighter down to 95 knots (109mph), allowing him the maneuverability to fire one burst of 20mm cannon fire. "I observed a burpgun (sic) fire from the bogey and 12.7-mm fire from the ground. I lost the bogey and headed south," Capt. Long said. TADC informed Long and Buckingham that the PO-2 was following them and the Tigercat pilot made another 360-degree turn and fired a 50-round burst, scoring hits on the enemy aircraft. "Contact with the bogey was then lost by 'Dentist' and myself. However, shortly afterward, I observed an elongated explosion and fire on the ground." It was the PO-2, which had crashed on the banks of the Han River near Seoul, giving the squadron its first of ten aerial victories.[5]

The squadron's first kill by an F4U-5N Corsair occurred when a PO-2 fell to a F4U-5N flown by Capt. Donald L. Fenton 12 July 1951. At 0035 hours, Fenton received word of a bogey from "Dentist." Fenton made contact 12 minutes later, with the PO-2 flying at an altitude of 3,000 feet at a speed of approximately 90 knots (104mph). The biplane's back seat gunner fired at the approaching F4U-5N with his 7.62mm machine gun as Fenton opened fire at a range of 1,000 feet. Hits from the Corsair's 20mm ammunition tore the right two wings off the PO-2, immediately followed by the aircraft's gas tank exploding as the little fabric-covered night heckler plummeted to earth. Fenton's kill was the last by a Marine F4U-5N pilot for nearly a year.

The next two enemy aircraft shot down went to VMF(N)-513 Tigercat crews. A third PO-2 fell victim to an orbiting F7F-3N during the dark morning hours of 23 September 1951. Maj. Eugene A. Van Gundy and his R/O, MSgt. Thomas H. Ullom, standing strip alert at K-13 (Suwon) in their Tigercat, were scrambled at 0040 hours to intercept an incoming bogey approaching Seoul. After friendly antiaircraft batteries failed to bring down the hostile aircraft, TADC vectored Van Gundy and Ullom towards it. The teamwork between ground control and the night fighter worked perfectly, as it guided Van Gundy towards the target by giving him changes in course, altitude, and airspeed. MSgt. Ullom took over from GCI when he established contact with the target at a range of one-and-a-half miles and guided the Tigercat's pilot in for the kill. According to Maj. Van Gundy, "He (MSgt. Ullom) accurately directed me to a point where I established visual contact of the bogey at approximately 500 feet. I made a firing pass, expending 100 rounds of 20mm ammunition. The bogey instantly burst into flames, and as we pulled away we observed the entire enemy aircraft ablaze." The PO-2 crashed still carrying its two occupants, who had no time to bail out of their burning aircraft.[6]

The second and last Marine F4U-5N kill came 7 June 1952, when 1st Lt. John W. Andre of VMF(N)-513 scored his only aerial victory of the war by shooting down a North Korean Yakovlev Yak-9, a soviet-built fighter, the only such aircraft brought down by an American night fighter. He lifted his F4U-5N from K-8 at 2125 hours to attack targets of opportunity after they were illuminated by flares provided by an accompanying flare plane. While attempting to vector towards the flare plane, GCI with the call sign "Dentist" called him and asked if he had good radar equipment aboard. The Corsair's pilot replied he had excellent radar gear and Dentist gave him a vector of 120 degrees to intercept a bogey, which was 20 miles ahead. After closing within 12 miles, he called again to request range. "Dentist" urgently replied, "Break it off! We have a night fighter in the area!" The alert surprised Andre, who assumed that "Dentist" was referring to his night fighter; however, he broke off anyway and returned to his primary mission.[7] Less than two hours later, while engaged in attacking a convoy of trucks illuminated by flares, he came under attack from the Yak-9 from the rear. The enemy's tracers passed over his left wing, then under the aircraft, and finally over the right wing. The Yak passed the F4U-5N to the starboard side at a speed estimated at 30 to 40 knots (35/46mph) faster than the Corsair's. Andre made a steep bank and came in on the unsuspecting enemy's tail, where he opened up with a short burst of 20mm cannon fire. The Yak shuddered from the impact from the Tigercat's cannon fire, and as it dived over a hill on fire, it hit the ground and exploded. This kill, along with four Japanese aircraft brought down while in the Pacific during WWII, earned him the title ace. His victory over the YaK-9 was the last scored by a squadron F4U-5N, but it was not the last aerial victory using that model. A year later, Navy pilot Lt. Guy Bordelon engaged and successfully downed five enemy aircraft piloting a night-flying Corsair while attached with the Fifth Air Force.

First Lt. John Andre (left) and MSgt. Carl E. Myers of Marine Night Fighter pictured in front of an F7F-3N Tigercat in Korea, 17 February 1952. Andre shot down a North Korean Yak-9 on 7 June 1952 while flying an F4U-5N Corsair. His one kill in Korea, along with four he made while serving with VMF(N)-541 in WWII, made him an Ace. (Emil Buehler Library, NMNA)

FADE INTO HISTORY

The era of prop-driven night fighters began drawing to a close with the introduction of the Douglas F3D Skyknight, the first turbo-jet all-weather fighter to operate in the Korean Theater. The training of Marine pilots and ROs training for operating the Skyknight in Korea with VMF(N)-513 lasted from late February to late May 1952. After the conclusion of training, 15 F3Ds flew to San Diego 1 June and loaded onto USS *Windham Bay* (TCVE 92), with the aircraft arriving at Itami airfield, Japan, 18 June. Col. Peter D. Lambrecht, the commanding officer of the Bat Eyes of VMF(N)-541 during WWII, led the first flight of four Skyknights to Kunsan Airbase 24 June, with another eight aircraft arriving within the next three days. Lambrecht assumed command of -513 upon his arrival at Kunsan. The arrival of the F3D in Korea changed VMF(N)-513's primary mission from close air support and interdiction missions to bomber escort for night raids over North Korea. Lambrecht and his radar operator died in a crash of their F3D-2 15 August 1952. In the capable hands of a pilot and RO, the Skyknight had six confirmed victories between November 1952 and January 1953. VC-4 Detachment 44 arrived in Korea with its complement of Skyknights in June 1953, joining -513 at Pyontaek, with a crew scoring one probable kill, but that crew in turn was lost. The Skyknight was the only jet night fighter used in Korea, although two other jet night fighters had become available during the war: the F2H-2N and F2H-3 Banshee. VC-4 operated twelve F2H-2N Banshee fighters beginning in mid-1951 and the F2H-3 by mid-1953, but only during Mediterranean cruises.

Flight crews of VMF(N)-513 pose in front of an F7F-3N and the Douglas F3D-2 Skyknight. The squadron began operating the Skyknight in June 1952, but still maintained its complement of Tigercats until the following May. (Garry Cleveland)

F4U-5N (WF-20, BuNo 12318) assigned to VMF(N)-513 at K-1 (Pusan West) South Korea during 1951. This aircraft is armed with eight five-inch High Velocity Air Rockets (HVARs) for close air support. (NMNA via Thomas E. Doll)

Snow blankets a South Korean airfield during the winter of 1952-53, with the wing and tail surfaces of Tigercat WF-18 covered by a heavy canvas tarp. In the right background are drop tanks and beyond, in the distance, a pair of Skyknights. (Robert F. Dorr)

VMF(N)-513 Skyknight aircrews provided bomber escort missions, while those flying Tigercats conducted most of the squadron's close air support sorties as peace negotiations between the UN Command, China, and the two Koreas dragged on. During March 1953, the First Marine Division was located along a 35-mile defensive line less than five miles from Panmunjon, the site of truce negotiations. North Korean and CHICOM forces began a massive series of attacks along this line to gain leverage at the negotiations, with fighting continuing until the Armistice took effect 27 July. The squadron's mission during this time was providing close air support for the Fifth Marines defending a hilly area with a series of outposts called the Nevada complex, located just below the 38th Parallel, 1,500 yards north of the MLR and approximately ten miles west of Panmunjon. Nevada consisted of five outposts named Boulder City, Carson, Elko, Reno, and Vegas. CHICOM forces began attacks against the outposts 26 March, marked at times by vicious hand-to-hand fighting. Squadron aircraft flew 364 combat missions during March and 399 in April against enemy artillery and machine gun positions, bunkers, ammunition dumps, trench systems, and troop concentrations.

A new tactic employed during the period involved the use of searchlights at night to pinpoint enemy positions for strikes by Tigercats. The tactic employed two or more ground-controlled 24-inch searchlights located on prominent terrain along the MLR. Intersecting searchlight beams pinpointed enemy locations, in some cases less than 500 yards from Marine positions. A tactical airborne observer in a light liaison aircraft directed the searchlight teams and controlled the missions. The long, pencil-like beams created an excellent artificial horizon, allowing Tigercat pilots to make bombing and strafing runs with a high degree of accuracy. A week of experimentation and trial runs to perfect the night close air support/searchlight concept was conducted under the direction of Col. Jack R. Cram and Marine Air Control Group Two (MACG-2). Combat operations began 12 April, with Maj. Charles L. Schroeder and 2nd Lt. Thomas F. St. Davis flying the first two strikes. The squadron flew 58 such sorties between 12 April and 5 May, with results exceeding all expectations.[12]

The Flying Nightmares officially retired the F7F-3N Tigercat at the end of May 1953, and it became an entirely all-weather jet fighter squadron with the F3D-2. NCAP and bomber escort took up the majority of combat operations, with an occasional interdiction strike, as the war in Korea entered its final phase. The squadron distinguished itself by shooting down 10 North Korean and CHICOM aircraft between 30 June 1951 and 31 January 1953, ranging from antiquated fabric-covered biplanes to the most advanced Soviet jet fighter of the period. The squadron scored air-to-air victories with all three aircraft models in its inventory, with six going to F3D pilots and radar operators, while F7F crews destroyed two more and F4U-5N pilots claimed the other pair. The final weeks of the conflict saw five more enemy aircraft fall to an American night fighter – all to one naval aviator in an F4U-5N Corsair.

This photograph of F7F-3N *Nuckle Head* of VMF(N)-513 at K-8, Korea, was taken by Sgt. "Bud" Page circa 1952-53. Behind the aircraft on the right are two of the squadron's F3D-2 Skyknights. (Robert F. Dorr)

Chapter 11

U.S. Navy F4U-5N/NL Corsair Korean Operations

Don't try to win this war all by yourself
- senior naval officer to pilot Lt. James Brown of VC-3

The Navy operated the F4U-5N (and the NL variant) almost exclusively for close air support and interdiction strikes. The Corsair's primary function was night defense of the task force, and since there was no real aerial threat to U.S. surface forces, they were often released to attack ground targets inside Korea during daylight hours. A number of former WWII USN night fighter pilots served in Korea, including Cmdr. Chick Harmer, skipper of VC-3, and Lt. Cmdr. Bill Henry, the highest scoring night fighter ace of WWII, in charge of the squadron's Detachment C. VC-3 lost seven pilots in Korea, including Lt. Robert Humprey, another WWII night ace, killed in action while flying an F4U-5N for Detachment E aboard USS *Princeton* (CVL 23).

Conducting night operations at sea during a Korean winter typically mirrored those of land-based units stationed in either Korea or Japan during the conflict; that of operating in extreme cold, often combined with snow, ice, and poor visibility. But Navy composite squadrons had the added problem of launching from and landing on a moving aircraft carrier at sea. That, however, is where the similarity ended, as many carrier-based night fighter pilots taking off and landing on a short flight deck, in extreme weather conditions, experienced mind-numbing stress, gut-wrenching takeoffs and landings, loneliness, anger, and bitterness. F4U-5 night and all-weather aircraft were assigned to a detachment or detachments belonging to a larger composite squadron that operated a variety of fighters and fighter-bombers. A night fighter detachment typically consisted of five F4U-5N/L Corsairs, five pilots, and some 30 to 40 maintenance and ordnance personnel. Lt. James Brown, serving aboard the aircraft carrier USS *Oriskany* (CVA 34) and assigned to Detachment "George" of VC-3 during the winter of 1952-53, experienced first-hand the stress of flying a F4U-5NL during harsh winter conditions.

The arrival of the all-weather Corsair into the Navy and Marine Corps inventory did not completely solve the problems of operating aircraft in extreme wintery conditions, as was the case of a Navy F4U-5NL detachment.

On one particular evening in the Sea of Japan, as Brown remembers, four of the detachment's Corsairs prepared to leave *Oriskany*'s deck to fly a night interdiction mission. The planes they were to fly had been stored on the warm hangar deck located below before being raised on the carrier's elevator to the frigid flight deck for a catapult launch. The first, flown by the team leader, launched without difficulty, but a second preparing to take off suffered a ruptured oil line as it went to full power and the pilot aborted. The third Corsair's catapult cable broke as it started down the flight deck, and not having enough power for a successful launch, the pilot jammed on the brakes, causing both tires to blow out. The fully-loaded aircraft slid sideways and skidded towards the edge of the deck. Miraculously, the aircraft came to a stop within inches of falling into the sea or catching on fire. Meanwhile, the team leader orbited above the ship, his aircraft burning fuel, as the fourth Corsair ran into trouble, with one of its wings locking pins. One wing

went down and locked without a problem, but the other, frozen solid, would not move. After several unsuccessful attempts to lock the wing into position, a plane handler, in total darkness, climbed out onto the wing, which extended over the deck 50 feet above the sea, and jumped up and down until he broke the pin free and it slid into place. This Corsair was launched successfully and joined up with the team leader; only two out of the four aircraft VC-3 had planned for the mission made it into the air that night.[1]

An F4U-5N of Utility Squadron Three (VC-3) in 1950. VC-3 operated detachments of night and all-weather variants of the F4U-5 from several carriers during the Korean War, providing Combat Air Patrol (NCAP) over the fleet and conducting interdiction and close air support. (Emil Buehler Library, NMNA)

F4U-5Ns of VC-3, probably of Det F, fly past USS *Boxer* during the ship's 2 March to 24 October 1951 deployment to Korea. (National Archives)

Deck crew sweeping snow from USS *Valley Forge* (CV-45), stationed off Korea in January 1951 during its 6 December 1950 to 7 April 1951 deployment. On the left stand a trio of F4U-5N Corsairs of VC-3 before the unit received the winterized version F4U-5NL. (National Archives)

Snow and ice being cleaned from the flight deck of USS *Oriskany* (CVA 34) after a snow storm during operations off the Korean coast, winter 1952-53. You can imagine that flight operations during such conditions were extremely dangerous. (National Archives)

A THANKLESS JOB

There was quite a bit of bitterness and anger among some naval aviators during the Korean War when their accomplishments as members of naval night fighter detachments were ignored by higher authorities, who often did not believe the statements they made in after action reports. Most North Korean and Chinese equipment and troops moved at night, and that's when night fighters of VC-3 struck. Each night, a pair of Corsairs went on night interdiction strikes and often destroyed multiple numbers of enemy vehicles, and caused, according to the night fighter pilots, countless enemy casualties that unequalled the numbers claimed by day fighters and fighter-bombers. The problem with claiming such action lay with the problem of verification. Often when daylight dawned, the enemy had already cleaned up all traces of the damage inflicted upon them by night fighters, and the enemy rapidly rebuilt bridges blown up the night before.

VC-4 NA-58 winterized F4U-5NL (BuNo124681) moves forward after trapping aboard USS *Bon Homme Richard* (CVA-31) during its 20 May 1952 to 8 January 1953 Korean War cruise. It was only the second deployment of a VC-4 Det to Korea. (William T. Larkins Collection via Nicholas Veronico)

Since scorched earth was not viewed as a reliable means of verification, the Navy brass viewed after action reports submitted by the pilots with a good deal of skepticism. Navy and Marine Corps night fighter pilots saw most of the action and became understandably angry and bitter, since they received very little recognition for their accomplishments. Therefore, as a result of their frustration, and since their reports were often ignored, pilots began under-reporting enemy contacts. Lt. Brown voiced his frustration and bitterness in the aftermath of having conducted two missions flown 31 January 1953 and 23 March 1953. In a letter to his father, he wrote:

> My wingman and I caught and attacked 500 to 1,000 trucks heading south to the front lines. As we strafed at headlight level and bombed with fragmentation bombs, they left their headlights on, and those that were not destroyed or burning. The Navy did not believe us. The next time we began to reduce our claims. Finally, on 23 March 1953, it happened again, and like the others, we attacked with cannon fire and anti-personnel bombs. Many trucks and possibly hundreds of enemy troops were immolated or torn apart by fragmentation bombs. We did not report (it) to the carrier as before. However, as usual, we mentioned it at the debriefing. Apparently, American troops were attacked by these surviving enemy troops and senior commanders on the ground wanted to know why they (the enemy) had not been reported.

Later in the day, a Marine guard went to Brown's cabin, woke him, and escorted him to the Admiral's cabin. In his pajamas, the young pilot explained why he failed to report the enemy contacts. "I told him that no one believed us when we had reported this twice before, and it was not apparently important to report it. After a severe and public reprimand by the admiral, an order was given by him to never disregard night fighter reports again. Promptly, we became even more isolated. One senior officer called me aside after the admiral had no doubt reprimanded him for their disbelief of our reports. He warned, 'Don't try to win the war all by yourself, Brown.' I had to remain silent with my rage," said Brown. Carrier F4U-5N night fighter pilots such as Lt. Brown continued to fly close air support and interdiction missions, causing as much destruction against NKPA and CHICOM forces as their ground-based Marine Corps brethren of VMF(N)-513.[2]

F4U-5NL Corsairs of VC-3 in the foreground aboard USS *Philippine Sea* (CV-47) off Korea. Detachments from VC-3, nicknamed "The Night Hawks," operated from this carrier on four separate occasions from 5 July 1950 to August 1953. (Robert A. Rice via Nicholas Veronico)

Fully loaded Night Hawk NP-5 aboard *Philippine Sea*, prepared to conduct an interdiction strike in Korea. The F4U-5 series could carry up to eight 5-inch rockets and 4,000lbs of bombs or ordnance on centerline and pylon racks. (Robert A. Rice via Nicholas A. Veronico)

Engine run-up on VC-3 NP-5 aboard *Philippine Sea*. Vought modified 101 F4U-5Ns to the -NL configuration. The -NL saw extensive service in the Korean conflict, primarily with VC-3 and VMF(N)-513. (Robert A. Rice via Nicholas A. Veronico)

VC-3 F4U-5NL named "Nite Mare" over Korea. The all-weather -NL was introduced in early-1951 in response to the need for a fighter aircraft capable of operating in the extreme cold conditions of Korea. (Robert A. Rice via Nicholas A. Veronico)

The deck crew aboard *Philippine Sea* battles the flames of a burning F4U-5NL that crashed after returning from a mission. (Robert A. Rice via Nicholas A. Veronico)

A flight of VC-3 F4U-5Ns from USS *Boxer* (CV 21), possibly during the carrier's spring-summer 1953 deployment, with 4-NP displaying the overpainted wing and tail codes to obscure visibility. (Emil Buehler Library, NMNA)

Aircraft of VC-3 with NP-12 (BuNo 124467) in the foreground, parked aboard an aircraft carrier at an unknown location during the Korean War. (Emil Buehler Library, NMNA)

NP-5 of VC-3 being transferred from the deck of *Philippine Sea* after a tour of flying interdiction missions over Korea. (Robert A. Rice via Nicholas A. Veronico)

Ensign F.E. Blum, attached to VC-3 based on USS *Boxer* (CVA-21), piloting his F4U-5NL named "Vibrating Virgin" in 1953. Here again, typical of night fighters in Korea, a light coat of paint has been applied to the squadron code, designator, and "Navy" title. (Emil Buehler Library, NMNA)

Lt. Guy P. Bordelon, Jr. of VC-3 smiling next to his F4U-5N (BuNo 124453) named "ANNIE-MO," after his wife. Note the engine exhaust dampeners to the left of the in-squadron number 21 and another where the pilot's hand rests. (DOD)

Navy Night Fighter Ace

The Navy and Marines produced only two pilots with five or more aerial kills during the Korean War: Lt. Guy Pierre Bordelon of the Navy and Maj. John F. Bolt of the Marines. Maj. Bolt scored six kills flying the North American F-86 Sabre while attached to an Air Force fighter squadron; he scored six victories in the Pacific during WWII while serving with VMF-214. However, his victories in Korea occurred during daylight hours. Bordelon of VC-3 was the only naval aviator operating a night fighter during the conflict to hold the title of ace, with all five aerial kills occurring between June and July 1953. He spent the first part of the war aboard the cruiser USS *Helena* (CA-75) as a staff member for Commander Cruiser Division Three until orders sent him to VC-3's Dog Detachment aboard the USS *Princeton*.

A VC-3 Night Hawk F4U-5N/NL (NP-6) aboard an unknown carrier during Korean operations being towed into position for launching. The aircraft is armed with HAVRs for for a typical close air or interdiction strike. (NMNA)

During May and June 1953, NKPA and CHICOM aircrews went back to night heckling raids using the same type of slow flying, difficult to pick up on radar PO-2s and other types of Soviet-built training aircraft. Those aircraft caused minimal damage and few casualties two years before, but this time they had become increasingly bold, and there came the fear that such attacks could potentially inflict serious damage, especially on aircraft parked at South Korean airfields. An attack by an estimated six PO-2s shortly after midnight 27 May dropped four 100-pound bombs and eight artillery shells on K-14 airfield, hitting a fuel pipeline. A nine-aircraft attack the evening of 8 June against Seoul killed two people and injured eight. On the night of 16 June, the Communists sent 15 aircraft and succeeded in bombing a fuel dump near Inchon that torched 52,000 gallons of petroleum products.

Neither the Fifth Air Force nor the ground-based VMF(N)-513 had any night fighters at their disposal that could fly slowly enough to shoot down the Bedcheck Charlies. VMF(N)-513, the only Marine night fighter squadron in Korea, had retired its F4U-5Ns and F7F-3Ns in exchange for the turbojet Douglas F3D-2. However, like the Air Force's F-94B, Skyknight crews found it quite difficult to intercept such slow-moving enemy aircraft.

"When I learned about these enemy night raids," said Vice Adm. J. J. "Jocko" Clark, Commander Seventh Fleet, "I asked my staff if there wasn't something the Navy could do to lend the Air Force a helping hand. The operations officer for CarDivOne (Carrier Division One), Cmdr. John P. Conn, suggested that we send Corsair F4U5N night fighters ashore to assist in combating these nuisance raids. Since our planes were Corsairs, and the Marines had an airfield at K-8 from where they operated Corsairs, the F4U5Ns could be based at that airfield, which was 35 miles south of Seoul." The admiral contacted Lt. Gen. S.E. Anderson, commander of the Fifth Air Force, and told him that Navy detachments of F4U-5Ns from VC-3 would operate from Kimpo under the command of the Air Force in an effort to knock down the enemy night hecklers. When the detachment of four aircraft and pilots, including thirty-one-year-old Lt. Guy P. Bordelon, Jr., arrived at K-14 17 June, the Navy pilots received a week of familiarization, then were sent to K-6 airfield at Pyongtaek, since K-6 was a Marine Corps airbase and could better maintain the Corsairs.[3]

Bordelon trained as a fighter pilot during the last phases of WWII, but missed seeing combat. Most of his service during the Korean War was on the cruiser USS *Helena*, and he hated every minute of it. One day at Yokuska, Japan, Marshall Foreman, then a young Ensign serving as a member of VC-3, Detachment D aboard the carrier USS *Princeton*, went to pay a social call to one of the officers aboard the *Helena*. Foreman was introduced to Bordelon, and the former suggested he look into joining VC-3. "I told him to look into VC-3 because in night fighters we flew in groups of two planes, we didn't have to follow around behind the CAG (Carrier Air Group), and we were pretty much on our own. He liked the idea, applied for it, and was assigned to VC-3."[4] During the early morning hours of June 30th, two VC-3 pilots, including Bordelon, were given instructions to scramble their aircraft:

> Local radar had picked up aircraft in the area. Two of us were launched. The other aircraft had some radar trouble, but I had good radar placed on the enemy. It was a nice moonlit night and I had a good chance to see the exhaust stack pattern. When I finally got a visual – we had to get a visual because there were friendly aircraft in the area too – I soon reported that it was obviously an enemy aircraft, a Yak-18. So they said "go shoot," and I shot. He immediately banked hard right, and I kept right on him and poured about fifty or sixty rounds into him and he exploded. I was using high explosive incendiary 20mm cannon fire. One of those rounds could have blown him out of the air. The Yak-18 was a utility aircraft they had equipped with a gun mount in the rear seat. This aircraft had a rear gunner who was firing off to the right, whereas I was to his left.[5]

Shortly thereafter, ground control radar vectored Bordelon on to another target, which he identified as another Yak-18. "I got in back of him and he started firing right away," Bordelon said, "but he was firing in the wrong direction again. I let loose with a long burst of 20mm and he caught fire, his wing came off, and he exploded on the ground."[6]

During the night of 30 June-1 July, Bordelon again encountered enemy aircraft. He was running a control barrier north of Seoul to keep the enemy from flying aircraft into the area. While patrolling seaward off Inchon, JOC (Joint Operations Center) vectored him towards a bogey:

> When I got in, there were several aircraft. I got back of one (an La-11) and managed to shoot him down. It sounds easy, but it wasn't. They were twisting and turning [while pursuing the second aircraft of the same type], and we ended up over North Korea. When I finally shot him down, I was being fired on by antiaircraft. I had pulled in close enough to him, under 200 yards, that when he finally leveled out I gave him a long burst.[7]

Lt. Bordelon's aircraft parked at Kimpo Airbase (K-14), undergoing engine maintenance in June-July 1953, has light blue overpaint applied to the white markings. (Emil Buehler Library, NMNA)

In two days, the Navy night fighter pilot had downed four Bedcheck Charlies. His success immediately went up to the Navy's highest echelon, and the brass was biting at the bit to award the service's first night fighter pilot to down an enemy aircraft. As Adm. Clark related:

> Adm. Briscoe told me about this (Bordelon's two kills) when I arrived in the office on the 30th for a routine visit. I immediately decided to award Lt. Bordelon a Silver Star Medal for his feat, and since I was scheduled to fly back to Korea that night, I decided to go to K-6 to witness the operations of our night fighters and to lend encouragement to their efforts.[8]

The admiral's aircraft flew to K-6, but was turned away as it approached the field because of an air raid, during which, unknown to the admiral at the time, Bordelon was involved in the process of downing two more North Korean aircraft. According to Adm. Clark, "...we learned that the reason for the alert at K-6 had been another enemy raid. Lt. Bordelon had shot down two more night fighters. Then and there, I decided to present him with a gold star in lieu of a second Silver Star." Although Air Force radar tracking confirmed both kills, but wreckage from the aircraft was not recovered, Clark flew down to K-6 for a luncheon in the pilot's honor and to award the night fighter pilot with the two Silver Star Medals. "In a traditional ceremony I presented Bordelon with both awards at the same time, promising him, or anyone else who shot down five planes at night, a Navy Cross," he said.[9]

Nearly two weeks later, on the evening of 17 July, Bordelon earned his fifth and final kill of the war and a place in naval aviation history:

> I was in the air heading north to go up to Seoul when one of our aircraft reported he had a bogey. Shortly thereafter he reported that his radar had gone out, so I was vectored in to take over, picked him up, and had a long chase. I finally got on his tail. It was dark, black dark, but I was able to pick up the exhaust pattern. It was the same exhaust pattern as the previous two aircraft, Lavochkin La-11a, which are high-performance fighters. He again led me right over the antiaircraft positions at Kaesong. They started firing and I pulled in closer, because they were firing to the rear of the aircraft. The closer I was to him the safer I was. I pulled up and started firing, and he made a turn to the right, as if he was going to really give me fits trying to get away, then exploded. The blast took my night vision away. I had to reach up and grab the autopilot switch, switching it on. I had really set it so that the autopilot would come in easily, and it cracked right in and I could have given her a kiss! She was so good to me. I flew around until I got my eyesight back and the plane (the enemy's) was burning on the ground. I probably put more rounds into my last kill than the others combined. I was down to about 50 rounds, and I carried a total of 200 rounds for each of the four guns."[10]

Adm. Clark acted upon his earlier promise of awarding the Navy Cross if a naval aviator earned a fifth confirmed kill. He recounted:

> On the night of July 17th, Lt. Bordelon succeeded in bagging his fifth enemy plane. Since his operations were conducted under Gen. Anderson, commanding the Fifth Air Force, after obtaining authority from the Secretary of the Navy, I asked the General to make the presentation of the Navy Cross at once. This he did at an appropriate ceremony at Fifth Air Force headquarters. Lt. Bordelon had attained for himself the distinction of being the first and only night ace in the U.S. Navy. As a result of his effort enemy night raids on Seoul ceased and the city was able to sleep once more.[11]

SUMMARY

Ten days after Lt. Bordelon's last kill, the Korean Armistice went into effect, ending the conflict, which also marked the end of the F4U-5N/NLs' combat career with the U.S. Navy and Marines. Combat operations for night fighter squadrons changed from the primary mission of providing NCAP for U.S. forces in the Pacific during WWII to mainly engaging in close-air support missions in Korea. There was little need for night fighters in Korea during the conflict's first two years. However, the growing menace of communist aircraft operating during the evening hours over the Seoul area beginning in late 1951 necessitated the need for night fighters to be available for interception. Through fine airmanship, Marine and Navy pilots were able to throttle-down on several occasions to shoot down slow-moving North Korean aircraft. FEAF, to tackle MIGs flying over South Korea and to protect UN bombers, brought in the F3D-2 Skyknight and the Air Force's F-94B. However, when it came to intercepting Bedcheck Charlies, jet pilots found it difficult, if not downright dangerous in throttling-down to engage such very slow and highly maneuverable aircraft as the PO-2. The F4U-5N and F7F-3N were vastly superior then those used during WWII, yet they did not make a significant impact on the course of the Korean conflict in terms of night interception. In other aspects of their contribution it cannot be understated. Navy and

ANNIE-MO with five red stars, each representing an aerial victory scored within a few weeks between 30 June and 17 July 1953. To the right of the stars are fifteen white bomb symbols, indicating the number of air support and interdiction strikes. (Robert F. Dorr)

Lt. Bordelon left ANNIE-MO at Kimpo and returned to the USS *Princeton*. Not long after the Navy's only Korean War ace left, an Air Force pilot crashed the aircraft on take-off. (National Archives)

Marine Tigercat and Corsair units contributed significantly in close air support of UN ground forces and in carrying out interdiction strikes against NKPA and CHICOM forces, and were major contributors to the success of the evacuation of UN forces in North Korea during December 1950. A year after the Korean War, only VC-3 and VC-4 were the last active duty Navy squadrons to operate the F4U-5N/NL Corsair, with the latter squadron turning its F4U-5N/NLs in during December 1955. Corsairs remained in the Naval Reserve until 1957, but continued to operate with a variety of air forces around the world, most notably in Latin America.

The Navy finally found a suitable carrier-based night/all-weather jet fighter with the F2H-2N and F2H-3/4. The McDonnell Aircraft Corporation entered jet aircraft development with the FH-1 Phantom, continuing with the F2H Banshee series, which included night and all-weather variants. The Banshee was a single-seat fighter derived from the FH-1 Phantom. Development began in mid-1945, and three prototypes, designated XF2H-1, were ready by late 1946, with the first test flight occurring in January 1947. The same engines powered the Banshee as the early F3D – two 3,000-pound Westinghouse J34-WE-22 turbojet engines. McDonnell produced 56 units, all conventional fighters, before switching over to producing the F2H-2, an improved version of its predecessor with Westinghouse J34-We-34 turbojets with increased fuel stores in detachable wingtip tanks and eight underwing pylons for external weapons stores. Four 20mm nose-mounted cannons were the standard defensive armament for the series. The maximum speed of 575mph exceeded that of the Skyknight by approximately 45 miles per hour.

VC-4 received twelve single-seat F2H-2N night versions equipped with the AN/APS-19 radar located in a slightly elongated nose. The F3H-3 with a redesigned tail, lengthened fuselage, and the Westinghouse AN/APQ-41 radar followed in March 1952, with VC-4 receiving them in the spring of 1953. Pilots considered the new radar equipment unreliable, with the major problem being the ability to maintain radar contact with an enemy fighter while maneuvering. The F2H-4 was an improved night variant with the Hughes AN/APG-37 radar system; superior to the APQ-41, and powered by 3,600-pound thrust Westinghouse J34-WE-38 turbojet engines. The total production run for the F2H-3 was 250 units and 150 for the -4. Although the Banshee night fighter variant arrived too late to see action in the Korean War, they did establish themselves as the Navy's front-line all-weather fighter until the late 1950s.

F4U-5N and S2F-1 Tracker aircraft aboard USS *Leyte* (CV 32) circa 1954-55. (Photo by Photographer's Mate 1st Class Louis T. Sereda via Nicholas A. Veronico)

Chapter 12

Night Cats and Corsairs in Foreign Service

Good airplanes are more important than superiority in numbers
- **Air Vice-Marshall J.E. Johnson,** RAF

The British Royal Navy (RN) received approximately 240 F6F-5N Hellcats between January and May 1945 designated as the Hellcat NF II. No. 891 and 892 Squadrons received the aircraft and were training for combat operations when the war ended. No. 892 received a compliment of 16 aircraft in April at Eglington, Northern Ireland, and embarked briefly aboard HMS *Premier* (D-23), with night fighter training continuing at Drem, Scotland, until VJ Day. The squadron continued operating the aircraft aboard HMS *Ocean* from November 1945 to April 1946. No. 891 received 16 such aircraft, with training occurring at Eglington and Nutts Corne, Northern Ireland, between June and September.

The French Fleet Air Arm received 15 F6F-5N Hellcats between 1951 and 1953 from the U.S., five of them converted back to the original -5 day fighter configuration. The French aircraft carrier *LaFayette* arrived in France 11 September 1951, carrying the first batch of aircraft, consisting of 16 F6F-5, 4 F6F-5N, and 12 radar-equipped TBM-3E Avengers. Flotilla 1F was the first squadron to receive the Hellcat, operating 24 F6F-5 and 6 F6F-5N. Three training squadrons (Squadron 54S, 57S, and all-weather training squadron 59S) operated the day and night variants until the late 1950s. The French did not operate true F6F-5Ns in the French Indochina War, but a few were used in Algeria to monitor militant movements and weapons traffic. Night landing qualification or French pilots took place on USS *Saipan* (CVL 48) 22 August 1951 off Norfolk, Virginia, with each pilot making seven landings, followed by two more on the French carrier *Lafayette* 29 August. Carrier qualification and the training of French deck-landing officers, since none were qualified, were conducted in the Mediterranean Sea on USS *Franklin D. Roosevelt* 19 October and USS *Tarawa* (CV 40) 20 December 1951. One of the Americans selected to train them was Lt. Guy Bordelon. Night deck landings on the *LaFayette* continued from May to July 1952.

Honduras and Argentina acquired F4U-5, F4U-5N, and F4U-5NLs from the U.S. under the Mutual Defense Assistance Plan (MDAP). The Honduran Air Force, *Fuerza Aerea Hondurena* (FAH), purchased 10 former F4U-5N/NL Corsairs from the U.S. in a 1956 MAP. It appears the FAH converted them to standard day fighters by removing the radar pod and associated cockpit gear. Some of these aircraft were operational with *Escuadrón de Caza-Bombardeo* during a brief conflict between El Salvador and Honduras known as the 1969 Soccer War (10-27 July); both nations were equipped with former American Mustangs and Corsairs. FAH Capt. Fernando Soto in F4U-5N FAH609 (BuNo 124715) scored three aerial victories 17 July against the El Salvadoran Air Force (*Fuerza Aerea Salvadorena* - FAS) during the brief conflict, shooting down an F-51 Mustang and a pair of FG-1D Corsairs.

FAH F4U-5N/NL

F4U-5N	
FAH 603	123168
FAH 604	122179
FAH 605	122184
FAH 606	124486
FAH 607	124692
FAH 608	124493
FAH 609	124715

F4U-5NL	
FAH 600	124724
FAH 601	124560
FAH 602	124447

One of approximately 240 RN Hellcat NF IIs provided by the United States to the Royal Navy at an airfield in Great Britain. The last two digits (65) visible near the tail identifies this aircraft as either JX965 or JZ965. (Author's Collection)

The following three photographs are from the collection of Lt. Cmdr. Donald McQueen, Senior Deck Landing Control Officer (DLCO), who served aboard HMS *Ocean*. A Hellcat II NF (left), a trio of Fairey Fireflys (center), and a Grumman TMF/TBM Avenger (named the Tarpon by the British) aboard HMS *Ocean*, docked at Malta in 1946. (Lt. Cmdr. Donald McQueen via the author)

Landing sequence of a Hellcat II NF of 892 Squadron as it approaches HMS Ocean between November 1945 and April 1946. (Lt. Cmdr. Donald McQueen via the author)

One of five French Navy Grumman F6F-5N Hellcat of *Flottile 11F*, which was converted back to the standard day fighter configuration on the deck of French carrier *Bois Belleau* during operations in the Gulf of Tonkin 8 June 1954. (Emil Buehler Library, NMNA via Tailhook Association)

The Argentine Navy (*Commando Aviacion Naval Argentina* - CANA) acquired approximately 26 flyable F4U-5, -5N, and -5NL, 16 of those -5N and -5NL, between 1956 and 1959. The unit assigned the aircraft was *Flotilla de Combate*, consisting of *Escuadrilla Nocturna* and *Escuadrilla Aeronaval de Ataque de la Escuadra Aeronaval. Escuadrilla Nocturna* conducted carrier operations with the F4U-5N/NL from the carrier *Independencia* (V-1). The unit, later renamed *2° Escuadrilla Aeronaval de Ataque* and then finally integrated into *Escuadra Aeronaval N° 3*, continued flying the Corsair until 1966.

ARGENTINIAN F4U-5N/NL

F4U-5N	
3-C-8	123203
3-C-10/2-A-210/3-A-210	122183
2-A-215/3-A-215/3-A-214	124701

F4U-5NL	
AG Code	USN Code
3-C-1/3-A-201	124705
3-C-2	124699
3-C-3/2-A-203/3-A-206	124514
3-C-4/2-A-204/3-A-204	122206
3-C-5/2-A-205/3-A-205	122192
3-C-6/2-A-206/3-A-203	124703
3-C-7/2-A-207	122038
3-C-8/2-A-208/3-A-208	124685
3-C-9/2-A-209/3-A-209	124559
2-A-202/3-A-204	124541
2-A-203/3-A-206	124514
2-A-213/3-A-213	124707
2-A-223/3-A-202	124678

The Argentine Navy acquired 26 F4U-5s, including this F4U-5NL (former BuNo 124705). They operated from the Argentine carrier *Indepencia* and were also shore-based at Punta de Indio. (Robert F. Dorr)

Appendices

Appendix A: Aircraft Specifications

	F4U-2	F4U-5
LENGTH	33ft 3in	33ft 5in
HEIGHT	16ft 10in	14ft 7in
WING SPAN	40ft 9in	same
EMPTY WEIGHT	8,962Lbs	9,863Lbs
GROSS WEIGHT	14,009lbs	14,670Lbs
POWER PLANT	Pratt & Whitney R-2800-8	Pratt & Whitney R-2800-32W
MAXIMUM SPEED AT ALTITUDE	425mph	470mph
CRUISING SPEED	182mph	227mph
RATE OF CLIMB	3,100ft/min	3,870ft/min
MAX RANGE	1,120 miles	1,120 miles
SERVICE CEILING	37,000ft	41,400ft
INTERNAL FUEL	178gal	234gal
EXTERNAL FUEL	two-150 or 170gal drop tanks	two-150gal drop tanks
ARMAMENT (STANDARD)	Five-.50cal machine guns	Four-20mm cannon
	-	Eight 5-inch HVAR rockets
	-	One 2,000lb bomb
	-	Two 1,000lb bombs
	-	Two 11.75 rockets

*Figures based on pilot's handbook for F4U-5, -5N, -5NL, and -5P dated 15 February 1952.
Figures for the F4U-2 from Vought Heritage History Center.

	F6F-3N	F6F-5N
LENGTH	33ft 7in	same
HEIGHT	11ft 1in	same
WING SPAN	42ft 10in	same
EMPTY WEIGHT	9,023Lbs	9,238Lbs
GROSS WEIGHT	12,771Lbs	12,483Lbs
POWER PLANT	Pratt & Whitney R-2800-10	Pratt & Whitney R-2800-10W
CRUISING SPEED SEA LEVEL	312mph	318mphMaximum Speed
MAXIMUM SPEED AT ALTITUDE	388mph	410mph
RATE OF CLIMB	3,050ft/min	3,150ft/min
SERVICE CEILING	39,400ft	38,800ft
INTERNAL FUEL	250gal	same
EXTERNAL FUEL	150gal	same
MAXIMUM RANGE	1,085 miles	1,300 miles
ARMAMENT (NIGHT FIGHTER)	Six .50-caliber machine guns	same*
	Six-5 inch HVAR rockets	
	Two 1,000lb bombs	
	Four 500lb bombs	

*Some F6F-5N equipped with 4x .50-caliber machine guns/2x 20mm cannon

F7F Tigercat (specifications based on data from Grumman)

	F7F-1	**F7F-2** (day variant)
LENGTH	45ft 6in	same
HEIGHT	13ft 9in	same
WING SPAN	51ft 6in	same
EMPTY WEIGHT	15,681Lbs	16,028Lbs
GROSS WEIGHT	21,381Lbs	21,690Lbs
POWER PLANT	two-2100-hp Pratt & Whitney R-2800-22W	same
MAXIMUM SPEED	445mph	same
CRUISING SPEED	190mph	same
RATE OF CLIMB	5,300ft/min	5,200ft/min
SERVICE CEILING	40,900ft	40,600ft
MAXIMUM RANGE	1,850 miles	1,790 miles
ARMAMENT	Four nose-mounted .50-caliber machine guns	same
	Four wing-mounted 20mm cannon	same
	One 2,000-pound bomb (centerline rack)	One 2,150lb torpedo (centerline)
	Two 1,000-pound bombs (centerline rack)	same
	-	Two 11.75 inch Tiny Time rockets (centerline)
	-	Eight 5-inch HVAR rockets (wing-mounted)

	F7F-3	**F7F-3N**
LENGTH	45ft 5in	46ft 5in
HEIGHT	13ft 9in	16ft 7in
SPAN	51ft 6in	same
EMPTY WEIGHT	16,396lbs	16,592lbs
GROSS WEIGHT	21,906lbs	21,738lbs
POWER PLANT	two 2,100-hp Pratt & Whitney R-2800-34W	same
MAXIMUM SPEED	460mph	447mph
CRUISING SPEED	190mph	same
RATE OF CLIMB	6,000ft/min	same
SERVICE CEILING	40,400ft	40,600 feet
RANGE	1,900 miles	1,750 miles
ARMAMENT	Same as F7F-2N	Four wing-mounted 20mm cannon

Appendix B: World War II Air-to-Air Credits by F4U and F6F Night Fighter Units

VF(N)-41

DATE	TIME	PILOT	TYPE
09/12/44	0755	Ens. Robert W. Klock (0.5)	G4M Betty
		Ens. George W. Obenour (0.5)	
09/12/44	1846	Lt. William E. Henry (0.5)	Ki-46 Dinah
		Ens. Jack Berkheimer (0.5)	
09/13/44	0812	Ens. Wallace E. Miller (0.333)	G4M Betty
		Ens. Reuben F. Peterson (0.333)	
		Ens. James A. Barnett (0.333)	
09/21/44	0935	Lt. Jesse T. Barker (0.25)	Ki-61 Tony
		Ens. Irvin H. Lee (0.25)	
		Ens. Gayle V. Williams (0.25)	
		Ens. Wallace E. Miller (0.25)	
09/21/44	0935	Ens. Robert R. Fegraeus	A6M Zeke (probable)
09/21/44	-	Lt. William E. Henry	Ki-43 Oscar (probable)
09/21/44	0940	Ens. Jack Berkheimer	Ki-57 Topsy
09/21/44	-	Ens. Floyd A. Fisher	Ki-57 Topsy (damaged)
09/21/44	-	Lt. Jesse T. Barker	Tony (damaged)
09/22/44	0810	Lt. William E. Henry	D3A Val
09/22/44	0815	Lt. William E. Henry	D3A Val
09/22/44	-	Ens. Joseph F. Moore	D3A Val
09/22/44	0830	Ens. Jack Berkheimer	A6M Zeke
09/22/44	0845	Ens. Reuben F. Peterson	F1M Pete (damaged)
09/24/44	0845	Ens. William T. Howard	E-13A Jake
10/12/44	1855	Lt. William E. Henry	G4M Betty
10/12/44	1900	Lt. William E. Henry	G4M Betty
10/12/44	-	Ens. James A. Barnett	G4M Betty
10/13/44	0500	Ens. Jack Berkheimer	H8K Emily
10/13/44	-	Ens. Jack Berkheimer	H8K Emily
10/13/44	-	Ens. Robert W. Klock	H8K Emily
10/15/44	0250	Lt. William E. Henry	H8K Emily
10/24/44	0215	Ens. Jack Berkheimer	H8K Emily
10/24/44	0335	Ens. Jack Berkheimer	H6K Mavis
10/24/44	1000	Ens. Wallace E. Miller	E13A Jake
10/24/44	1010	Lt. Erwin J. Becker (0.5)	P1Y Frances
		Ens. Wallace E. Miller (0.5)	
10/27/44	0230	Ens. Irvin H. Lee	H6K Mavis
11/05/44	1105	Lt. (jg) Robert R. Fegraeus (0.5)	D4Y Judy
		Ens. Joe S. Allen (0.5)	
11/06/44	0445	Lt. William E. Henry	Ki-57 Topsy
11/06/44	-	Ens. James A. Barnett	Ki-57 Topsy

11/19/44	0205	Lt. William E. Henry	H8K Emily
11/19/44	0545	Ens. Jack Berkheimer	Ki-43 Oscar
11/19/44	-	Ens. Floyd A. Fisher	Ki-57 Topsy
11/19/44	-	Ens. Floyd A. Fisher	Ki-57 Topsy
11/19/44	1800	Ens. Wallace E. Miller	G4M Betty
11/19/44	-	Ens. Wallace E. Miller	G4M Betty
11/19/44	-	Ens. Wallace E. Miller	G4M Betty (probable)
12/14/44	0415	Lt. William E. Henry	H8K Emily
12/15/44	0615	Lt. Baker A. Bradenbaugh	Ki-45 Nick
12/16/44	0145	Ens. Reuben F. Peterson	E13A Jake
12/16/44	0150	Ens. Reuben F. Peterson	unidentified fighter
12/16/44	0450	Ens. Lester H. Diskosky	Ki-57 Topsy
01/06/45	0800	Lt. (jg) James A. Barnett	Ki-43 Oscar
01/06/45	1715	Lt. Kyle H. Morris	Ki-43 Oscar
01/06/45	1720	Ens. Emmett R. Edwards	Ki-44 Tojo
01/06/45	1725	Ens. Emmett R. Edwards	G4M Betty
01/06/45	-	Ens. Emmett R. Edwards	unidentified
01/06/45	-	Lt. Kyle H. Morris	Ki-44 Tojo
01/10/45	0610	Ens. Arthur Hansen	Ki-21 Sally
01/10/45	0647	Lt. (jg) Robert R. Fegraeus	Ki-21 Sally
01/10/45	0709	Ens. Arthur Hansen	Ki-45 Nick
01/16/45	1845	Lt. William E. Henry	Ki-43 Oscar
Squadron Totals:	46/3/3		

VF(N)-53

DATE	TIME	PILOT	TYPE
02/21/44	1650	Lt. Raymond W. Luke	A6M Zeke
02/21/44	-	Ens. Lewis C. Radford, Jr.	A6M Zeke
02/21/44	-	Ens. Constantine Szymborski	A6M Zeke
02/21/44	-	Ens. John P. Nelson	A6M Zeke
Squadron Totals:	5/0/0		

VF(N)-75

DATE	TIME	PILOT	TYPE
10/31/43	2300	Hugh D. O'Neill, Jr.	G4M Betty
12/11/43	2300	Hugh D. O'Neill, Jr.	G4M Betty
12/13/43	2015	Lt. John S. Hill	unidentified floatplane (probable)
12/15/43	2350	Lt. John S. Hill	A6M2-N Rufe
12/16/43	0105	Lt. John S. Hill	A6M2-N Rufe
12/19/43	0235	Lt. Reuben L. Johns	A6M-2N Rufe
01/01/44	2139	Lt. Charles L. Penner	D3A Val
01/01/44	2156	Lt. Charles L. Penner	D3A Val (probable)
01/13/44	0415	Lt. Reuben L. Johns	D3A Val
Squadron Totals:	7/2/0		

VF(N)-76

DATE	TIME	PILOT	TYPE
02/22/44	0730-0745	Lt. Cdr. Evan P. Aurand	G4M Betty
02/22/44	0645-0800	Lt. Cdr. Evan P. Aurand	A6M Zeke
02/22/44	-	Lt. (jg) Norman L. Davisson	A6M Zeke
02/22/44	-	Ens. John R. Bertie	A6M Zeke
02/22/44	-	Ens. John R. Bertie	A6M Zeke
02/22/44	-	Ens. John R. Bertie	A6M Zeke
04/23/44	1030	Lt. (jg) Fred L. Dungan	G4M Betty
06/15/44	1857	Lt. Cdr. Evan P. Aurand	D4Y Judy
06/19/44	1415	Lt. Cdr. Evan P. Aurand	B6N Jill
06/19/44	1545-1615	Lt. Russell L. Reiserer	D3A Val
06/19/44	-	Lt. Russell L. Reiserer	D3A Val
06/19/44	-	Lt. Russell L. Reiserer	D3A Val
06/19/44	-	Lt. Russell L. Reiserer	D3A Val
06/19/44	-	Lt. Russell L. Reiserer	D3A Val
06/19/44	-	Ens. William E. Levering	Val Val
06/19/44	-	Lt.(jg) Fred L. Dungan	B5N Kate
06/19/44	-	Lt. (jg) Fred L. Dungan	A6M Zeke
06/19/44	-	Lt. (jg) Fred L. Dungan	B5N Kate (probable)
06/24/44	1000	Lt. (jg) John W. Dear, Jr.	B5N Kate
06/24/44	-	Lt. (jg) John W. Dear, Jr.	B5N Kate
06/24/44	-	Lt. (jg) John W. Dear, Jr.	B5N Kate
06/24/44	-	Lt. Russell L. Reiserer	B5N Kate
06/24/44	-	Lt. Russell L. Reiserer	B5N Kate
07/02/44	0008	Lt. Warren H. Abercrombie	G4M Betty
07/03/44	1600	Ens. Thomas H. Cunningham	A6M Zeke
07/03/44	-	Ens. Thomas H. Cunningham	A6M Zeke
07/03/44	-	Ens. Thomas H. Cunningham	A6M Zeke
07/33/44	-	Ens. Thomas H. Cunningham	A6M Zeke (probable)
07/04/44	0530	Lt. (jg) John W. Dear, Jr.	A6M2-N Rufe
07/04/44	-	Lt. (jg) John W. Dear, Jr.	A6M2-N Rufe
07/04/44	-	Lt. (jg) John W. Dear, Jr.	A6M2-N Rufe
07/04/44	-	Lt. (jg) Fred L. Dungan	A6M2-N Rufe
07/04/44	-	Lt. (jg) Fred L. Dungan	A6M2-N Rufe
07/04/44	-	Lt. (jg) Fred L. Dungan	A6M2-N Rufe
07/04/44	-	Lt. (jg) Fred L. Dungan	A6M2-N Rufe
07/07/44	2019	Ens. William E. Levering	G4M Betty
07/07/44	2105	Lt. Russell L. Reiserer	G4M Betty
09/13/44	1415	Lt. (jg) Jackson E. Conner	G4M Betty
09/22/44	0630	Lt. (jg) John W. Dear, Jr.	B6N Jill or B5N Kate
Squadron Totals:	37/2/0		

VF(N)-77

DATE	TIME	PILOT	TYPE
06/20/44	0350	Ens. George L. Tarleton	D3A Val
06/20/44	0410	Ens. George L. Tarleton	D3A Val
06/20/44	-	Lt. Cdr. Robert M. Freeman	D3A Val
07/04/44	0600	Ens. Joseph H. Rohde	A6M2-N Rufe
07/11/44	0333	Lt. Anthony C. Benjes, Jr.	G4M Betty
07/11/44	0508	Ens. Charles A. Soderlund	G4M Betty
07/16/44	unstated	Lt. John H. Boyum	unidentified
09/01/44	0330	Lt. Anthony C. Benjes, Jr	H8K Emily
Squadron Totals:	8/0/0		

VF(N)-78

DATE	TIME	PILOT	TYPE
08/31/44	0230	Cdr. James Seton Gray, Jr.	G4M Betty (damaged)
09/12/44	1110	Lt. William H.B. Miller (0.5)	P1Y Francis
		Lt. Donald P. Matheson (0.5)	
09/22/44	0615-0925	Lt. William B. Thompson (0.5)	A6M Zeke (damaged)
		Ens. William A. Herpich (0.5)	
09/22/44	0615-0925	Lt. William B. Thompson (0.5)	A6M Zeke
		Lt. William H.B. Miller (0.5)	
Squadron Totals:	2/0/2		

VF(N)-90

DATE	TIME	PILOT	TYPE
01/06/45	1700	Lt. Carl S. Nielsen	Ki-46 Dinah
01/06/45	1708	Lt. Carl S. Nielsen	A6M Zeke
01/06/45	1710	Lt. Carl S. Nielsen	Ki-43 Oscar
01/16/45	1900	Ens. Robert C. Wattenburger	Tojo Ki-44
01/21/45	2245	Lt. James J. Wood	P1Y Frances
02/19/45	1926	Lt. James J. Wood	Helen Ki-49
02/24/45	2055	Lt. Kenneth D. Smith	Ki-49 Helen
03/18/45	0030	Ens. Robert C. Wattenburger	Ki-49 Helen
03/18/45	0320	Lt. (jg) Wesley R. Williams	unidentified single-engine aircraft
03/18/45	0410	Ens. Glen R. Earl	P1Y Frances
03/18/45	0430	Lt. (jg) James P. Purcell, Jr.	L2D2 Tabby (probable)
03/18/45	0620	Lt. (jg) Will J. Squires	E13A Jake
03/19/45	0445	Ens. James R. Perkins	G4M Betty (probable)
03/19/45	0500	Lt. (jg) Lamar F. Harrison (0.5)	G4M Betty
		Lt. (jg) Layton E. Robison (0.5)	
04/07/45	1505	Lt. Dallas E. Runion	P1Y Frances
04/09/45	1908	Lt. (jg) Will J. Squires D3A Val	
04/11/45	1905	Lt. Dallas E. Runion	Ki-61 Tony
04/11/45	2130	Lt. Kenneth D. Smith	G4M Betty
04/12/45	0200	Lt. (jg) Joseph C. Gallant	G4M Betty

04/12/45	0230	Lt. James J. Wood	Ki-67 Peggy
04/12/45	0510	Ens. James R. Perkins	G2M Jack
05/12/45	0410	Lt. Owen D. Young	Ki-61 Tony
05/12/45	0515	Lt. Kenneth D. Smith	Ki-61 Tony
05/12/45	0520	Lt. Owen D. Young	E13A Jake
05/12/45	0522	Lt. Owen D. Young	E13A Jake
05/12/45	0525	Lt. (jg) Charles H. Latrobe	E13A Jake
05/12/45	0530	Lt. Owen D. Young	E13A Jake
05/12/45	0533	Lt. Owen D. Young (0.5)	F1M1 Pete
		Lt. (jg) Charles H. Latrobe (0.5)	
05/12/45	0545	Lt. (jg) John R. Kenyon, Jr.	Ki-43 Oscar
05/13/45	2300	Lt. (jg) George A. Oden	Ki-46 Dinah
05/14/45	0100	Lt. (jg) Charles H. Latrobe	G4M Betty
05/14/45	0530	Lt. (jg) Lamar F. Harrison	Ki-43 Oscar
05/14/45	0615	Lt. (jg) George P. Taylor	A6M Zeke
Squadron Totals:	31/2/0		

VF(N)-91

DATE	TIME	PILOT	TYPE
07/25/45	1823	Ens. Kenneth J. Baldwin	K5Y Willow
07/25/45	-	Ens. J.C. Stires	K5Y Willow (probable)
07/25/45	1850	Lt. (jg) Robert M. Kloze	B7A Grace
08/09/45	1833	Ens. J.C. Stires	D4Y3 Judy
08/09/45	-	Ens. J.C. Stires	D4Y3 Judy
08/13/45	1835	Lt. Robert T. Kieling	Ki-45 Nick
08/13/45	-	Ens. Philip T. McDonald	Ki-45 Nick
08/13/45	1850-1910	Ens. Philip T. McDonald	P1Y Frances
08/13/45	-	Ens. Philip T. McDonald	P1Y Frances
08/13/45	-	Ens. Philip T. McDonald	P1Y Frances (probable)
08/13/45	1915	Ens. Philip T. McDonald	Ki-45 Nick
SquadronTotals:	9/2/0		

VF(N)-101

DATE	TIME	PILOT	TYPE
02/19/44	0600	Lt. Cdr. Richard E. Harmer	G4M Betty (damaged)
04/24/44	2010	Lt. Cdr. Richard E. Harmer	Ki-21 Sally*
04/24/44	-	Lt. Cdr. Richard E. Harmer	Ki-21 Sally* (damaged)
06/15/44	1905	Lt. Cdr. Richard E. Harmer	Ki-21 Sally* (damaged)
06/15/44	-	Lt. (jg) R. F. Holden	Ki-44 Tojo (probable)
06/27/44	2035	Lt. (jg) R. F. Holden	Ki-21 Sally
06/28/44	2015	Lt. (jg) R. F. Holden	G4M Betty
06/28/44	2130	Lt. (jg) R. F. Holden	G4M Betty
06/28/44	2245	Lt. Cdr. Richard E. Harmer	G4M Betty
			*type of aircraft not verified
Squadron Totals:	5/1/3		

VMF(N)-532

DATE	TIME	PILOT	TYPE
04/14/44	0036	1st Lt. Joel E. Bonner	G4M Betty (probable)
04/14/44	0111	1st Lt. Edward A. Sovik	G4M Betty
04/14/44	0112	Capt. Howard W. Bollman	G4M Betty
Squadron Totals:	2/1/0		

VMF(N)-533

DATE	TIME	PILOT	TYPE
05/16/45	0015-0440	1st Lt. Alfred F. Branham	Francis (probable)
05/16/45	0300	1st Lt. Robert M. Wilhide	G4M Betty
05/18/45	2210	1st Lt. Robert E. Wellwood	G4M Betty
05/18/45	2230	1st Lt. Edward N. Le Faivre	A6M3 Hamp
05/18/45	-	1st Lt. Robert E. Wellwood	G4M Betty
05/18/45	2300	1st Lt. Edward N. Le Faivre	G4M Betty
05/18/45	2353	1st Lt. Robert E. Wellwood	G4M Betty
05/24/45	2105	1st Lt. James E. Smurr	G4M Betty
05/24/45	2115	1st Lt. Thomas B. Trammell	G4M Betty
05/24/45	2140	1st Lt. Albert F. Dellamano	G4M Betty
05/24/45	2200	1st Lt. Albert F. Dellamano	E13A Jake
05/24/45	2220	1st Lt. Albert F. Dellamano	Ki-21 Sally
05/27/45	2025	1st Lt. James E. Smurr	E13A Jake
05/28/45	0200	1st Lt. Forris M. Hollowell	G4M Betty
05/28/45	0315	1st Lt. Robert S. Hemstad	J1N1 Irving
05/28/45	0320	1st Lt. Richard M. Moore	J1N1 Irving
06/09/45	0430	1st Lt. Jay A. Stokes	Ki-61 Tony
06/09/45	2130	Capt. Robert Baird	E13A Jake
06/16/45	0351	Capt. Robert Baird	G4M Betty
06/16/45	0501	Capt. Robert Baird	G3M Nell
06/19/45	0135	1st Lt. William T. Treynor	G4M Betty
06/19/45	0157	1st Lt. Robert S. Hemstad	G4M Betty
06/22/45	0045	Capt. Robert Baird	P1Y Frances
06/22/45	0057	1st Lt. Karl B. Witte	Ki-21 Sally
06/22/45	0230	1st Lt. John R. Mahoney	Ki-21 Sally
06/22/45	0233	Capt. Robert Baird	G4M Betty
06/22/45	2245	Maj. Marion M. Magruder	G4M Betty
06/24/45	0157	1st Lt. Robert S. Hemstad	Ki-21 Sally
06/26/34	0125	1st Lt. Johnny W. Peacock	E13A Jake
06/26/45	0205	1st Lt. Rayln C. Parkhill	A6M2-N Rufe
06/30/45	0105	1st Lt. Charles S. Stitt, Jr.	E13A Jake
07/14/45	0441	Capt. Robert Baird	G4M Betty
07/18/45	2136	1st Lt. John R. Mahoney	B6N2 Jill
07/18/45	2140	Capt. George A. Hanna	G6N2 Jill
07/19/45	0215	1st Lt. Karl B. Witte	A6M Zeke

07/30/45	0206	2nd Lt. Irving B. Hardy	G4M Betty
Squadron Totals:	35/1/0		

VMF(N)-534

DATE	TIME	PILOT	TYPE
02/02/45	1030	1st Lt. Brett E. Roueche	C6N Myrt
Squadron Totals:	1/0/0		

VMF(N)-541

DATE	TIME	PILOT	TYPE
10/31/44	1945	Maj. Norman L. Mitchell	E13A Jake
12/05/44	0630	2nd Lt. Rodney E. Montgomery, Jr.	Ki-43 Oscar
12/07/44	0145	T. Sgt. John W. Andre	Ki-45 Nick or Ki-48 Lily
12/07/44	0610	Capt. Harlin J. Morrison	Ki-48 Lily
12/12/44	0720	T. Sgt. John W. Andre	A6M Zeke
12/12/44	-	1st Lt. Harold T. Hayes, Jr.	A6M Zeke
12/12/44	-	1st Lt. Harold T. Hayes, Jr.	D3A Val
12/12/44	-	2nd Lt. Karl T. Keller	A6M Zeke
12/12/44	-	2nd Lt. Karl T. Keller (0.5)	A6M Zeke
		2nd Lt. Paul L. Martelli (0.5)	
12/12/44	-	2nd Lt. Paul L. Martelli	A6M Zeke
12/12/44	-	1st Lt. Fletcher D. Miller, Jr. (0.5)	Ki-32 Mary
		T. Sgt. Francis A. Ratchford (0.5)	
12/12/44	-	T. Sgt. Francis A. Ratchford	Ki-48 Lily
12/12/44	-	Capt. David W. Thompson	Ki-43 Oscar
12/12/44	-	Capt. David W. Thompson	A6M Zeke
12/12/44	-	Capt. David W. Thompson	Ki-43 Oscar (damaged)
12/15/44	0805	1st Lt. Lyle R. Whitner	D3A Val
12/15/44	0840	2nd Lt. Robert F. Marr	A6M Zeke
12/15/44	-	Capt. Harlin J. Morrison	B6N2 Jill
12/15/44	-	1st Lt. Carl D. Williams	B6N2 Jill
12/22/44	1915	T. Sgt.	John W. Andre
12/22/44	-	T. Sgt. John W. Andre	J2M Jack
12/26/44	1900	2nd Lt. Rodney E. Montgomery, Jr.	unidentified
12/26/44	-	2nd Lt. Rodney E. Montgomery, Jr.	Ki-84 Frank (probable)
01/03/45	0715	2nd Lt. Harold T. Hayes, Jr.	A6M Zeke
01/03/45	0720	2nd Lt. Harold T. Hayes, Jr.	A6M Nick
Squadron Totals:	23/1/1		

VMF(N)-542

DATE	TIME	PILOT	TYPE
04/16/45	1845	2nd Lt. Arthur J. Arceneaux	A6M Zeke
04/16/45	-	2nd Lt. William W. Campbell	Ki-84 Frank
04/22/45	0230	1st Lt. Herbert Groff	G4M Betty
04/27/45	2220	2nd Lt. George J. Collins	B5N Kate
04/28/45	0015	Capt. Wallace E. Sigler	Ki-61 Tony

04/30/45	0335	2nd Lt. Delno W. Carlton	A6M Zeke
05/13/45	2030	2nd Lt. Lloyd J. Parsons	P1Y Frances
05/16/45	2315	2nd Lt. William W. Campbell	unidentified
05/20/45	1940	2nd Lt. Arthur J. Arceneaux (0.5)	E13A Jake
		2nd Lt. Gordon L. Coles (0.5)	
05/20/45	2030	2nd Lt. Gordon L. Coles	E13A Jake
05/22/45	2052	2nd Lt. George J. Collins	Ki-61 Tony
05/27/45	2330	2nd Lt. Gordon L. Coles	D3A Val
06/03/45	0230	1st Lt. William E. Smith	J1N1 Irving
06/10/45	1420	1st Lt. Fred Hiliard, Jr.	unidentified
06/15/45	2118	Maj. Robert B. Porter	Ki-45 Nick
06/15/45	2225	Maj. Robert B. Porter	G4M Betty
06/27/45	2330	1st Lt. Delno W. Carlton	F1M1 Pete
08/08/45	0308	2nd Lt. William E. Jennings	Ki-61 Tony
Squadron Totals:	18/0/0		

VMF(N)-543

DATE	TIME	PILOT	TYPE
04/15/45	1855	Capt. James A. Etheridge	Ki-84 Frank
04/17/45	2130	2nd Lt. Charles A. Engman, Jr.	Ki-21 Sally
05/04/45	0345	Capt. William P. Mitchell	A6M Zeke
05/10/45	0530	2nd Lt. Edgar F. Gaudette, Jr.	Ki-61 Tony
05/22/45	2020	2nd Lt. Richard T. Ward	A6M2-N Rufe
05/24/45	2345	1st Lt. Carl M. Davis	G4M Betty
05/27/45	2400	Capt. James A. Etheridge	E13A Jake
05/27/45	-	2nd Lt. Ruford P. Covington, Jr.	A6M3 Hamp
06/07/45	1905	1st Lt. Edwin Pendrey	D3A Val
07/03/45	0345	1st Lt. Gerald P. Anderson	Ki-61 Tony
07/12/45	0420	2nd Lt. Louis J. McGowan	Ki-21 Sally
07/29/45	0117	2nd Lt. Thomas H. Danaher	G4M Betty
07/29/45	0205	2nd Lt. Paul Moser, Jr.	Betty
07/29/45	0205	2nd Lt. Thomas H. Danaher	G4M Betty (probable)
08/07/45	0245	2nd Lt. Henry A. Berck	G4M Betty
08/07/45	2331	2nd Lt. Thomas H. Danaher	G4M Betty
Squadron Totals:	15/1/0		

Appendix C: Top WWII Night Fighter Scores

NAME	CREDITS	SQUADRON
Lt. William E. Henry	(6.5+4)	VF(N)-41
Capt. Robert Baird	(6+0)	VMF(N)-533
Lt. (jg) John Orth	(6+0)	VF-9
Ens. Jack S. Berkheimer	(5.5+2)	VF(N)-41
Lt. Robert J. Humphrey	(5+.333)	VF-17
Lt. Donald E. Umphres	(4+2)	VF-83
Ens. L. Bowman	(4+0)	VF-6
Lt. John W. Dear	(4+3)	VF(N)-76
Lt. Fred L. Dungan	(4+3)	VF(N)-76
Ens. James M. Barnes	(4+2)	VF-83
Ens. Philip I. McDonald	(4+0)	VF(N)-91
Lt. (jg) Kenneth D. Smith	(4+0)	VF(N)-90
Maj. R.B. Porter	(2+6)	VMF(N)-542

Note: Lt. R.L. Reiserer scored 1 night kill and 7 day kills with VF(N)-76, and 1 day kill with VF-10. Maj. R.B. Porter scored 2 night kills with VMF(N)-542 and 3 day kills with VMF-121.

Appendix D: USN/USMC Korean War Air-to-Air Victories by F4U-5N and F7F Aircraft

SQUADRON	DATE	PILOT/RO	AIRCRAFT	AIRCRAFT DESTROYED
VMF(N)-513	07/01/51	Capt. Edwin B. Long	F7F-3N	PO-2
		CWO Robert C. Buckingham		
VMF(N)-513	07/12/51	Capt. Donald L. Fenton	F4U-5N	PO-2
VMF(N)-513	09/23/51	Maj. Eugene A. Van Gundy	F7F-3N	Yak-9
		MSgt. Thomas H. Ullom		
VMF(N)-513	06/05/52	Lt. John W. Andre	F4U-5N	YaK-9
VC-3/Det D	06/30/53	Lt. Guy P. Bordelon Jr.	F4U-5N	YaK-18
VC-3/Det D	06/30/53	-	F4U-5N	YaK-18
VC-3/Det D	07/05/53	-	F4U-5N	PO-2
VC-3/Det D	07/05/53	-	F4U-5N	PO-2
VC-3/Det D	07/16/53	-	F4U-5N	PO-2

Appendix E: Unit Codes

WWII USN Night Fighter Squadrons

SQUADRON	TAIL CODE IDENTIFIER
VF(N)-41	Circle with in-squadron number
VF(N)-53	Inverted white "V"
VF(N)-76	Diagonal white bar
VF(N)-77	Diagonal white bar
VF(N)-78	White circle
VF(N)-90	White arrow
VF(N)-91	White SS
VF(N)-101	None

Korean War Night Fighter Unit Codes

SQUADRON	AIRCRAFT	TAIL.CODE IDENTIFIER
VC-3	NP	
VC-4	NA	
VMF(N)-513	WF	
VMF(N)-542	WH	

Appendix F: Korean War USN F4U-5N/NL Deployments

VC-3	CARRIER	DATES
Det C	Valley Forge (CV 45)	1 May 1950-1 Dec 1950
Det 3	Philippine Sea (CV 47)	5 Jul 1950-26 Mar 1951
Det ?	Boxer (CV 21)	24 Aug 1950-11 Nov 1950
Det F	Princeton (CV 37)	9 Nov 1950-29 May 1951
Det ?	Valley Forge	6 Dec 1950-7 Apr 1951
Det F	Boxer	2 Mar 1951-24 Oct 1951
Det ?	Philippine Sea	28 Mar 1951-9 Jun 1951
Det G	Bon Homme Richard(CVA 31)	10 May 1951-17 Dec 1951
Det ?	Princeton	31 May 1951-29 Aug 1951
Det B	*Essex* (CV 9)	26 Jun 1951-25 Mar 1952
Det D	Antietam (CV 36)	8 Sep 1951-2 May 1952
Det H	Valley Forge	15 Oct 1951-3 Jul 1952
Det C	Philippine Sea	31 Dec 1951-8 Aug 1952
Det A	Boxer	8 Feb 1952-26 Sep 1952
Det E	Princeton	21 Mar 1952-3 Nov 1952
Det I	*Essex*	16 Jun 1952-6 Feb 1953
Det F	Kearsarge (CVA 33)	11 Aug 1952-17 Mar 1953
Det G	Oriskany (CVA 34)	15 Sep 1952-18 May 1953
Det B	Valley Forge	20 Nov 1952-25 Jun 1953
Det M	Philippine Sea	15 Dec 1952-14 Aug 1953
Det D	Princeton	24 Jan 1953-21 Sep 1953
Det H	Boxer	30 Mar 1953-28 Nov 1953

VC-4	CARRIER	DATES
Det 3	USS Leyte (CV 32)	6 Sep 1950-3 Feb 1951
Det 4	Bon Homme Richard	20 May 1952-8 Jan 1953

Endnotes

INTRODUCTION:

1. Joe G. Taylor, *Development of Night Air Operations 1941-1952* (Air Historical Studies No. 92, 1953), 7.
2. Taylor, *Development of Night Air Operations*, 18.

CHAPTER 1:

1. Roy A. Grossnick, et al, *United States Naval Aviation 1910-1995* (Washington, DC: Naval Historical Center, 1997), 104. Ibid, 108.
2. Ibid, 109.
3. Warren Thompson, "Wait Until Dark," *Wings*, October 1989, 24 and W.E. Scarborough, *F7F Tigercat in Action* (Carrollton, TX: Squadron/Signal Publications, 1986), 4.
4. Scarborough, *F7F Tigercat in Action*, 4-5.
5. Ibid.
6. Ibid.
7. See Howard L. Turner and George E. Cooper, *Partial Measurements in Flight of the Flying Qualities of a Grumman XF7F-1 Airplane with a Modified Vertical Tail NACA Research Memorandum A7D15* (National Advisory Committee for Aeronautics, Bureau of Aeronautics) and Corky Meyer, "F7F Tigercat: The Untold Story," *Flight Journal*, August 2002: 48–56, 58.
8. Meyer, "F7F Tigercat: The Untold Story," 49.
9. Ibid.
10. Capt. W.E. Scarborough, *F7F Tigercat in Action* (Carrollton, TX: Squadron/Signal Publications, 1986) 5.

CHAPTER 2:

1. Robert Sherrod, *History of Marine Corps Aviation in World War II* (Combat Forces Press, 1952), 159
2. Ibid.
3. Lt. Col. Harry W. Edwards USMC (Ret), *A Different War: Marines in Europe and North Africa* (Marines in World War II Commemorative Series, 1994), http://www.nps.gov/history/history/online_books/npswapa/extContent/usmc/pcn-190-003125-00/sec5b.htm.
4. Bureau of Aeronautics, *Interview of Lt. Colonel Edward A. Montgomery, USMC. Night Fighter Operations in Great Britain*, 9 June 1943.
5. Sherrod, *Marine Corps Aviation in World War II*, 161.
6. "Night Fighters," *Naval Aviation News*, Jul 1945, 22-26.
7. Sherrod, *Marine Corps Aviation in World War II*, 162.
8. Ibid, 162-163.
9. Ibid.
10. Ibid, 167.

CHAPTER 3:

1. Action Report of USS *Enterprise* (CV 6), *Operations as a Unit of Task Group 50.2 from 10 November to 27 November 1943, Enclosure 22*, 16 December 1943.
2. *Randolph* Bartlett, "The Big E's Impatient Virgins," *Naval History Magazine*, Dec 2006, http://www.usni.org/magazines/navalhistory/2006-12/big-es-impatient-virgins.
3. VF(N)-101 After Action Report, 15 June 1944.
4. VF(N)-77 After Action Report, 20 June 1944.

CHAPTER 4:

1. "Bogey at 2 miles, twelve o' clock," VF(N)-41 After Action Report, 14 December 1944.
2. "A solid sheet of AA," VF(N)-41 After Action Report, 14 December 1944.
3. Peterson heard his fellow night fighter pilot utter, "Peter...," VF(N)-41 After Action Report, 15 December 1944.
4. "I'll never make it," VF(N)-41 After Action Report, 16 December 1944.

CHAPTER 5

1. Commander Task Force FIFTY-EIGHT (First Carrier Task Force) to Commander in Chief, United States Fleet, *Action Report of operations of U.S.S. Enterprise in support of amphibious assault on Iwo Jima, 10 February to 23 February 1945-Phase I* (File No. A16-3, Serial 0343, 11 April 1945).
2. Commander Fifth Fleet to Commander in Chief, United States Fleet, *Action Report of operations of U.S.S. Enterprise in support of amphibious assault on Iwo Jima, 10 February to 23 February 1945-Phase I* (File No. A16-3 (2e-A), Serial: 0331).
3. A Peggy and Betty, both twin-engine aircraft, were destroyed near Kasonohara (Kanoya East airfield) at approximately the same time according to Japanese sources.

CHAPTER 6:

1. Thomas E. Doll, *Night Wings: USMC Night Fighters, 1942-1953* (Carrolton, TX: Squadron/Signal Publications, 2000), 13
2. E.A. Sovik, "Two Nights in the Pacific," *Marine Night Fighter Association* (Paducah, KY: Turner Publishing Company, 1999), 87-88.
3. Japanese sources do not substantiate the claim of a high-ranking Japanese officer or official on board the Myrt.
4. Sherrod, *Marine Corps Aviation in World War II*, 275.
5. Ibid, 281.
6. Ibid, 282-283.
7. Maj. Charles W. Boggs, Jr., USMC, *Marine Aviation in the Philippines* (Washington, DC: Historical Division Headquarters U.S. Marine Corps, 1951), 42.
8. Sherrod, *Marine Corps Aviation in World War II*, 286.
9. Boggs, *Marine Aviation in the Philippines*, 46.

CHAPTER 7:

1. Benis M. Frank and Henry I. Saw, Jr., History of Marine Corps Operations, *Victory and Occupation*, Vol. V (Washington, DC: U.S. Marine Corps Historical Branch, 1968), 181.
2. Doll, *Night Wings*, 31.
3. Ibid.
4. Sherrod, *Marine Corps Aviation in World War II*, 400-401.
5. Barrett Tillman, *Hellcat: The F6F in World War II* (Annapolis, MD: Naval Institute Press, 1979), 185.
6. Sherrod, *Marine Corps Aviation in World War II*, 401.
7. Colonel R. Bruce Porter, USMCR (Ret) with Bruce Hammel, *Ace: A Marine Night-Fighter Pilot in World War II* (New York: Jove Books. Berkley Publishing Group, 1987), 259.
8. Ibid, 259-260.
9. Ibid, 271.
10. Doll, *Night Wings*, 44.
11. Mark A. Magruder, *Nightfighter Radar Intercept Killer* (Gretna. LA: Pelican Publishing Company, Inc., 2012), 254.
12. Pilots MIA during that period were: Capt. August L. Aendt (14 May), 1st Lt. Amor L. Towns (5 June), 1st Lt. Donald M. Steele (9 June), and 2nd Lt. Ruford P. Covington (11 June).
13. Magruder, *Nightfighter Radar Intercept Killer*, 267.
14. Sherrod, *Marine Corps Aviation in World War II*, 372 and 403.

CHAPTER 8:

1. Charles H. Brown, *Dark Sky, Black Sea: Aircraft Carrier Night and All-Weather Operations* (Annapolis, MD: Naval Institute Press, 1999), 41-43.
2. "Planes Sinks Battleships," *Naval Aviation News*, October 1948, 11.

3. For a detailed analysis of external fuel tank design for the F7F, see Turner and Cooper, NACA Research Memorandum A7A07.
4. "F4U Goes into Production," *Naval Aviation News*, July 1947, 16 and "New Corsair F4U-5," *Naval Aviation News*, October 1948, 18-19.
5. "Night Fighters get Mark 8 Gun Sight," *Naval Aviation News*, June 1947, 37.
6. Nicholas A. Veronico with John M. and Donna Campbell, *F4U Corsair: Combat, Development, and Racing History of the Corsair* (Osceola, WI: Motorbooks International, 1994), 84.
7. See VMF(N)-513 squadron diaries for the period of September to December 1950.
8. VMF(N)-513 Commander's Report dated January 1951.
9. Ibid.
10. "Corsair is Winterized in 'Crash' Job," *Naval Aviation News*, 28.
11. Ibid.

CHAPTER 9:

1. Warren Thompson, "Wait Until Dark," Wings, 18.
2. Email from Mr. Garry Cleveland to the author.
3. Lynn Montross, Nicolas A. Canzona, et al. U.S. Marine Corps Operations in Korea. The Chosin Reservoir Campaign, Vol. 3.
4. Thompson, "Wait Until Dark," Wings, 20.
5. The other pilots on the mission were Capt. Edwin Pendry, 1st Lt. Warren J. Beyes, and 1st Lt. William E. Jennings.
6. Malcom W. Cagle and Frank A. and Manson, "Wall of Fire around Hungnam. The Hungnam Redeployment," Ch.6. The Sea War in Korea.

CHAPTER 10:

1. VMF(N)-513 Monthly Diary, May 1951.
2. VMF(N)-513 Monthly Diary, October 1951.
3.Email from Mr. Cleveland to the author.
4.Colonel Jack R. Cram, *Evaluation of Night Close Air Support System using Searchlights, Report of 1st Marine Aircraft Wing*, FMF. FF14/1stMAW, A1:04, JRC:ddp, Serial: 005238, dated 24 April 1953. Also See VMF(N)-513 War Diaries from August 1951 onward concerning squadron installation and use of the MPQ-14.
5. Email from Mr. Cleveland to the author.
6. VMF(N)-513 Monthly Diary, September 1951.
7. VMF(N)-513 Monthly Diary, June 1952.

CHAPTER 11:

1. Email from James Brown to the author.
2. Ibid.
3. Email attachment from Nicholas A. Veronico to the author. Also see: Veronico et al, "The Navy's Only Korean War Ace," F4U Corsair: The Combat, Development, and Racing History of the Corsair.
4. Email from Marshall Foreman to the author.
5.Email attachment from Veronico, *The Navy's Only Korean War Ace.*
6. Ibid.
7. Ibid.
8. Cagle and Manson. "Bedcheck Charlies." Ch.13, On the Line: The Sea War in Korea.
9. Ibid.
10. Email attachment from Veronico, *The Navy's Only Korean War Ace.*
11. Cagle and Manson, *Bedcheck Charlies.*
12. Cram, *Evaluation of Night Close Air Support System using Searchlights, Report of 1st Marine Aircraft Wing.*

Bibliography

BOOKS

Brown, Charles H. Dark Sky, *Black Sea: Aircraft Carrier Night and All-Weather Operations*. Annapolis, MD: Naval Institute Press, 1999.

De Chant, John A., Capt. USMCR. *Devilbirds: The Story of United States Marine Corps Aviation in World War II*. New York and London: Harper & Brothers Publishers, 1947.

Doll, Thomas E. *Night Wings: USMC Night Fighters, 1942-1953*. Carrollton, TX: Squadron/Signal Publications, Inc., 2000.

Hallion, Richard P. *The Naval Air War in Korea*. The Nautical and Aviation Publishing Company, Baltimore, MD, 1986.

Magruder, Mark A. *Night Fighter Radar Intercept Killer*. Pelican Publishing Company, Gretna, LA, 2012.

Marine Night Fighter Association. Turner Publishing Company. Paducah, KY, 1999.

Morison, Samuel Eliot. *A History of U.S. Naval Operations in WWII*. Little, Brown and Co., Boston, 1960

--Vol. XII *Leyte*

--XIV *Victory in the Pacific*

Porter, R. Bruce., Colonel (USMCR (Ret) with Bruce Hammel. *Ace: A Marine Night-Fighter Pilot in World War II*. Jove Books. Berkley Publishing Group. NY, NY, 1987.

Scarborough, W.E. Capt., USN (Ret). *F7F Tigercat in Action*. Squadron/Signal Publications. Carrollton, TX, 1986.

Sherrod, Robert. *History of Marine Corps Aviation in World War II*. Combat Forces Press, 1952.

Sullivan, Jim. *F4U Corsair in Action*. Squadron/Signal Publications, Inc. Carrollton, TX, 1994.

--*F6F Hellcat in Action*, 1979.

Thruelsen, Richard. *The Grumman Story*. Praeger Publications, New York, NY, 1976.

Tillman, Barrett. *Corsair:The F4U in World War II and Korea*. Naval Institute Press. Annapolis, Maryland, 1979.

---. *Hellcat: The F6F in World War II*. Naval Institute Press. Annapolis, Maryland, 1979.

Veronico, Nicholas A., with John M. and Donna Campbell. *F4U Corsair: Combat, Development, and Racing History of the Corsair*. Motorbooks International. Osceola, WI, 1994.

PERIODICALS

Bartlett, *Randolph.* "The Big E's Impatient Virgins." *Naval History Magazine* December 2006. Electronic.

Caldwell, Turner F, Jr., Cdr. USN. "We Put the Flattops on the Night Shift." Jr. *Saturday Evening Post* 11 Aug 1945: 26-27, 41-42.

Daniels, C.M. On the Track of the Tigercat. Wings, Vol. 3 No.4, August 1973

Fuller, Curtis. Killer in the Night. Flying Magazine, August 1951

Gray, James Seton, Jr., Cdr. USN. "Development of Naval Night Fighters in WWII." *U.S. Navy Proceedings Magazine* Jul 1948. Electronic.

Meyer, Corky. The Legendary Bob Hall. Flight Journal, Vol. 5, No. 5, October 2000.

--"F7F Tigercat: The Untold Story". *Flight Journal*, Aug 2002.

Odell, William C., Col. USAF (ret). "The Development of Night Fighters in World War II." *Navy History Magazine* Winter 1989, Vol. 3, No. 1. Electronic.

Thompson, Warren. Wait Until Dark. Wings Magazine, Vol. 19 No. 5, October 1999.

GOVERNMENT SOURCES

"Air War at Night." *Naval Aviation Confidential Bulletin* May 1953.

Boggs, Charles W. Jr., Major (USMC). Historical Division Headquarters U.S. Marine Corps. Marine Aviation in the Philippines. Washington, GPO, 1951.

Bureau of Aeronautics. Interview of Lt. Colonel Edward A. Montgomery, USMC. Night Fighter Operations in Great Britain in the Bureau of Aeronautics, 9 June 1943.

Commander Fifth Fleet to Commander in Chief, United States Fleet. Action Report of operations of U.S.S. *Enterprise* in support of amphibious assault on Iwo Jima, 10 February to 23 February 1945-Phase I. File No. File No. A16-3 (2e-A), Serial: 0331.

Commander Task Force FIFTY-EIGHT (First Carrier Task Force) to Commander in Chief, United States Fleet. Action Report of operations of U.S.S. *Enterprise* in support of amphibious assault on Iwo Jima, 10 February to 23 February 1945-Phase I. File No. A16-3, Serial 0343. Dated 11 April 1945.

"Corsair is Winterized in 'Crash' Job." *Naval Aviation News* 1951, 28.

Cram, Jack R., Colonel USMC. Colonel Jack R. Cram, *Evaluation of Night Close Air Support System using Searchlights, Report of 1st Marine Aircraft Wing,* FMF. FF14/1stMAW, A1:04, JRC:ddp, Serial: 005238, dated 24 April 1953.

Edwards, Harry W., Lt. Col. USMC (Ret), A Different War: Marines in Europe and North Africa: Marines in World War II Commemorative Series. U.S. Marine Corps Historical Center, Washington DC, 1994.

"F4U-5 Goes Into Production." *Naval Aviation News* Sept 1947, 16

"F7F Tigercat." *Naval Aviation News* Jul-Aug 1998.

Frank, Benis M., and Henry I. Saw, Jr., History of Marine Corps Operations, Victory and Occupation, Vol. V (Washington, DC: U.S. Marine Corps Historical Branch, 1968).

Grossnick, et al. United States Naval Aviation 1910-1995. Washington, DC: Naval Historical Center, Washington, 1997. "New Corsair F4U-5, *Naval Aviation News* October 1948, 18-19.

"Night Fighters." *Naval Aviation News* Jul 1945: 22-26.

"Night Fighters Get Mark 8 Gun Sight." *Naval Aviation News.* June 1947, 37.

"Planes Sinks Battleships," *Naval Aviation News*, October 1948, 11.

Squadron Diaries and After Action Reports: VF-9, -17, -20, -74, VF(N)-41, -53, -75, -76, -77, -78, -90, -101, VMF(N)-513,-532, -533, -534, -541, and -542

Taylor, Joe G. Development of Night Air Operations 1941-1952. Air Historical Studies No. 92, 1953.

Turner, Howard L. and George E. Cooper. Partial Measurements in Flight of the Flying Qualities of a Grumman XF7F-1 Airplane with a Modified Vertical Tail. National Advisory Committee for Aeronautics, Bureau of Aeronautics.

Index

— A —

— B —

— C —

— D —

—E—

—F—

—G—

—H—

—I—

—J—

—K—

—L—

—M—